THE BUSINESS FORECASTING REVOLUTION

WHARTON EXECUTIVE LIBRARY
Yoram J. Wind, Editor
The Wharton School, University of Pennsylvania

F. Gerard Adams:
The Business Forecasting Revolution: Nation—Industry—Firm

Leonard M. Lodish:
The Advertising and Promotion Challenge:
Vaguely Right or Precisely Wrong?

David Solomons:
Making Accounting Policy:
The Quest for Credibility in Financial Reporting

Other titles to be announced.

THE BUSINESS FORECASTING REVOLUTION

Nation–Industry–Firm

F. Gerard Adams

New York • *Oxford*
OXFORD UNIVERSITY PRESS
1986

Oxford University Press

Oxford   New York   Toronto
Delhi   Bombay   Calcutta   Madras   Karachi
Petaling Jaya   Singapore   Hong Kong   Tokyo
Nairobi   Dar es Salaam   Cape Town
Melbourne   Auckland

and associated companies in
Beirut   Berlin   Ibadan   Nicosia

Copyright © 1986 by Oxford University Press, Inc.

Published by Oxford University Press, Inc.,
200 Madison Avenue,
New York, New York 10016

Oxford is a registered trademark of Oxford University Press

Library of Congress Cataloging-in-Publication Data
Adams, F. Gerard (Francis Gerard), 1929–
The business forecasting revolution
(Wharton executive library)
Includes bibliographies and index.
1. Business forecasting—Data processing.
2. Economic forecasting—Data processing.
I. Title. II. Series.
HD30.27.A33   1986   338.5'442   85-18943
ISBN 0-19-503700-6

Printing (last digit): 9 8 7 6 5 4 3 2 1

Printed in the United States of America
on acid-free paper

To Courtney

Series Foreword

The Wharton Executive Library is designed to fill a critical need for a new kind of book for managers. The rapidly changing business environment poses a major challenge to senior executives that cannot be met by the traditional strategies that produced yesterday's and today's winners. Technological advances and their diffusion, dramatic changes in the structure of key industries that result from government deregulation, the rising tide of mergers and acquisitions, the change in consumer lifestyles, and the internationalization of business are some of the forces management must contend with.

Modern business schools are aware of these challenges and much current business research is concerned with finding concepts and methods to help managers solve their new range of problems. However, it can take as long as five years for useful academic work to reach managers—progressing through presentations at academic meetings, limited circulation of working papers, publication of scholarly journals, and finally perhaps reaching publication in one of the nontechnical journals directed at practicing managers. Given the nature of the current business environment, this is too long a delay.

The Wharton Executive Library provides executives with state-of-the-art books in key management areas without the usual time-lag. To enhance their usefulness, each book is:

- Up to date; reflects the latest and best research
- Authoritative; authors are experts in their fields

- Brief; can be read reasonably quickly
- Nontechnical; avoids unnecessary jargon and methodology
- Practical; includes many examples and applications of the concepts discussed
- Compact; can be carried easily in briefcases on business travel

Senior managers will find the volumes in the series to be especially valuable. Because of the books' readability, top management can use them to assess whether their key managers are aware of and using the latest concepts in, for example, marketing, forecasting, financial accounting, finance, strategic planning, information systems, management of technology, human resources, and managing multinational corporations. Given the strong interdependency among the various management functions, it is essential that senior executives be aware of the best academic thinking in the areas for which they are ultimately responsible.

The qualities that make these books useful to managers should make them equally valuable as assigned reading in executive development programs in colleges and universities and management training programs in industry. They can also be used as supplementary reading in academic business courses where their state-of-the-art content should nicely complement theoretical material in standard textbooks.

It is appropriate that this new series should originate in the Wharton School, the first business school founded in the United States—and probably in the world. Its faculty is at the top of its profession, and its graduates fill the management ranks at all levels in all parts of the world. The school's academic focus is on the functional areas of management with an analytic and empirical approach. This quality and approach are clearly evident in these books.

We, the series editor and the publisher, hope that you, the reader, will share our enthusiasm for the series and find the advice of some of the leading scholars in their fields, as presented in these books, of value to you.

We also welcome any suggestions and comments from our readers that will help us to find new and useful titles and achieve the widest possible audience for the books.

Yoram (Jerry) Wind
The Lauder Professor
The Wharton School
University of Pennsylvania
Series Editor

Preface

This book is about business forecasting using the tools of econometrics. No business forecaster can ignore the economic environment in which future business activity will take place. Inflation, interest rates, personal income, and the unemployment rate are among the economic forces that have a decisive impact on business performance.

Econometrics—the use of statistical and mathematical models to predict future economic activity—provides the tools for business forecasters to account for changes in the economy on their forecasts. This book seeks to bridge the gap between econometric forecasting as an academic discipline and the application of these techniques to the world of business. It explores the latest techniques by which business economists can get a handle on the economic environment, today and tomorrow.

We are in the middle of a revolution in forecasting. Models that run at long distance on giant mainframe computers are on the way out. The microcomputer has placed the task of forecasting squarely on the desk of business planners and managers. This fits well with the growing use of computer models in business for marketing studies, investment analysis, financial planning, inventory and production decisions, and the like. The microcomputer opens vast new horizons for business forecasting and this book looks at the range of choices that are open to forecasters.

The book is organized in a logical progression. It starts with a survey of the field of econometrics using reasonably non-technical language. It moves to the application of econometric models to the economy as a whole. Then it narrows its focus to the level of a specific industry. Finally it looks at forecasting in a single firm—where, after all, the business forecaster is located and which is the forecaster's ultimate concern. It thus provides business planners with the kind of perspective on their tasks that should make their strategic planning more accurate.

But it is important to remember that there are no easy solutions in business forecasting. Those who forecast are accustomed to the constant changes in the economic environment. In recent years the difficulties of forecasting have increased as the economy has been exposed to new pressures from abroad, as new economic institutions have emerged, as the priorities of economic policy have changed, and as views about appropriate economic theories have evolved. In this brave new world, hundred billion dollars plus budget and trade deficits, deregulation, rational expectations, Reaganomics and all that create new uncertainties. And the greater the uncertainty, the more the need to look ahead and to anticipate the future.

This book, which was itself repeatedly modified as the world changed while it was being written, reflects my own work and that of my colleagues in the field of econometric forecasting. As the reader will note in many places, I have relied heavily on the experience of the Wharton Econometrics forecasting group with whom I have been associated since its beginning, more than twenty years ago.

Econometric forecasting is a craft and cannot be learned in isolation. Many people—colleagues, associates, and students—have contributed to my experience with model building and forecasting. I appreciate the help of the entire Wharton Econometrics team over many years, especially Lawrence Klein, George Schink, Michael McCarthy, Enrique Sanchez, Don Straszheim, Robert Wescott, Roger Bird, Jonathan Francis, Howard Howe, John Green, Vijaya Duggal, and Abel Beltran del Rio. Bruce Lippke's insights into the role of the business forecaster were most helpful. Alvin Karchere and John Qualls made valuable comments on earlier versions of the manuscript. Many of my students have contributed directly and indirectly to this book, but, as with one's children, it is better to thank them all and not to single out anyone for special praise. Parts of the manuscript were written while I was at Confindustria in Rome, associated with Massimo Tivegna and Antonio Martelli. Lynnmarie Costello ably typed many drafts.

Thanks go to all of you.

Philadelphia   F. G. A.
January 1986

Contents

THE BUSINESS
FORECASTING REVOLUTION

❖ 1 ❖

The New
Economic Environment:
Challenge to Business

The world of business forecasting is undergoing a fundamental revolution. Techniques of modeling and simulation that have served many economic forecasters in government and in business for the past twenty years are being adapted to today's changed economic environment and economic thinking. Interestingly enough, a technological revolution—the microcomputer and all its promise for low cost data manipulation and business applications—is likely to lead to the most significant changes. Large-scale models run at long distance on giant mainframe computers are on the way out. The microcomputer has placed the task of forecasting squarely on the desk of business planners and managers. Model-based forecasting is being stretched from the model of the nation to models of industries and firms. Model systems link the company's financial planning model, marketing studies, and inventory and production scheduling to the national economic environment. And in this work the industrial engineer and planner are taking the place of the formally trained business economist.

The microcomputer has opened vast new horizons for business forecasting. This book is an update on these developments. What is the shape of the new environment for business forecasting? How is the econometric model approach being adapted to new conditions and new ideas? How is macroeconomic forecasting being extended into the realms of industrial and business forecasting? What are the implications of the mi-

3

crocomputer for the method and organization of business forecasting and planning?

The Business Forecasting Challenge

The economic environment of the 1980s is very different from the golden age of economic growth faced by American business until the early 1970s. The long postwar cycle of economic expansion in the United States and other industrial economies is over. With its passing has come a world of industrial transition: slower growth; regional and industrial disparities; and more serious cyclical swings. The United States has lost its dominant role in world markets and has become increasingly dependent on foreign suppliers of energy, some essential raw materials, and most recently, mass production products. Even the unexpectedly rapid United States economic recovery of 1983–84 can be seen as an episode in an increasingly uncertain economic prospect.

Along with a new environment have come significant changes in public policy. Traditional Keynesian policy prescriptions no longer seem to apply. The inability of economic policymakers to achieve hoped for objectives of growth, full unemployment, and price stability—perhaps an impossible dream—has turned economic policy in most western democracies in a conservative direction. The current view, which seeks to reduce the role of government, makes for a very different economic prospect than the policies aimed toward macroeconomic stabilization that prevailed in previous decades. However, conservative philosophy has not been matched by a turn toward fiscal responsibility, and the unresolved question of the federal budget deficit hangs like a dark cloud over the economic outlook.

Labeling activist fiscal policy as Keynesian is unfair to the memory of Lord Keynes. If Keynes were still alive, he would undoubtedly make different policy recommendations today.

From the business executive's point of view, this new world carries new and greater risks. With slower and more uncertain growth, continuously expanding demand cannot be expected to bail out the overextended inventory holder. Inflation and low interest rates no longer validate risky investments. Foreign competition threatens traditionally American industries such as automobiles and steel. Uncertain prospects for interest rates, exchange rates, and commodity prices must be factored into business decisions. Rapid changes in economic conditions, particularly unexpected changes, may have a profound impact on the success or failure of business ventures—as many business executives caught by rising interest rates or falling prices have discovered.

In an uncertain and risky world, information is at a premium. The information required is both for today and about tomorrow. More than ever, forecasting is an essential ingredient for business planning and decision making. The fact that increasing uncertainty has made forecasts seem less accurate does not make them any less useful. Just the opposite. Greater uncertainty increases the need for forward planning and testing the plan against alternative forecasts. This is the heart of business forecasting.

The scope and detail of informational inputs required by business are broad, and have been increasing, ranging from aggregate measures describing the economic environment as a whole (e.g., GNP, inflation, and so on) down to detailed information (e.g., sales, costs, interest rates, and so forth) which impinge specifically on particular business decisions. For perspective, it is important to remember that the business executive does not want this information for its own sake. Ultimately, narrowly specific forecasts relating to particular business ventures are required to factor into investment decisions, to determine how capital funds are to be raised, to influence the marketing plan, and to support capital budget allocations.

Fortunately, as needs for detailed forecasts have increased, improved forecasting techniques have been developed. Modern econometrics has become a mainstay of business forecasting. Computer systems drawing on national data banks and large-scale econometric models feed into every major business enterprise. In recent years, the original focus of econometric forecasting on national macroeconomic variables has been extended in the direction of more detailed industry and product statistics, regional data, prices and wages, interest rates, financial flows, and so forth. Information from computerized data banks and econometric models is an important input into corporate planning and decision making in nearly every major corporation. It is now beginning to flow even into smaller enterprises. This material offers an empirical picture of history and a most probable forecast. Perhaps most important, it offers the opportunity to look at alternative forecast scenarios and to consider many of the risks affecting business decisions.

This book is concerned with econometrics and business forecasting—the latest techniques used by business economists to get a handle on current and future economic trends. As such, it seeks to bridge the gap between econometric forecasting as (1) an academic discipline and (2) a business technique. It also seeks to understand the new world of business econometrics and to project its future.

The Changing Economic Environment

Even if managers feel relatively secure in their control of internal business variables, the outcomes of their decisions are affected by the changing external economic environment. Factors such as aggregate economic demand, the markets for particular products, wage rates, interest rates, exchange rates, and costs of material inputs seem to be more uncertain and less predictable than in the immediate postwar decades.

The Domestic U.S. Economy

The performance of the U.S. economy during the 1970s and early 1980s was disappointing. In place of rapid and stable growth came a period of stagnation and wide cyclical swings. The recession of 1973–74, triggered by the oil embargo and price increase, was the most serious cyclical downturn since the Depression. The double dip recessions of 1980 and 1981–82 represented an extended period of bad times. Industries like steel, automobiles, rubber, and machinery—which had long been considered the mainstays of the American economy—found themselves in serious difficulty. Even the strong recovery of 1983–84 did not bring many of these sectors back to buoyant health. The failing international competitiveness of American industry, in part a reflection of the overvalued U.S. dollar, shows up in the burgeoning international trade deficit. Productivity showed only small increases during the 1970s at an annual rate of 0.5% with actual declines toward the turn of the decade. Although the business cycle upswing of 1983–84—particularly the improvement in unemployment and inflation—should not go unnoted, the 1980s saw widespread fears that the United States was past its high water mark as a leader in the world of modern high technology industry and that the coming decade would be difficult and uncertain.

Since this book is concerned primarily with forecasting, a lengthy discussion of the sources of the U.S. growth problem is not appropriate. Suffice it to say that research has yielded a number of explanations, including the impact of high energy prices, the effect of pollution control and other government regulations, the effect of high marginal tax rates, the shifts in the composition of the labor force, and the structural change from industry to services. Yet, there remains an important "unexplained residual" factor.[1]

Along with slower growth has come more serious cyclical instability: business cycle swings have become wider, recessions deeper, and episodes of inflation more heated. Again, the explanation is multifaceted—greater exposure to the international economy, errors in the management of stabilization policy, and more responsive inflationary expectations, for example. The recent cyclical upswing brought improved growth and price and productivity performance, but it would be imprudent to say that problems are a thing of the past.

While we may not have a full explanation for the slower economic growth and cyclical instability, there is little question about the implications for forecasting. Business executives must now take into account a wider range of possibilities, including rapid recovery on one extreme and stagflation, recession, or even depression on the other. The slowness of the underlying growth trend has tended to make recessions more serious. In a rapidly growing world, business can tolerate a temporary slowdown; in a stagnant world, periods of recession can be disastrous. Slow growth and instability are a risky combination for business enterprise.

Another major economic change has been the increasing uncertainty about inflation. This comment may come as a surprise at a time when the inflation rate is down to less than 4%. Paradoxically, after people have begun to accept inflation as the norm, stable or declining prices can also be a source of difficulty. In the Midwest, many farmers and oilmen are in serious trouble because they are unable to meet loan obligations that were taken in the expectation of ever-rising wheat and oil prices.

In the 1960s and 1970s, it appeared that inflation was built into the economy. Cost-of-living adjustment clauses for wages, escalation for inflation even without formal mechanisms, and indexing of Social Security benefits and government payrolls were the grease that allowed the wage-price spiral to turn. Inflationary expectations, learned from personal experience, fueled further price increases. An initial inflationary impulse, like the oil shocks, caused inflation to continue for an extended period as wages chased prices and prices reacted to wages. And unless extended periods of recession and growing imports were accepted, as in the early 1980s, there was little occasion for downward readjustments in inflationary pressures. In the twenty years from 1960 to 1980, we came out of each successive recession with a higher underlying inflation rate. Growth of productivity offset some of the increase in production costs, but the productivity slowdown of the 1970s tended to aggravate the problem. The dilemma of the economy thus became neither unemployment or inflation, but both problems at the same time—stagflation.

At long last, some signs are pointing in a more favorable direction. From 1983 to 1985, there was a significant slowdown in the rate of inflation and wage increase. Givebacks reduced labor costs to some hard-pressed firms and unions were more willing to adjust working practices to improve productivity. Foreign competition, facilitated by the overvaluation of the dollar, prevented firms in many industries from getting higher prices.

It would be optimistic to translate these developments into a new world where inflationary pressures have vanished permanently. It is too soon to say that inflation is dead. Union labor is much less powerful today than only five or ten years ago, but workers have not forgotten the inflationary experience. They may seek to regain their past real incomes. Business executives, too, call for rebuilding profit margins. Indeed, the slow growth of the 1970s and early 1980s has resulted in less—not more—investment per worker! While inflation is under control, in the short run, the economy may actually be more inflation prone than in the past once full employment is reached. With the economy more affected by influences from abroad, inflation depends on international forces as well as domestic policies. If the economic expansion encounters capacity constraints or, alternatively, if the dollar drops sharply on foreign exchange markets, inflationary pressures might reoccur.

This creates an environment of considerable uncertainty for the business decision maker. Expectations about inflation affect what kinds of assets should be held and what contracts should be signed. In the short run, variations in prices affect production and inventory planning. Accounting for taxes and profits is influenced by changes in the price level. Inflation also affects long-term decisions: a long-term interest rate of 12% may not loom large in a world of double digit inflation, but such an interest rate may suddenly be very burdensome when inflation comes down to more moderate levels. Inflation is an unpredictable and uncertain tax!

The U.S. and the World Economy

Undoubtedly one of the most important changes in the U.S. economy in recent years has been its internationalization. Even today, imports and exports barely account for 10% of the nation's GNP, about double what they were 20 years ago. But we can no longer proceed on the assumption that the U.S. economy moves along a forecast path independently of what goes on in the outside world. The sharpest reminder of this fact was in the two oil shocks that took place in the 1970s. The sudden quadrupling of oil prices in 1973–74 and the almost equally sharp increase in 1979–80 resulted in major recessions. Even much smaller shocks have had perceptible impacts—the Soviet harvest failure in 1972 increased U.S. grain exports and drove up the price of wheat, causing an upsurge of inflation in the United States.

> On the occasion of the Soviet harvest failure, this author confided to a sociologist colleague that in order to forecast the U.S. economy it was necessary now to keep track of the weather in the Soviet Union. The sociologist responded that he had thought all along that economic forecasts had little more basis than weather forecasts!

The rapid expansion of world trade has slowed. Today, American industry is competing on less favorable terms with new high technology industries in Japan, Europe, and the newly industrialized countries. The result is a burgeoning trade deficit now approaching $150 billion, which has taken much of the steam out of U.S. economic expansion.

The system of floating exchange rates that replaced the rigid Bretton Woods exchange-rate regime which had operated during the first 25 postwar years also contributed to the U.S. economy's sensitivity to foreign influences. Fluctuations in the international value of the dollar greatly influence the cost of imported goods. It is likely that some of the inflationary pressures of the late 1970s reflected the decline of the dollar exchange rate, while some of the easing of inflation in 1982–84 must be related to the strength of the U.S. dollar.

The volatility of the world economy poses particularly significant problems for multinational enterprises and foreign investors. The profitability of foreign investments depends on both their success as a business venture and the exchange rate at which foreign earnings can be converted into dollars. International trade is affected by widely swinging exchange rates because of (1) capital movements and (2) a tendency for expectations to "overshoot" the underlying structural factors. The problem of accumulated foreign debts, particularly by the less developed countries and by the Eastern European economies, poses a threat to the operation of the international banking system. This is, thus, a much more uncertain international world for American business than the one which prevailed in the first postwar generation.

Changes in Government Regulations

Institutional changes have had and will continue to have profound effects on the economy. These institutional changes make the task of forecasting more difficult since they affect the economy's behavior in fundamental ways.

The 1970s witnessed a significant increase in the government's role in the economy. The magnitude of government spending as a share of economic activity increased sharply. Perhaps the changes in the role of government regulatory agencies, for example, in pollution control and safety on the job, have been even more important. Some observers have charged that excessive regulation contributed to the slowing productivity performance of the U.S. economy. There is no doubt that the reallocation of resources toward mandated pollution controls and occupational safety has diverted investment and entrepreneurial effort from alternative objectives. From the perspective of the business decision maker, these regulations are burdensome. Safety standards on the job must be met. Automobiles and smokestacks must not exceed specified pollutant emissions. And sometimes the precise way to meet the standards is not known until regulations are written—often in an arbitrary and costly manner. However, the consumer benefits from cleaner air and the worker benefits from greater safety represent improvements even if they are not measured in the GNP.

Recently, the climate with respect to regulation has begun to turn in the direction of an easing of regulatory standards toward more realistic objectives though, ideally, not toward their elimination. Moreover, since the late 1970s, we have seen a widespread new deregulation strategy with regard to the traditionally regulated industries such as transportation, communications, and banking and finance. These fields are undergoing fundamental structural changes: new competition in air transportation and trucking; the breakup of the American Telephone and Telegraph Company after an antitrust settlement; and wide-ranging institutional changes in banking and finance. These developments introduce new uncertainties. They may affect behavior of the participants in the economy in far-reaching ways.

An illustration of how significant small changes can be on the behavior of the economy as a whole is provided by the impact of some of the first steps in the restructuring of the financial system. Until the late 1970s the savings and loans associations (S&Ls) were under fairly tight restrictions with respect to the interest rates they could charge for mortgages and those they could pay to depositors. Consequently, when short-term market interest rates rose in times of tight money, funds would be diverted from the S&Ls into short-term financial paper where higher returns could be obtained. The result was a shortage of funds for mortgages, and an abrupt decline in residential construction. This process, called "disintermediation" after the movement of funds out of the intermediary S&L institutions, was a regular feature of the postwar business cycle.

Even the first limited steps toward deregulating financial institutions significantly altered this phenomenon. Usury ceilings on mortgage rates were lifted. At the same time S&Ls were permitted to issue high interest rate savings certificates and to participate in the certificate of deposit (CD) market with short-term CDs competitive with other short-term financial instruments. Disintermediation was no more! In place of a sudden shortage of mortgage money when the Fed tightens its monetary screws, funds remain available—sometimes at sky high rates. Nor surprisingly, this has altered behavior in the housing market. The decline in housing starts in 1981–82 was much slower in coming and required much higher interest rates than in previous recessions. Forecasters were forced to adjust their models to take account of the impact of this institutional change.

The changes in financial institutions in the past few years are small compared to the coming revolution of financial mechanisms. Electronic funds transfer and money machines may make money balances well-nigh obsolete. S&Ls are being turned into full service banks, commercial banks are extending into brokerage, and the "financial supermarket" is likely to replace them all. No one knows yet what will be the implications for the economy and for the behavior of investors as a result of the changes that will be taking place in financial markets over the next few years.

Changes in Government Policy

The fundamental philosophy underlying government policy has changed significantly. These changes are not just the ordinary shifts in tax rates and expenditure plans that take place over any period of years. Econometric models are well adapted to consider the impacts of moderate shifts in fiscal and monetary policy. In fact, the study of alternative policy scenarios, so-called "what if" simulations, is one of the most important uses of econometric models. The type of policy change that has occurred in recent years is a change in the underlying philosophy likely to persist to some degree across Republican and Democratic administrations alike.

With the apparent ineffectiveness of macroeconomic policy to meet the objectives of full employment and price stability during the 1970s has come the recognition that a policy of economic stabilization by means of fiscal and monetary measures may no longer work well. Some economists following old-fashioned conservative precepts have interpreted this to mean that government should not attempt counter-cyclical policies. Others continue to recognize the political necessity of taking policy action when unemployment is high or when runaway inflation threatens. In general, we are now willing to stand for deeper and longer periods of recession than we were willing to tolerate in the immediate postwar period. Such a rightward shift in priorities has occurred in Europe as well as in the United States. In the future, a more positive view of counter-cyclical policy, perhaps combined with incomes policies or other approaches, may be taken. But a realistic appraisal of the options leads to the conclusion that the dream of "fine tuning" the

"Remember the good old days when all the economy needed
was a little fine-tuning?"

Drawing by Dana Fradon; Copyright © 1983, the New Yorker Magazine, Inc.

economy for stable growth did not work out and that economic swings may be wider in the coming decades in part because of less vigorous counter-cyclical stabilization policy.

Another story of increased uncertainty due to changes in the philosophy of policy can be told with regard to the international exchange rates. Until 1971, international exchange rates were stabilized under the Bretton Woods Agreement. To be sure, the rates were not quite fixed even then since exchange rate readjustments occurred whenever there was a so-called "fundamental disequilibrium." In 1971, however, the United States devalued the dollar and the world went to a system of floating exchange rates. The uncertainty in the international economy has increased considerably since then.

This is not simply a change in institutions or in approach. Instead, it reflects a fundamental change in policy, a decision that floating exchange rates might be more effective than intervention. Indeed, the Reagan Administration has indicated that it prefers not to intervene in foreign exchange markets to stabilize exchange rates (i.e., the "dirty float" practiced by many other countries). Some economists in the monetarist tradition dream of a return to fixed exchange rates in the framework of a gold standard, but it is not likely that such an objective can be achieved. Thus, business decisions must be made in an uncertain world without the benefit of government efforts to stabilize exchange rates at fixed parities.

Implications for Business Decision Making

What are the consequences of these profound changes for business decision making? Clearly, they imply a continuation of much uncertainty, probably greater uncertainty than our earlier postwar experience. For the business executive who must make decisions in the face of this uncertainty, the need for forecasts is all the greater. Econometrics for business forecasting and planning can help to reduce these uncertainties.

Modern econometrics is not the esoteric field that it once was. It is being widely applied in the business world. The time-shared computer and, more recently, the business planner's own personal computer have made vast data bases accessible. Statisti-

---

Weather forecasters have developed a useful way of presenting uncertain forecasts—probability. Forecasts are presented as "a 90% probability of sunshine and a 10% probability of rain." On the basis of this kind of information, we decide whether to carry an umbrella. In either event, however, the weather forecaster can never be said to be wrong!

cal estimation, modeling, and visual presentation techniques are readily available in most business economics and planning departments. The potential for using these new methods for forecasting and for studying alternative scenarios is virtually without limit. But we must remember that decisions must be made in an uncertain world. This uncertainty can be reduced, but it cannot be eliminated.

Plan of the Book

This book presents two main focuses:

- From the model of the economy to forecasting for the industry and firm.
- From the central mainframe computers to the microcomputer on the executive's desk.

The first part of the book, Chapters 2 to 6, is concerned with the macro economy—that is, the underlying theories, measurement, structure, and forecasting performance of the macromodel. This material is of general interest. Its particular appeal is to people who are concerned, privately or professionally, with the economy as an aggregate.

The second half of the book, Chapters 7 to 9, focuses on forecasting for the industry and the firm. Inevitably, the material is somewhat more narrow and technical than in the first part of the book. These chapters appeal particularly to practicing business planners and to the executives who rely on their work. Finally, Chapter 10 develops some perspectives on the future of business forecasting and how it will be organized in the age of the microcomputer.

Further Readings

The annual *Economic Report* of the Council of Economic Advisers provides a convenient starting point for appraising recent developments and the implications of institutional change and economic policy. The Brookings Institution also published many books and papers that are concerned with current economic issues, for example, Alice

M. Rivlin, ed., *Economic Choices 1987* (Washington, D.C.: Brookings, 1986). On a more technical level, the *Brookings Papers in Economic Activity*, which appear twice yearly, consider the most important current questions of economic performance, theory, and policy. *The Reagan Record*, edited by John L. Palmer and Isabel V. Sawhill (Washington: Urban Institute Press, 1984), presents a comprehensive evaluation of the success or failure of recent economic policy. The same issues are viewed from a more conservative perspectives by scholars of the American Enterprise Institute and the Hoover Institution.

Note

1. Denison, Edward F., *Accounting for Slower Economic Growth* (Washington: Brookings, 1979); and *Trends in American Economic Growth, 1929–1982* (Washington: Brookings, 1985).

*". . . First I was a Keynesian . . . Next I was a monetarist
. . . Then a supplysider . . . Now I'm a bum . . ."*
Drawing by Bill Schorr, 1982 Los Angeles Herald Examiner

❖ 2 ❖

Economic Theories:
"Old" and "New"—
The Implications
for Economic Forecasting

The ideas of economists and political philosophers, both when they are right and when they are wrong, are more powerful than is commonly understood. Indeed, the world is ruled by little else. Practical men, who believe themselves to be quite exempt from any intellectual influences, are usually the slaves of some defunct economist.[1]

Behind the forecast lies a theoretical perception of how the economy operates. Without some theory of how the conscious and implicit forces guiding the economy's path work, forecasting would become mere intellectual dart throwing. So, what are the theoretical underpinnings of the forecasting process? This is all the more important since, justifiably or not, many "new" theories may be crowding out some of the older views.

The substantial consensus on Keynesian aggregate demand theory of the 1960s has evolved into a number of new doctrines—monetarism, supply side economics, and rational expectations, for example—which compete for the forecaster's attention. Are these new theories necessary or appropriate? Has economic behavior changed? Are new theories widely used to forecast and, if so, are they a more effective basis for forecasting than the old ones? These questions are the concern of this chapter.

There have, indeed, been new developments in economics during the 1970s and 1980s. Some are useful, but others are speculative and, in some cases, confused. There have also been behavioral, institutional, and policy changes with important implications. However, the macroeconometric model approach to economic forecasting, which was first developed using Keynesian theory, has not been replaced by a new orthodoxy. Changes in the economy and in theory are not being disregarded. Econometrics offers a scientific approach to testing and measuring competing theoretical hypotheses. As they are validated, they are being incorporated into the forecast models. Thus, new ideas extend—but do not replace—traditional econometric forecasting methods.

The Total Demand Approach

Modern economic theory and forecasting developed largely in the Keynesian tradition with emphasis on demand. The current academic vogue of the new classical economics notwithstanding, Keynesian economics—much maligned, frequently misunderstood, and greatly modified—remains the basis that lies behind most macroeconometric models. Keynesian theory has been called "depression economics" and, indeed, it developed as a response to the inability of classical economic theory to deal with the 1930s phenomenon of long periods of unemployment and underutilization. But the focus on demand as a determinant of output and on the cyclical movements of business activity is not just a matter of depressions. It applies as well at the boom phase of the cycle. It has become the central emphasis of business forecasters and of government policy makers.

Today, we better understand the essential elements of the Keynesian framework, how it must be augmented to deal with the world of inflation as well as recession, and its limitations. Keynesian theory brings together the determination of output in the economy's market for goods and services, the interest rate in its money market, and the production and labor sectors. It is a comprehensive theory of how the economy operates.

The determination of the economy's level of operation is dominated by demand. In other words, within the limits of production capacity, businesses produce in response to what they can sell. If demand is insufficient to absorb what the econ-

Drawing by J-C Suares, originally published in the Atlantic Monthly, September 1985.

omy is producing, inventories pile up, and production schedules are cut back. The result is a recession or a depression. The
business cycle experience of the postwar period illustrates this
phenomenon repeatedly.

Business cycle swings have been dominated by demand side
forces, some originating outside the system (the technical term
is *exogenous*) such as the Korean and Vietnam wars and the
OPEC oil shocks, fiscal and monetary policy changes, and other
factors originating within the dynamic of the economy itself, for
example, in inventory and investment cycles.

Postwar business cycles have been more moderate than the
depressions and crises of the prewar period. This may reflect
improved institutions, better understanding by business and
government of how demand forces operate, and, until recently, a greater commitment to stabilization policy.

Fiscal and Monetary Policy

The original emphasis of Keynesians was on stabilization
through counter-cyclical fiscal policy—that is, increasing gov-

ernment expenditures and implementing tax cuts during recessions and imposing spending cuts and tax increases at times
when the economy is bumping against its capacity ceilings. But
even the most traditional Keynesians have long recognized the
importance of monetary policy as an influence on demand. The
critical linkage in the Keynesian system between demand and
the monetary sector is the rate of interest that impacts on the
real economy by way of its effect on business fixed investment,
inventory accumulation, residential construction, and consumer durable purchases. In turn, the interest rate is determined by equilibrium in the money market and by the need for
money balances as contrasted to the supply of monetary reserves made available by the Federal Reserve (the Fed).

The Fed's management of monetary policy, an important force
in influencing the economy, is focused on (1) the growth of
money supply and (2) interest rates. However, the Fed weighs
heavily economic conditions in general—unemployment, inflation, growth, and the international situation of the dollar—in
reaching its policy decisions.

The business executive sees the immediate impact of Fed policy
in the credit markets. Questions typically asked by financial executives of their economic consultants are: What are prospects
for long- and short-term interest rates? Will there be a "win-
dow" during which it will be advantageous to go to financial
markets? What is the condition of equity markets?

Labor Markets and Supply

Keynesian theory recognizes that there can be periods of unemployment, when the economy operates below its full production potential. The wage-employment mechanism does not
quickly tend to adjust toward a full employment (or, in modern
terminology, to a natural unemployment rate) equilibrium. This
is not to say that Keynesians assume away the operation of
market forces in labor markets. Rather they observe the slowness of labor market adjustments and recognize that wage adjustments cannot be expected to greatly affect employment over
the course of a business cycle.

The Keynesian system does not, as some people charge, lack

a supply side. The supply mechanism in the model represents the constraint to production imposed by the output potential of the economy. That in turn is limited by the available stock of capital, the labor force, and productivity. Inflation occurs in the system as aggregate demand rises relative to the supply constraint.

The concept of aggregate supply, that is, the economy's production capacity, has been quite elusive. In the 1970s, inflationary price increases as a consequence of demand pressures began to mount long before the economy was at full capacity. Thus, it is necessary to look at the composition of industry output where bottlenecks can develop before the total economy is fully employed. Business executives are often well aware of the building up of demand pressure strains. These strains can be seen through growing order backlogs, delivery delays, declining quality, and, sometimes, rising prices as the economy approaches its full capacity.

A similar phenomenon can be seen in labor markets where wage pressures relate inversely to the unemployment rate. In tight labor markets wages are bid up. As will be noted in more detail later, a critical consideration in this regard is how much workers adjust their demands for higher wages to their expectations about prices. Post-Keynesians have introduced a cost markup mechanism that makes it possible for prices to rise when the economy is operating well below full capacity as a result of cost pressures originating from excessive labor union wage settlements or from oil price increases, for example.

Implications for Forecasting

What are the implications of Keynesian theory for forecasting? The focus on demand provides an important initial handle for forecasting. In the short term, business activity responds largely to demand and short-term forecasts can be built around a detailed analysis of demand. In effect, the forecaster is asking: what is the level of aggregate production that can be supported by the expected purchasing of consumers, investors, government, and foreign markets?

The importance of public policy in influencing demand does

Business forecasters worth their salt will look first at the demand for their product. The worst situation is to have product and no market!

not go unrecognized. The budget and its implications are central to most forecast analyses. The issue in most political controversies is not whether macro policies have an impact but rather whether they have been managed so as to achieve counter-cyclical (rather than pro-cyclical) results.

Supply phenomena and inflation have been a difficult challenge for Keynesian forecasters. The long-run growth of GNP can be seen as a supply side phenomenon. The economy's output potential is determined by the available labor force and its productivity. Productivity trends, in turn, reflect the impact of numerous interrelated forces, the capital intensity of production, technology, the makeup of the labor force, and the composition and scale of production. At times, when the economy is in a recession and when there is ample capacity, supply limits may not be operational and demand forces have free play. But, as seen during the 1960s and 1970s, specific sectoral supply constraints produce inflation even when an economy is substantially below full capacity. The forecaster must watch these inflationary forces closely whether they originate from domestic wage pressures or from external events.

Money and interest rates are drawing increasing attention. When interest rates were traditionally quite low, it was customary to assume that expenditures were insensitive to interest rates. This is no longer true. The cost of capital has perceptible impact on investment and even on consumer spending, when interest rates are as high as in the recent past. Consequently, monetary factors play an important role in the real forecast as well as in the financial forecast. That is why there has been a rising chorus of concern about the inconsistencies of recent American monetary and fiscal policy. Loose fiscal policy—that is, large deficits—along with monetary restraint is a recipe for high interest rates. To the typical forecaster, these represent dark clouds on the economic horizon.

The simplest Keynesian model must be enlarged to deal with the internationalization of the U.S. economy. Some economists argue that the United States is still managing its domestic policy as if the outside world did not matter. However, the forecaster must recognize the important role of foreign economic activity and of the exchange rate on the competitiveness between American and foreign products. In a more or less open economy, the important interactions of interest rates and exchange rates also affect the forecast. The Keynesian theoretical framework has been considerably broadened to take these factors into account.

A final point must be made here. In this context, the Keynesian or aggregate demand approach is presented as a way of analyzing economic forces and of forecasting. It does not follow that one must go along with what, perhaps unjustifiably, have been called Keynesian policy prescriptions for demand management and "fine tuning." Moreover, in many respects, modern econometric forecasting methods are a far cry from the old-fashioned Keynesian approach, incorporating new theoretical concepts in important ways. Many practitioners of aggregate demand forecasting would be unhappy indeed to see themselves called Keynesians.

The aggregate demand approach had become the workhorse method for economic forecasting. Some business economists use simple short-cut methods, others rely on complex econometric models. But no matter what the theoretical philosophy, most economists approach the short-term forecast with demand side tools. On the other hand, as we will see in more detail in Chapter 5, long-term projections are based principally on growth of the production potential of the economy—that is, on the supply side.

The New Approaches

A number of new ideas have drawn the attention of economists and forecasters. It would be too strong to say that these ideas have revolutionized the field, but they have certainly caused all of us—conservatives and liberals alike—to rethink our approach. New ideas do not spring like Venus out of a clamshell. They have their foundation in the failure of old approaches to explain what is going on, specifically, the combination of inflation and economic stagnation that characterized the economy in the 1970s. We now turn our attention to what the principal new economic theories attempt to explain and to their strengths and weaknesses.

Monetarism

The monetarist approach to analysis and forecasting has its roots in the old empirical generalization known as the quantity theory of money. This approach relates the nominal growth of demand to the expansion of the money supply and, given a fixed real output, it translates monetary growth into inflation. Friedman makes a broad generalization: "Faster monetary growth tends to be followed after some three to nine months by economic expansion; slower monetary growth by economic contraction" (Milton Friedman in *Business Week*, July 12, 1982, p. 64). There is no mention of inflation here, but monetarists typically correlate inflation with rapid monetary expansion.

The monetarist view led in two directions, one of them related to forecasts and the other to policy prescription. The monetarist view of forecasts was translated into the empirical forecasting equations of the St. Louis Federal Reserve Bank by simply relating economic activity to money supply. This provided verification for Friedman's statement quoted above. With respect to prescription, there is the notion that (1) money supply should grow more slowly than the growth of nominal demand so as to slow down inflation and (2) monetary growth should be steady so as to steady the course of economic expansion. The first implies high interest rates and economic stagnation. The second is difficult to achieve because money growth is volatile and hard to keep within fixed bounds.

As noted above, forecasters have increasingly recognized the need to follow monetary developments and to integrate them into their models. At most times, the movements of the principal monetary aggregates are pretty good indicators of prospects for consumer and business spending. And economists, even those who would be most unhappy to be called monetarists, see at least a long-run tie between the money supply and the potential for inflation. Certainly an uncontrolled expansion of money supply can set the stage for rapid inflation, as has been demonstrated time and time again in many parts of the world. A structural view of the role of money comes out with a rather more complex picture than the "too many dollars chasing too few goods" notion of inflationary processes. Structurally, money balances do influence spending perhaps even in part directly, but, more largely, the effect of money is through interest rates and availability of credit. These are the mechanisms that immediately influence consumer purchases of cars, other durables, houses, and business investments.

Money Supply and Monetary Policy The Federal Reserve has found it extremely difficult to maintain the desired steady path of money supply. Every year, the Fed announces ranges for its monetary growth targets—between 4½ and 9% for demand deposits and currency for the year starting in late 1984, for example—but monetary growth has a habit of straying out of even these broad limits. Measurement of the monetary aggregates is imprecise. Business credit demands fluctuate over the year in accord with seasons, tax deadlines, business failures, and so on. Finally, the very definition of money is threatened as a result of institutional and behavioral changes such as the creation of money market funds and NOW accounts. We write checks against our savings accounts! We receive interest on our checking deposits! We can overdraw these accounts and automatically establish credit as needed. Not only does this change the velocity of money—each dollar of money balance can support a larger value of transactions—it challenges the liquidity concept that enters into the monetarist equation. In any case, the

---

An interesting sidelight on this issue is being posed by the transition to electronic funds transfer and "gold" credit cards. Once these technologies reach universal use, there will be no need for money balances. What then is the definition of money? Whither monetarism?

Federal Reserve has found it extremely difficult to smooth out the growth of money supply, however defined. We will consider the alternate ways of measuring of money supply in the next chapter

Despite a "steady as you go" policy, monetary growth has tended to fluctuate so that the strictest monetarists have charged the Fed with doing an inadequate job. The consequences for interest rates were even more serious: the rates became unstable and spiked up to record levels in 1982 while the Fed had adopted a policy of strict monetarism. When the Fed eased its policy stance, interest rates dropped, though real interest rates— that is, the nominal interest rate less inflationary expectations—have remained high. But there are continued fears that that the Fed's efforts to limit monetary growth in the face of large federal deficits mean that interest rates will continue to be high and even that further monetary restraint might cause interest rates to soar again.

On one side is sentiment toward a flexible monetary policy. The preamble to the Federal Reserve Act of 1913 calls for the creation of an "elastic currency" to meet the needs of business and finance. On the other side are those who would argue that the Federal Reserve has little or no leeway. Once committed to a stated set of monetary growth targets, deviations from these target levels cause markets to react. Thus, if monetary growth is allowed at rates above the upper target level, the market will assume either that this growth is inflationary—that is, the Fed is going to stoke the fires of inflation—or that the Fed will sharply reduce monetary growth at a later point in order to meet its targets. In either case, higher interest rates result. A Catch 22 world like this one leaves little scope for discretionary monetary policy.

Monetarism and Forecasting   What then are the implications of monetarism for forecasting? Clearly, money must be taken seriously. It has had—and will continue to have—significant influence on the economy. Just as clearly, monetary policy must be taken into account in the forecasting process. If the Federal Reserve is firmly committed to a policy of steady monetary growth, this policy, and the responses of consumers and investors to it, must be built into the forecast. On the other hand, this does not mean that the forecast must either be developed out of a simple monetarist equation linking GNP growth to a fixed monetary growth path or that the forecaster can assume a fixed monetary growth path. The Fed's aim of smoothing the path of money supply must be considered, but that is clearly not the Fed's only, or even its most important, objective. The minutes of the Federal Reserve's Open Market Committee, puslished with some weeks' time delay in the Federal Reserve Bulletin, show that Federal Reserve deliberations typically take into account many dimensions of the economic outlook, for example, retail sales and inventories, unemployment, inflation, interest rates, the foreign exchange rate, the situation of the banking system, and the growth of monetary aggregates.

Numerous factors, not the least of which would be consumer and investor expectations, influence the economic outlook, even if the Federal Reserve followed a strict monetarist rule. Consequently, relying only on the monetarist approach is not a very effective way to forecast. Most economists and forecasters recognize the importance of money, however, and monetarism has had profound implications for how and what we predict.

Supply Side Economics

The ideas of supply side economics are also a response to economic conditions. For many years, there has been concern about the failure of the U.S. economy to achieve rapid growth of productivity and to maintain its competitiveness in international markets. There has also been considerable uncertainty about the cause of the productivity lag. The consensus is, however, that to put the economy back on a fast track of economic growth the United States needs to both invest more in new machinery and equipment to modernize its industrial capacity and introduce new labor-saving technologies such as robots. From this perspective, we are all supply siders! The proposals for investment incentives and rapid depreciation considered by the Carter Administration and incorporated by the Reagan Administration into its Capital Recovery Act (the so-called 15-10-5-3 tax lives proposal) fall into this tradition.

In response to the dissatisfaction of the American middle class—heavily burdened by rising taxes—the supply side ideas were merged with the Kemp-Roth proposals for large reductions in personal income taxes. The notion of the Laffer curve, which held that economic activity was being greatly impeded by high marginal tax rates, had considerable appeal. Some optimists believed along with Arthur Laffer that lower tax rates would actually bring in more tax revenues. Even people who did not believe that the effects were as important as Laffer and the Kemp-Roth proponents maintained were led to support the idea that marginal tax rates were too high and that tax rate reductions, particularly at the upper end of the income scale, would significantly increase work effort and savings and investments. Thus, reductions in *personal* tax rates, became the keynote of Reagan's supply side policy. There was hope that cuts in tax revenues could be matched by cuts in government spending, but these expenditure cuts have not been realized.

Much empirical work was carried out in an effort to verify the supply side hypotheses (i.e., there would be large increases in work effort and in savings and investment as a result of the personal income tax cuts). It has been possible to measure some impacts, though so far not of the magnitudes that had been hoped for. It is difficult to test the effect of changes in the progressivity of the income tax schedule. Most economists would argue, moreover, that the returns are not yet in, that it might take a long time for consumers and investors to adjust to the tax law changes. However, the fiscal results of the last three years show clearly that the revenue impacts of supply side change in personal income tax rates are not so great as to offset the rate reductions. There have been large declines in tax receipts and, in the absence of corresponding expenditure cuts, there are big deficits!

Supply Side and Forecasting   What then are the implications of supply side for model builders and forecasters? In the early phases of the Reagan Administration it was widely argued that the old models no longer worked, that the Keynesian model did not contain a supply side, and that new "supply side" models were required to forecast the optimistic new world that was about to unfold. Much of that misguided enthusiasm has faded. There is a grain of truth—but only a grain—to the contention that the old models no longer worked. The traditional model has had difficulty in explaining and forecasting some of the complexities of the current world (the cost and supply problems associated with the oil crisis, for example). And it must be recognized that the supply side in Keynesian models was frequently rudimentary and that traditional modelers, concentrating largely on short-run business cycle forecasts, paid little attention to the determinants of supply.

It is not clear that "supply side only" models can be built or, for that matter, that they would be useful. Both supply and demand play a role. It is clear, however, that the dialogue about the supply side has caused model builders to look for supply side effects wherever the data would support them. As a result most models are more supply-oriented today than they were 10 years ago.

At the beginning of its term, the new Reagan Administration turned to a new model that emphasized rational expectations and the supply side—the Rutledge model built at the Claremont Graduate School in California. But the predictions of this model were so unrealistically rosy that the Council of Economic Advisers (CEA) toned them down. Murray Weidenbaum, chairman of the CEA at that time, claimed subsequently that no model was used to make the forecasts for 1981 and 1982.

Conventional macromodels recognize the personal income tax changes, but there may still be some need for adjustment to fully allow for the marginal effects of the tax cuts, with respect to both work effort and savings and investment. Only the most detailed models take into account the income distribution effects of changes in the tax structure. Moreover, it takes elaborate structural representation of the financial sectors to recognize the impact of saving on the availability of funding for capital investment. This is not fully represented in many models currently in use.

Consequently, while a lot has been done, there may still be some way to go to integrate the effects of tax incentives into the supply side of econometric forecasting models. This work is proceeding. In the meantime, forecasters have adjusted their predictions as best as possible to capture the full impact of supply side changes. The impact of these developments can be focused in narrow parts of the model structure. Can one expect changes in labor supply and over what kind of a time horizon? Can increases in saving be anticipated? Do they translate into increased investment? What is the effect of the large deficits on financial markets and how may they impede the sought-after investment? What is likely to be the impact of investment on the growth of capital stock and the nation's productive potential? These questions can be addressed with the macromodels and taken into account in the forecast.

Rational Expectations and the "New Classical" Economics

It goes almost without saying that expectations are critical in explaining economic behavior—consumers' expectations about their future income streams influence their spending and investors' expectations about the economic environment influence their investment decision. Expectations are individual forecasts about the future. They may reflect a variety of forces: the recent economic situation, expectations about outside pressures (e.g., oil prices in the Middle East), known or anticipated policies by the public sector, and even personal optimism and pessimism. In a sense, expectations are "what it is all about."

To this complex field a new concept has been added in recent years, that of "rational expectations." The term is undeniably attractive. Technically, it means that economic agents appraise the future correctly on average. Taking all known facts into account, they may err on either side of the ultimate outcome, but on balance they will guess correctly. This is not a statement of fact, it is a theoretical hypothesis whose implications are being investigated widely. Yet it has already had considerable influence in the policy arena.

The introduction of rational expectations considerations into public policy is unique. This concept originated in the high altitudes of abstract theory. Unlike the other doctrines considered above, rational expectations did not arise as a response to public needs and concerns. The concept was invented to resolve a theoretical contradiction. Most economic theory is based on the assumption that economic decision makers maximize and that they make, on average, careful and logical decisions. But Keynesian theory assumes that workers do not act in the same logical way when they seek wage increases because they are not fully aware of the impact of higher wages on prices. This proposition served as an explanation for the fact that wages are sticky and that labor markets do not tend quickly toward full employment. That has been a problem for macro theory. Economists have sought for almost 50 years to find a way around it. The notion that workers might after all take properly into account all available information, leaving only unknown and presumably random forces, has tremendous appeal on theoretical grounds. Thus, rational expectations has had wide influence in the field of theoretical economics.

Rational Expectations and the Phillips Curve   An illustration of the implications of rational expectations for wages and prices is a good indication. Figure 2-1 shows the relation between wage increase and unemployment, the so-called Phillips curve. This relationship, a classic in economics, finds its way, in some form, into almost all macromodels. The relationship is nonlinear: when labor markets are tight, pressures for higher wage increases mount, but even when there is lots of unemployment, there is little if any tendency for wages to decline. The solid line assumes unrealistically that workers are not aware of the fact that wage increases translate into price increases; they are primarily concerned with money wages. According to the chart, at an unemployment rate of 4% wage demands are assumed to be at a rate of 6% (A). But since productivity typically only increases at an annual rate of 2%, prices must rise, roughly by the 4% difference. As a result of this inflation, workers who had expected an increase in pay of 6% are left with only a 2% increase in real purchasing power. The response might be to ask for a nominal increase sufficient to also offset the 4% price rise, say 10% (B) (10% less 4% inflation would yield real wage increase of 6%). This is shown in the dashed Phillips curve on the chart. But this does not represent a rational view of inflation *either* since

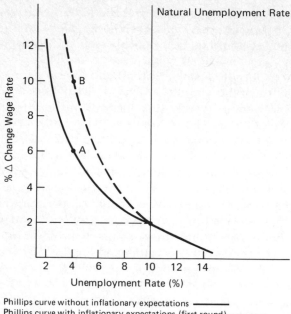

Phillips curve without inflationary expectations ━━━━━
Phillips curve with inflationary expectations (first round) ━ ━

Figure 2-1. The shifting Phillips curve.

it is obvious that 10% wage increases would result in a still higher
rate of inflation than the assumed 4%. We could draw a still
steeper Phillips curve as workers become increasingly aware of
the interaction between wage and price increases.

If workers were fully rational, they would immediately recognize that wage increases would result in price increases, and
they would demand ever higher nominal wage increases to offset the anticipated price increases. Carrying this idea to its logical extreme produces a vertical Phillips curve at an unemployment level, termed the natural unemployment rate. At that
unemployment rate, wage increases consistent with the growth
of productivity (2% in the assumed case) are possible without
causing inflationary pressure. Unemployment below the so-called
natural level would produce inflation (without limit). Stability
can be achieved only if unemployment increases until the natural unemployment rate is reestablished. The assumption of rational expectations has resurrected the world of the classical

economics, hence, "new classical" economics. If worker expectations are fully rational, the economy would be tied to a natural unemployment rate that public policy can do little about.

Rational Expectations and Policy   Economists have been hard at work developing the implications of the assumption that expectations are rational. These implications are far reaching, and may be damaging to the notion that public policy can consistently influence economic activity and employment. Carrying the rational expectations idea to its irrational extreme, some theorists have been using oversimplified models to prove that, if all aspects of expectations are in rational expectations equilibrium, fiscal policy cannot be effective except insofar as people are surprised or deceived. But this is an example of how extreme and unrealistic assumptions can produce extreme and unrealistic results. Other economists have been equally hard at work demonstrating that the assumption of rational expectations is extreme and that it is not supported by real world facts. In that case, there remains an important role for stabilization policy.

In mid-1982, this author was severely challenged during a talk to a business economics colloquium, held, incidentally, at one of the regional Federal Reserve banks. I had recommended that the Fed ease monetary policy, expanding money supply in order to bring down interest rates and stimulate investment. A member of the audience stood up and asked whether I was unaware of the "fact" that *increases* in the money supply were associated with *increases* in interest rates. A rational expectations view, he said, would suggest that more money would lead to inflationary expectations and, hence, to higher interest rates.

Only a couple of weeks later, in a move that was probably in the works before my talk took place, the Fed switched from its policy of strict monetarism to easier money. The stock market rallied and interest rates dropped sharply! This is not to suggest that expectations are not rational, only to say that what appears rational to one observer may not be rational to another.

The rational expectations notion was used in a unique way during 1981 to paper over some inconsistencies of the early Reagan economic program. The problem was that supply side policies without corresponding budget cuts were likely to lead to large budget deficits. Some people were arguing that together with restrictive monetary policy deficits would produce high interest rates and thwart the very investment the supply side program was intended to stimulate. It was said, at that time, that the key to making Reaganomics work was to persuade the public at large that the Administration and the Federal Reserve were truly serious about their anti-inflationary policy stance. If the public could be persuaded that these policies would effectively reduce inflation, inflationary expectations would be eased. In a rational expectations world, easing of wage pressures and price escalation would follow, the inflationary component of interest rates would be eliminated, and, to a significant extent, even the deficit would fade away.

But the public did not believe. On Wall Street, the Dow Jones index dropped by 200 points in the eight weeks following the passage of the tax cut legislation. In a hearing before a Congressional Committee in mid-1981, former Presidential economic adviser Alan Greenspan suggested that public fears that spending would not be cut sufficiently were because President Reagan had said there would be a safety net that would protect the needy and the aged. Senator Heinz responded that maybe the public did not believe because of plans to sharply increase defense spending. Surely both of them were partly right. In any case, the rational expectations argument did not work out as planned. The American consumer and investor are more rational than they had been given credit for after all!

Rational Expectations and Forecasting   What, then, are the implications of rational expectations for econometric models and forecasting? Does this represent a useful paradigm for business forecasting? The answer is "maybe." Even advanced econometricians are not yet in a position to estimate complex econometric models that fully embody the rational expectations assumption in all relevant structural components. But to do that would be inappropriate, in any case. Little is known about how expectations are formed. The critical issue is whether workers anticipate the full inflationary effect of any wage increase. Workers today are much better informed about inflation than they used to be. People do learn from experience and, as a consequence, the trade-off between inflation and unemployment today is even less favorable than it was before the inflationary binge of the 1970s. This must be recognized by the forecasting model. On the other hand, it is not clear that the inflationary implications of wage increases are fully predicted. After all, many wage adjustments are not in anticipation of inflation but simply to make up for last year's price increase. Economists are not in agreement that rational expectations, narrowly defined, exist in labor markets or in other aspects of economic decision making. There is no more reason to assume that economic agents are fully rational in their expectations than to assume that they are uninfluenced by expected future events and by the implications of policy.

There is still room to incorporate expectation effects into models—in fact, there is still much to learn about them. For the moment, model forecasters take expectational phenomena into account as best they can by drawing on recent experience to adjust the critical relationships where expectations play a role, by drawing on anticipation survey variables where available, and, most importantly, by not swinging their forecasts too far in the direction where the expectational "tail" might sway the structural economic "dog."

Postscript

Does this discussion mean that current forecasting practice ignores the new ideas of economics? This question can be safely answered in the negative. Insofar as the new hypotheses can be sustained, they belong into the forecasting models. And, as we have pointed out, steps have been and are being taken to put them there.

The reader should be reminded that it is not a single issue economy. Paying attention to the supply side does not mean that one can ignore demand. Emphasizing monetarism does not answer the questions about real economic activity and employment. The entire theoretical system is needed to consider the interrelated aspects of an exceedingly complex economy. As we will note in greater detail below, the tendency has been away from simplistic models, to complex systems that explicitly recognize numerous aspects of the economy. While these systems are complicated and costly to operate, they better meet the needs of forecasters than do models focused on a single issue or built around an overly simple theory.

Further Readings

A number of current textbooks provide a survey of macroeconomic theory. Among the most popular macro textbooks are Rudiger Dornbusch and Stanley Fischer, *Macroeconomics* 3rd edition (New York: McGraw-Hill, 1984), and Robert J. Gordon, *Macroeconomics,* 3rd edition (Boston: Little Brown, 1984). In striking contrast to traditional macro books, Robert J. Barro, *Macroeconomics* (New York: John Wiley and Sons, 1984), focuses entirely on the "new classical" economics and relegates Keynesian theory to Chapter 19! Elizabeth S. Johnson and Harvey G. Johnson, *The Shadow of Keynes* (Chicago: University of Chicago Press, 1979), provides an interesting look back at the development of Keynesian economics.

Numerous new books consider the revolution(s) in economic theory. Lester C. Thurow of MIT provides a good introduction to the various new lines of thought in *Dangerous Currents: The State of Economics,* (New York: Vintage books, Random House, 1983). Another survey with papers of many influential economists is Daniel Bell and Irving Kristol, eds., *The Crisis in Economic Theory,* (New York: Basic Books, 1981). Arjo Klamer, *Conversations with Economists,* (Totowa, N.J.: Rowman and Allenheld, 1983), contains interviews with leading Keynesian and neoclassical economists. Looking back historically, there is T. W. Hutchison, *The Politics and Philosophy of Economics,* (New York: New York University Press, 1984). Focusing on more recent theoretical issues is Jerome L. Stein, *Monetarist, Keynesian and New Classical Economics* (New York: New York University Press, 1984).

Post-Keynesian economics is surveyed in: A. S. Eichner, *A Guide to Post Keynesian Economics* (White Plains: M. E. Sharpe, 1979).

Monetarism has been surveyed in Thomas Mayer, ed., *The Structure of Monetarism* (New York: Norton, 1978) and in David Laidler, *Mone-*

tarist Perspectives (Oxford: Philip Allan, 1982). Friedman's most recent empirical study of the relation of money to income and prices is Milton Friedman and Anna Schwartz, *Monetary Trends in the United States and the United Kingdom* (Chicago: University of Chicago Press, 1982).

A bible of supply side economics is George Gilder, *Wealth and Poverty*, (New York: Basic Books, 1981). Empirical tests of supply side concepts are in Victor A. Canto, Douglas H. Joines, and Arthur B. Laffer, *Foundations of Supply Side Economics* (New York: Academic Press, 1983), and Michael K. Evans, *The Truth About Supply Side Economics* (New York: Basic Books, 1983). A report on the results of the policy change so far is John L. Palmer and Isabel V. Sawhill, *The Reagan Record* (Washington: Urban Institute Press, 1984).

Daniel K. H. Begg, *The Rational Expectations Revolution in Macroeconomics* (Baltimore: John Hopkins, 1982), and Stanley Fisher, ed., *Rational Expectations and Economic Policy* (Chicago: University of Chicago, 1980), cover the rational expectations question. A primer on this difficult subject is Rodney Maddock and Michael Carter, "A Child's Guide to Rational Expectations," *Journal of Economic Literature* (March 1982).

Note

1. Keynes, John Maynard, *The General Theory of Employment, Interest and Money* (New York: Harcourt Brace, 1936), p. 383.

"I think we can definitely say that things are looking up"

from Herblock Through the Looking Glass (W.W. Norton, 1984)

✤ 3 ✤

Measuring the
Economic Environment—
The Statistics

The greater the uncertainty of the economic outlook, the more important it is to ascertain the current economy's precise business cycle position. Measuring the workings of the economy is made more difficult by circumstances such as structural changes in the economy, the increased interdependence between the United States and the rest of the world, and the financial revolution. Yet, it is precisely because of such developments that special efforts must be made to measure the economy. Measurement of the economy's current performance is a necessary prerequisite to any econometric forecasting activity. Economic statistics, produced by federal and state governments, as well as by private agencies, capture the details though not always the spirit, of the economy's direction.

This chapter surveys the economic measures most important to the business forecaster. The economy can be compared to a ship traveling on an uncharted and frequently stormy sea: Even though we know approximately the forces operating on the vessel—the winds, the currents, and the power of the engines—we are not quite sure where we are and where we are heading. Measurements of the vessel's current course and future position are aided by the use of a sextant, the stars, and wind gauges. Many will argue that this analogy exaggerates our ability to control the path of the economic ship of state, but few will differ on the uncertainties.

Rough estimates of current conditions are always available.

Economic measures that help get a reading on the economy's position are:

Multidimensional: production, prices, interest rates, employment, and so on.

Varied in timing: daily, weekly, monthly, annual.

Collected from various sources: shipping ladings, census, tax returns, sample surveys, and so on.

Reported by many different agencies: Bureau of Economic Analysis (BEA), Bureau of Labor Statistics (BLS), Federal Reserve, United Nations, Organization for Economic Cooperation and Development (OECD), business associations and labor unions, corporations, among others.

The data must be interpreted with care to learn precisely where the economy is in the business cycle, and if possible, were it is likely to go.

Unless the economy is well into a broadly based boom or a serious recession, some of the available information will point up and some will point down. This phenomenon is well illustrated by some quotations from the *Wall Street Journal* at various points over the most recent business cycle.[1]

February 1983—The economy was still in a recession which, we can see on the basis of hindsight, had bottomed out toward the end of 1982.

The economy contracted at an adjusted 1.9% annual rate in the fourth quarter after inflation. The Commerce Department earlier said GNP declined 2.5% in the period.

U.S. car sales fell 13% in mid-February from a year earlier. Deliveries were far below industry expectations.

Industrial output rose 0.9% in January and housing starts soared a record 35.9%.

Producer prices, which fell a record seasonally adjusted 1% in January, may drop further. . . .

January's drop in unemployment to an adjusted 10.4% from 10.8% in December provides further evidence that the economy is beginning to recover.

August 1983—Only six months later the economic news was consistently pointing in the up direction. A bouyant recovery was under way as shown by many different indicators, though already there were fears of higher interest rates.

New car sales in the U.S. jumped to 790,000 units in July, up more than 31% from a year earlier.

Construction rose a strong 2.6% in June, to an adjusted $259.7 billion annual rate. The gain was the third consecutive monthly increase, but many economists fear the pace can't be sustained unless interest rates decline.

Factory orders rose 3.9% in June to an adjusted $176.78 billion. The increase, the largest monthly gain in nearly three years, should trigger higher industrial output, and employment, the Commerce Department's chief economist said.

Interest rates rose amid fears that the Fed is tightening credit conditions further, and the higher rates pushed stocks lower.

January 1985—In the third year of economic recovery, statistics provided mixed readings about whether the rapid growth would be maintained.

Production in the nation's factories, mines and utilities rose a strong 0.6% in December, following a 0.4% increase in November and declines in both September and October.

The Commerce Department reported that retail sales dropped 0.1% in December following a strong 2% increase in November.

A survey of consumers by the Conference Board did raise a warning signal in the economic outlook. The Board's index of consumer confidence fell sharply to 85.6 in December from 96.8 in November and its index of consumer buying plans dropped to 95.9 from 102.7.

In recent years, economic literacy has increased tremendously. Today, it does not take a trained economist to distinguish between the economic indicators or to find one's way among the alphabet soup of the different measures of money supply. This is fortunate because as business econometrics extends further down from major corporations to smaller firms, and from headquarters to the divisions, forecasting will increasingly become the task of executives and planners whose training is in management rather than in economics.

> Some business economists claim that an important change of the economic environment of the 1970s and 1980s has been an information overload! But in fact the increasing use of economic information and its integration into business planning and operations are an equally striking and positive development. We would argue that, in many respects, the available statistics have not kept up with rapidly expanding needs for detail and accuracy.

What then are the most important measures that describe economic performance? How sensitive and accurate are these measures? How useful are they? Our objective here is not so much to list these variables as to consider them from the perspective of the business forecaster.

The Major Measures of Aggregate Economic Activity

A sample of the most important variables describing economic activity is shown in the monthly Executive Summary tables distributed to clients of Wharton Econometrics (Tables 3-1 and 3-2). The Wharton quarterly model includes many more statistics than are shown here—in fact there are quarterly forecasts for more than 1,000 variables. But the statistics shown are the most important measures descriptive of the aggregate economy.

Increasing the Nation's Total Output

The single most important number describing the economy's performance is the *Gross National Product* (GNP). This figure sums up in dollar terms all the goods and services produced by Americans of the course of a year. The GNP can be viewed as the expenditures for goods and services by consumers, investors, and governments plus exports and less imports. As shown in Table 3-1, of the more than $3.6 trillion (1982$) of 1985, by far the largest share, about two-thirds was spent by consumers. Business fixed investment and residential construction accounted for 18%. And purchases of goods and services by federal, state, and local governments amounted to 20%. With imports growing rapidly and exceeding 10% of GNP, the role of the foreign sector is far greater than the 1984 figure for net exports ($−119.8 billion) would suggest. Change in business inventories, a small but volatile and imperfectly predictable component, has been a direct cause of many of the postwar business cycle swings.

GNP is a flow concept, so it must have a time dimension. Thus, it must be expressed as "so many" billion dollars per year. In fact, U.S. GNP statistics are quarterly, at annual rates. The figure of $4016.9 billion reported for the fourth quarter of 1985 means that the nation's total output of goods and services would have amounted to that figure if it had continued running at that rate for an entire year. Real GNP amounted to $3584.1 billion measured at 1982 prices.

National accounts data use seasonally adjusted annual rates (SAAR) to allow for normal seasonal variation. These rates are arrived at by using complex statistical procedures to disentangle the seasonal factor from the cycle and trend components of the data series.

But seasonals have a way of going out of whack. A good example is the delay in processing income tax refunds in the spring of 1985. Instead of being mailed in March, the refunds did not reach consumers until April or May. The result: a shift in consumer income and spending from the first to the second quarter that seasonal adjustment procedures could not handle. This was not a trivial matter; it was not clear whether the slow economy in the first quarter of 1985 was "for real."

Table 3-1 Selected Economic Indicators, SAAR (Quarterly Data, Seasonally Adjusted Annual Rates)

	History 1985 Q3	1985 Q4	1986 Q1	1986 Q2	1986 Q3	1986 Q4	Forecast 1987 Q1	1987 Q2	1987 Q3	1987 Q4	History Forecast 1985	1986	1987	1988
Economic Activity and Income														
Real GNP, Bil 82$	3584.1	3605.0	3630.2	3657.9	3693.3	3738.8	3776.7	3802.2	3836.1	3859.3	3573.6	3680.1	3820.1	3916.2
% SAAR	3.0	2.4	2.8	3.1	3.9	5.0	4.1	4.1	3.0	2.4	2.3	3.0	3.8	2.5
% Year Ago	2.1	2.5	2.3	2.8	3.0	3.7	4.0	4.1	3.9	3.2				
Nominal GNP, Bil $	4016.9	4075.1	4133.9	4195.8	4269.4	4356.2	4433.5	4503.1	4575.5	4642.6	3992.5	4238.8	4538.7	4830.2
% SAAR	5.8	5.9	5.9	6.1	7.2	8.4	7.3	6.4	6.6	6.0	5.8	6.2	7.1	6.4
% Year Ago	5.4	5.8	5.5	5.9	6.3	6.9	7.2	7.3	7.2	6.6				
Industrial Prod (77=100)	124.8	125.2	126.5	127.4	128.8	130.5	132.0	133.2	134.2	134.9	124.5	128.3	133.6	136.6
% SAAR	2.1	1.2	4.3	2.9	4.3	5.5	4.6	3.8	3.0	2.1	2.2	3.1	4.1	2.3
% Year Ago	1.2	1.7	2.2	2.6	3.2	4.3	4.3	4.5	4.2	3.4				
Civil Unempl Rate, %	7.2	7.0	7.0	7.1	7.0	6.9	6.8	6.6	6.5	6.4	7.2	7.0	6.6	6.5
Auto Sales, Mil	12.4	10.3	10.5	10.6	10.7	10.8	10.7	10.6	10.4	10.3	11.1	10.6	10.5	10.4
Housing Starts, Mil	1.67	1.73	1.81	1.83	1.84	1.88	1.92	1.86	1.81	1.77	1.74	1.84	1.84	1.73
Real Disp Inc, Bil 82$	2503.1	2517.9	2545.1	2566.7	2591.4	2617.1	2640.1	2660.3	2681.1	2704.0	2509.0	2580.1	2671.4	2755.6
% SAAR	-4.5	2.4	4.4	3.4	3.9	4.0	3.6	3.1	3.2	3.5	1.6	2.8	3.5	3.2
Personal Savings Rate, %	3.7	4.1	4.2	4.1	4.1	4.2	4.2	4.2	4.2	4.3	4.6	4.1	4.2	4.2
FRB Exch Rate (73=100)	139.2	129.3	128.3	120.9	118.7	117.2	116.9	112.1	111.1	110.1	143.6	121.3	112.5	106.0
% Year Ago	-1.8	-12.2	-18.0	-18.9	-14.7	-9.5	-8.9	-7.2	-6.4	-6.1	3.8	-15.5	-7.2	-5.8
Curr Acct Bal, Bil $	-121.8	-136.4	-127.9	-129.7	-122.9	-117.3	-119.7	-125.1	-127.8	-133.0	-116.5	-124.4	-126.4	-138.1
Aft-Tax Corp Prof, Bil $	141.1	147.7	148.8	152.4	157.0	166.9	171.7	173.9	175.3	172.9	140.4	156.3	173.5	173.5
% SAAR	14.5	20.0	3.1	10.0	12.7	27.7	12.1	5.2	3.2	-5.4	-2.5	11.3	11.0	0.0
% Year Ago	0.6	5.0	8.9	11.7	11.3	13.0	15.4	14.1	11.7	3.6				
Fed Surplus, NIA, Bil $	-201.3	-210.7	-202.4	-194.3	-177.7	-155.4	-142.4	-135.4	-130.4	-127.0	-195.9	-182.4	-133.8	-110.1
Components of GNP—Billions of 1982 Dollars														
Consumption Expenditures	2329.6	2328.7	2351.5	2370.0	2390.9	2412.9	2432.1	2450.2	2468.8	2487.8	2312.6	2381.3	2459.7	2538.8
% SAAR	4.6	-0.2	4.0	3.2	3.6	3.7	3.2	3.0	3.1	3.1	3.2	3.0	3.3	3.2
Bus Fixed Investment	473.7	485.4	488.4	493.6	501.6	509.9	519.6	527.8	535.5	542.8	471.8	498.4	531.4	558.4
% SAAR	2.4	10.3	2.5	4.4	6.6	6.8	7.8	6.5	6.0	5.6	9.7	5.6	6.6	5.1

Res Fixed Investment	173.1	176.7	179.8	181.7	184.9	188.3	192.1	195.9	199.4	202.0	171.5	183.7	197.4	206.3
% SAAR	8.5	8.6	7.2	4.2	7.4	7.5	8.4	8.0	7.4	5.4	1.9	7.1	7.5	4.5
Government Purchases	729.2	741.7	741.3	739.7	731.0	724.0	721.4	719.4	718.3	715.3	715.4	734.0	718.6	709.5
% SAAR	-8.2	7.0	-0.2	-0.9	-4.6	-3.8	-1.4	-1.1	-0.6	-1.6	5.9	2.6	-2.1	-1.3
Chg in Bus Inventories	-1.9	0.1	1.2	5.8	12.0	24.1	27.8	28.8	25.8	21.3	7.3	10.8	25.9	7.6
Net Exports	-119.8	-127.6	-131.8	-132.9	-127.0	-120.4	-116.3	-113.9	-111.7	-109.9	-105.1	-128.0	-112.9	-104.2
Inflation and Determinants														
GNP Deflator (82=100)	112.1	113.0	113.9	114.7	115.6	116.5	117.4	118.2	119.3	120.3	111.7	115.2	118.8	123.3
% SAAR	2.9	3.2	3.0	3.0	3.1	3.2	3.1	2.9	3.5	3.5	3.3	3.1	3.2	3.8
% Year Ago	3.2	3.1	3.1	3.1	3.1	3.1	3.1	3.1	3.2	3.2				
CPI All-Urban, % SAAR	2.4	4.1	1.7	2.6	2.7	3.4	3.3	3.5	3.6	3.7	3.5	2.8	3.3	4.0
% Year Ago	3.3	3.5	3.1	2.7	2.8	2.6	3.0	3.2	3.4	3.5				
Consump Defl, % SAAR	2.2	4.4	1.9	2.7	2.8	3.3	3.2	3.4	3.5	3.6	3.2	2.9	3.3	3.9
% Year Ago	2.9	3.2	3.0	2.8	2.9	2.7	3.0	3.2	3.4	3.5				
PPI, Finished, % SAAR	-0.7	4.2	-1.0	0.5	0.8	1.7	1.8	1.9	2.4	2.6	0.9	0.9	1.7	3.3
% Year Ago	0.6	1.6	1.2	0.7	1.1	0.5	1.2	1.5	1.9	2.2				
PPI, Indus Comm, % SAAR	-1.3	1.7	-2.1	-0.7	-0.2	0.7	1.1	1.6	2.1	2.2	0.4	-0.3	1.0	3.1
% Year Ago	0.1	0.5	0.2	-0.6	-0.3	-0.6	0.2	0.8	1.4	1.8				
Comp per Hour, % SAAR	2.8	3.7	3.6	3.6	3.8	4.0	4.2	4.4	4.4	4.4	3.7	3.6	4.2	4.4
Output per Hour, % SAAR	0.4	-1.9	1.1	1.1	2.0	2.9	2.7	2.5	2.3	2.2	0.0	0.6	2.4	2.2
Unit Labor Cost, % SAAR	2.7	5.4	2.7	2.5	1.8	1.1	1.5	1.9	2.1	2.2	3.7	2.9	1.7	2.2
Financial Markets														
Money Supply (M1), Bil $	604.5	617.8	632.3	644.7	656.6	668.8	681.8	692.9	702.9	713.2	617.8	668.8	713.2	755.8
% SAAR	-5.1	8.8	9.4	7.9	7.4	7.4	7.8	6.5	5.8	5.9	11.6	8.2	6.6	6.0
% Year Ago	-0.1	11.6	11.3	10.7	8.6	8.2	7.8	7.5	7.0	6.6				
Money Supply (M2), Bil $	2541.1	2547.6	2584.3	2622.9	2663.2	2706.8	2753.6	2800.6	2843.0	2885.4	2547.6	2706.8	2885.4	3057.1
% SAAR	-0.2	5.8	5.8	6.0	6.2	6.5	6.9	6.8	6.1	6.0	8.6	6.2	6.6	5.9
% Year Ago	9.5	8.6	6.9	7.1	6.1	6.2	6.5	6.8	6.7	6.6				
Federal Funds Rate, %	7.90	8.10	7.58	6.81	6.45	6.58	7.15	7.30	7.44	7.53	8.10	6.85	7.35	7.68
3-Mo T-Bill Rate, %	7.11	7.17	6.88	6.35	6.33	6.49	6.93	6.89	7.09	7.17	7.48	6.51	7.02	7.34
Bank Prime Rate, %	9.50	9.50	9.32	8.63	8.30	8.40	8.91	8.95	9.04	9.14	9.93	8.66	9.01	9.32
Moody AAA Seas Bond, %	11.03	10.58	9.96	9.37	8.91	8.98	9.14	9.19	9.37	9.49	11.37	9.31	9.30	9.66
Mort Rate, Exist Home, %	11.33	11.24	10.86	10.26	9.67	9.55	9.51	9.43	9.72	9.76	11.74	10.09	9.61	10.06

Source: Wharton Quarterly Model Outlook, February 1986, p. 3.

Table 3-2 Monthly Economic Indicators (Seasonally Adjusted)

	1984		1985											
	Nov.	Dec.	Apr.	May	Jun.	Jul.	Aug.	Sept.	Oct.	Nov.	Dec.	1982	1983	1984
Industrial Market Indicators														
Industrial Prod (77=100)	123.4	123.3	124.1	124.1	124.3	124.1	125.2	125.1	124.4	125.1	126.0	103.1	109.2	121.8
%	0.6	-0.1	0.1	0.0	0.2	-0.2	0.9	-0.1	-0.6	0.6	0.7	-7.2	5.9	11.6
% Year Ago	7.5	6.8	2.8	2.3	1.6	0.7	1.4	1.5	1.4	1.4	2.2			
Capacity Utiliz, FRB, %	81.2	80.9	80.5	80.3	80.1	80.1	80.7	80.1	79.5	79.9	80.3	70.3	74.0	80.8
Civil Unempl Rate, %	7.2	7.2	7.3	7.3	7.3	7.3	7.1	7.1	7.1	7.0	6.9	9.7	9.6	7.5
Empl, Hhold Surv, Mil	105.93	106.27	106.94	106.96	106.37	106.86	107.21	107.52	107.81	107.97	108.21	99.53	100.82	105.00
Change, Mil	0.283	0.341	-0.174	0.015	-0.590	0.492	0.348	0.309	0.294	0.156	0.237	-0.870	1.295	4.181
%	0.3	0.3	-0.2	0.0	-0.6	0.5	0.3	0.3	0.3	0.1	0.2	-0.9	1.3	4.1
% Year Ago	3.1	3.1	2.4	1.7	0.9	1.4	2.0	2.0	2.0	1.9	1.8			
Empl, Estab Surv, Mil	95.88	96.09	97.12	97.42	97.47	97.71	97.98	98.22	98.56	98.74	99.06	89.57	90.19	94.45
Change, Mil	0.309	0.210	0.210	0.301	0.052	0.234	0.270	0.240	0.342	0.180	0.320	-1.590	0.621	4.265
%	0.3	0.2	0.2	0.3	0.1	0.2	0.3	0.2	0.3	0.2	0.3	-1.7	0.7	4.7
% Year Ago	4.5	4.3	3.6	3.6	3.3	3.3	3.2	3.1	3.1	3.0	3.1			
Ldg Econ Indic (67=100)	165.2	164.1	166.9	167.3	167.5	168.5	170.0	170.6	171.6	172.0	173.6	136.8	156.0	165.7
%	0.6	-0.7	-0.5	0.2	0.1	0.6	0.9	0.4	0.6	0.2	0.9	-2.9	14.0	6.2
New Orders, Mfg, Bil $, MR	195.0	193.7	191.1	195.0	198.3	195.8	198.8	197.3	195.4	197.4		1884.6	2080.6	2299.0
%	4.4	-0.7	-0.2	2.1	1.7	-1.2	1.5	-0.7	-1.0	1.0		-6.4	10.4	10.5
Inventory Change, Mfg & Trade, Bil $, MR	2.5	2.2	1.4	-2.4	1.9	0.5	-1.9	0.7	3.3	1.2		-18.5	11.1	53.2
Merch Tr Bal, Bil $, MR	-10.2	-8.0	-11.8	-12.7	-13.4	-10.5	-9.9	-15.5	-11.5	-13.7	-17.4	-42.6	-69.3	-123.4
Consumer Market Indicators														
Real Disp Inc, Bil 82$	2481.1	2492.0	2530.9	2567.1	2498.5	2504.0	2501.4	2504.2	2510.2	2508.4		2261.6	2334.6	2468.3
%	0.0	0.4	2.9	1.4	-2.7	0.2	-0.1	0.1	0.2	-0.1		0.6	3.2	5.7
% Year Ago	3.8	3.5	2.8	4.4	1.4	1.1	0.9	0.8	1.2	1.1				
Personal Income, Bil $	3184.0	3207.4	3288.6	3271.2	3280.5	3290.0	3295.5	3309.9	3330.7	3347.4	3394.0	2670.8	2836.4	3111.9
%	0.5	0.7	0.9	-0.5	0.3	0.3	0.4	0.4	0.5	0.5	1.4	5.9	6.2	9.7
% Year Ago	8.5	8.3	7.0	6.2	5.9	5.3	4.8	4.6	5.2	5.1	5.8			
Personal Savings Rate, %	6.0	5.7	5.8	5.9	5.4	4.3	3.7	3.6	3.8	4.1		6.8	5.5	6.5
FRB Exch Rate (73=100)	144.9	149.2	149.6	149.9	147.7	140.9	137.5	139.1	130.7	128.1	125.8	116.6	125.3	138.3
% Year Ago	13.7	12.3	15.0	11.9	10.0	1.2	-1.9	-4.5	-11.4	-11.6	-15.7	12.9	7.5	10.4

Consump Exp'end, Bil $	2485.1	2503.4	2544.0	2575.5	2570.4	2575.5	2606.2	2636.6	2603.1	2621.6	2675.1	2050.7	2229.3	2423.0
%	1.4	0.7	0.5	1.2	-0.2	0.2	1.2	1.2	-1.3	0.7	2.0	7.1	8.7	8.7
% Year Ago	8.0	7.6	6.1	6.6	5.9	6.2	7.3	7.1	6.2	5.5	6.9			
Retail Sales, Bil $, MR	110.3	110.5	115.4	114.9	113.7	114.4	117.0	119.5	114.9	115.6	117.9	1070.4	1171.4	1293.9
%	1.2	0.2	3.1	-0.4	-1.0	0.6	2.2	2.2	-3.9	0.7	1.9	2.8	9.4	10.5
% Year Ago	7.9	7.4	7.4	6.4	4.3	6.4	8.9	10.3	5.4	4.9	6.6			
Auto Sales, Mil	10.0	10.9	11.1	11.3	10.3	10.3	12.6	14.4	9.6	9.8	11.5	8.0	9.2	10.4
Domestic	7.4	8.2	8.7	8.4	7.6	7.4	9.7	11.3	6.3	6.5	8.1	5.8	6.8	8.0
Foreign	2.6	2.7	2.4	2.9	2.7	2.9	2.9	3.1	3.3	3.3	3.4	2.2	2.4	2.4
Chg Cons Cred, Bil $, SAMR	6.1	6.8	8.3	9.0	5.2	6.2	6.3	11.5	8.1	4.9		1.1	4.0	6.4
Cons Conf (67-69=100)	96.8	85.9	93.1	87.2	91.5	92.1	89.8	88.2	89.9	91.5	86.0	55.9	81.0	93.9
Housing Starts, Mil	1.600	1.630	1.933	1.681	1.701	1.663	1.740	1.616	1.772	1.566	1.840	1.057	1.702	1.766
Housing Permits, Mil	1.616	1.599	1.704	1.778	1.712	1.694	1.784	1.808	1.688	1.661	1.844	0.999	1.623	1.688
Inflation Indicators														
CPI All-Urban, %	0.2	0.3	0.4	0.2	0.2	0.2	0.2	0.2	0.3	0.6	0.4	6.2	3.2	4.3
% Year Ago	4.0	4.0	3.6	3.7	3.7	3.6	3.3	3.2	3.2	3.6	3.7			
Consump Deflator, %	0.3	0.2	0.2	0.3	0.2	0.2	0.1	0.3	0.4	0.4		5.7	3.9	4.2
% Year Ago	4.1	4.0	3.4	3.4	3.3	3.2	2.8	2.7	2.9	3.1				
PPI, Finished Goods, %	0.3	0.0	0.4	0.2	-0.2	0.3	-0.3	-0.6	0.9	0.8	0.4	4.0	1.7	2.1
% Year Ago	2.0	1.7	0.7	1.0	0.8	0.9	0.8	0.2	1.1	1.6	2.0			
PPI, Industrial Comm, %	0.1	-0.2	0.4	0.5	-0.2	-0.1	-0.2	-0.4	0.6	0.2	0.1	2.7	1.1	2.2
% Year Ago	1.7	1.4	0.4	0.6	0.3	0.2	0.1	0.1	0.3	0.4	0.7			
Financial Market Indicators														
Money Supply (M1), Bil $	553.8	558.5	574.9	581.6	591.2	595.8	605.9	611.9	611.1	617.9	624.7	476.6	526.1	553.5
% SAAR	12.0	10.2	5.9	14.0	19.8	9.3	20.3	11.9	-1.6	13.4	13.2	8.7	10.4	5.2
% Year Ago	5.2	5.8	6.6	7.2	8.0	8.9	10.4	11.0	11.5	11.6	11.9			
Money Supply (M2), Bil $	2346.3	2371.7	2427.7	2444.9	2472.9	2490.6	2514.0	2528.8	2533.0	2547.1	2563.6	1939.9	2177.1	2345.8
%	14.0	13.0	-0.9	8.5	13.7	8.6	11.3	7.1	2.0	6.7	7.8	9.1	12.2	7.7
% Year Ago	7.7	8.4	8.3	8.4	9.0	9.2	9.6	9.5	9.2	8.6	8.1			
Federal Funds Rate, %	9.43	8.38	8.27	7.97	7.53	7.88	7.90	7.92	7.99	8.05	8.27	12.26	9.09	10.22
3-Mo T-Bill Rate, %	8.61	8.06	7.95	7.48	6.95	7.08	7.14	7.10	7.16	7.24	7.10	10.61	8.61	9.52
Bank Prime Rate, %	11.77	10.50	10.31	9.78	9.50	9.50	9.50	9.50	9.50	9.50	9.50	14.86	10.79	12.04
Moody AAA Seas Bond, %	12.29	12.13	12.23	11.72	10.94	10.97	11.05	11.07	11.02	10.55	10.16	13.79	12.04	12.71
Mort Rate, Exist Home, %	12.89	12.77	12.11	12.11	11.76	11.47	11.33	11.20	11.32	11.26	11.14	15.38	12.85	12.49

Source: Wharton Quarterly Model Outlook, February 1986, p. 4.

49

Before the GNP can be used as a measure of the economy's real product, it must be deflated. During the period 1973–85, U.S. GNP almost tripled in nominal terms from $1326 billion to $3992 billion—an annual rate of 9.6%. But much of this growth resulted from price increase. Real output, adjusted for inflation, advanced 2.4% per year, a rate which compares to the long-term trend of approximately 3% annually.

The "underground" economy presents another problem in economic statistics. Work done "off the books," illegal activities, and alien workers who do not have necessary papers are not recorded in the statistics. Some economists have argued that the national accounts statistics significantly understate economic growth in recent years since the underground economy has been growing much faster than conventional measured economic activity. Estimates of unrecorded activities, based largely on the circulation of currency, range from 5 to 15% of GNP.

Time is an important consideration for the business user of economic statistics. The U.S. data are available with extraordinary speed. Until recently a "flash" forecast of the current quarter's GNP was published in the middle of the third month of the quarter—before the quarter is complete. This figure, an estimate based on incomplete preliminary data, was notoriously inaccurate. An almost complete statement of the entire national accounts—omitting only the figure on corporate profits—is available on the 20th day following the close of the quarter. These estimates are also based on preliminary data. Some of the data used, such as automobile sales and retail sales, are available up to the end of the quarter, but others, such as government expenditures and investment, lag—thus causing the GNP estimate to be based on only two months of information. Revisions are made in the data one and two months after the preliminary release, and further annual revisions are made in mid-July. In addition, so-called benchmark revisions are made every five years or so, sometimes changing the details but hopefully not the substance of the national accounts figures for many years past.

The availability of national accounts data so quickly is a remarkable achievement and an important one from the point of view of business and government economists, who must know where the economy is as quickly as possible. But there is an inevitable cost in accuracy, since more complete and accurate data, available only with a time delay, often show that the preliminary data were in error. The critical issue here is not, however, a question of precision. It does not matter so much to business decisions whether growth really was 5% or 6%. The issue is whether the data properly signal the direction of movement of the economy and particularly the turning points of the business cycle. In recent years, experience has shown that they sometimes do not. For example, failure to measure the true extent of the inventory buildup in 1981 caused many business economists to miss the timing of the recession and to underestimate its dimension. Some have suggested that recent failures in this respect reflect, in part, inadequate resources devoted to the federal statistical establishment.

It is ironic that federal statistical services are being cut back just when data have become increasingly central to the business decision making. At the same time that business executives have been complaining about the cost and paperwork of supplying the federal government with statistics, there was a loud chorus of complaints when it was proposed to cut back data services, for example, the regional department store sales data. Andrew F. Brimmer, a private economic consultant, says wisely: "It must be recognized that in the private sector, businesses of all sizes and in all industries and sectors make their own plans and decisions on the basis of current and prospective economic data and statistics. Reduced availability and eroded quality of this information base can, therefore, have pervasively adverse effects on actual economic activity in the private sector."[2]

Nevertheless, the movement of real GNP is the broadest indication of what is happening in the economy. Since the GNP is measure of production, all the way from production of automobiles to waitress services, it is a coincident measure of the business cycle, reaching its peaks and troughs approximately the same time as the economy as a whole. Movements in GNP can, however, give a misleading picture of the underlying strength of demand. In the third quarter of 1984, the growth of GNP was recorded at 1.5%, slow but positive, but final sales (defined as the change in GNP less the buildup of inventories)

The "rule of thumb" measure to define a recession is two consecutive quarterly declines in GNP. But this is clearly not the only consideration taken into account by the National Bureau of Economic Research committee which dates business cycles. A recession is an economy-wide phenomenon that is picked up by many indicators. And just to show that rules of thumb do not always work, the sudden sharp drop of GNP when the Fed proposed consumer credit controls in mid-1980 lasted little more than a quarter but was nevertheless defined as a recession.

---

declined at an annual rate of 1%. In other words, (1) real GNP increased by $10 billion, but final sales declined by $3.9 billion and (2) inventories piled up at $30.6 billion rate compared to $20.3 billion the previous quarter. The final sales concept is a useful one since it is a measure of current demand, a critical factor in determining business production decisions.

Industrial Production

The Federal Reserve industrial production index is a more narrow and more sensitive measure of the economy's output. The components of this index record production in the various goods-producing sectors such as mining, manufacturing, and public utilities. Derived from data on employment, shipments, and electricity consumption, the industrial production index offers a sensitive gauge of the cyclical fluctuations of the economy. The components for electrical and nonelectrical machinery are particularly sensitive measures of the capital goods sectors.

The industrial production index is available monthly for many separate industries. A serious drawback is that it does not take into account the increasingly important service side of the economy. Because the goods-producing sectors are considerably more sensitive to demand than the service sectors, the industrial production figures display greater cyclical variability than does the overall economy. And as imports of merchandise have mounted, in recent years, industrial production has lagged more seriously than more general measures of economic activity.

Capacity Utilization

A related indicator, the Federal Reserve industrial capacity utilization index signals when demand pressures are building up and when inflationary pressures can be expected to mount. Unfortunately, the measurement of capacity utilization raises some difficult and imperfectly handled challenges. During the 1970s, much capital equipment became uneconomic because of high energy prices, obsolescence, and foreign competition. It is difficult to tell how much of the capital stock still standing and counted will never be put back into use and should not be counted as unused capacity. This problem is most severe in the older capital intensive industries such as steel and chemicals. The concept of capacity is also tenuous in high technology industries.

Personal Income and the Consumer

The income flows received by consumers and corporations are counterparts to production activity measured by GNP. An important measure is personal disposable income. Consisting principally of wage and salary receipts, personal disposable income also includes other personal income flows, most important Social Security and welfare payments. It excludes personal income tax payments. Over the business cycle, some of the swings in wage and salary payments are offset by unemployment compensation and welfare payments. To establish a measure of real consumer purchasing power, personal income can be deflated by the deflator for personal consumption or by the consumer price index (CPI).

Business economists keep close watch of personal income data that are available monthly and thus furnish a benchmark to which the model can be calibrated. Personal income is the principal determinant of consumer expenditure. The experience of the 1981 to 1984 tax cuts makes an interesting illustration. These tax cuts were originally conceived to stimulate savings as a part of a supply side program. In fact, however, as consumers saw improvements in their after tax income, they tended to spend rather than to save. This is apparent from the savings rate (shown on Table 3-1), which declined from an already low 5.7% in 1982 to 4.6% in 1985. The tax cuts served as a massive demand side stimulus, and this turned out to be an important contributor to the economic recovery. But experience also tells us that personal consumption spending will not always adjust quickly to fluctuations in income. Consumer expectations play an important role in influencing consumer spending particularly for durable goods. Important anticipatory variables for consumer spending are the Conference Board's and the University of Michigan Survey Research Center's measures of consumer sentiment.

Employment and Unemployment

From the point of view of the business forecaster, employment and unemployment statistics are indicators of the tightness of labor markets. A low unemployment rate, perhaps 6%, which is widely recognized as corresponding to normal labor turnover, indicates that labor markets are fairly tight. Such a situation could translate into inflationary wage pressures. A high unemployment rate does not mean that economy-wide wages will actually be dropping, but it does typically mean less pressure for higher wages. Following the 1982 recession when unemployment reached 10.8%, the decline in wage demands and the willingness of unions to give wage givebacks was striking. An encouraging sign pointing to continued price stability was the fact that wage pressures continued moderate despite con- siderable improvement in the labor market. Undoubtedly, one important factor was foreign competition. Large wage increases would simply have priced U.S. products out of the market.

It is useful often to look at the source of statistics closely, to see what they might really mean. The unemployment statistics are a good example. The familiar unemployment rate is a hazy indicator. The primary source of employment, unemployment, and labor force data is the Current Population Survey (CPS), a monthly survey of more than 50,000 households. The critical question is definitional: whether the respondent falls into one of the following three categories: employed, unemployed, or not in the labor force. The definitional distinctions are important. To be considered employed, the respondent must have been working or be only temporarily off the job for special reasons such as illness or vacation. To be considered unemployed, the respondent must be out of work, expecting to be recalled to a job, or reporting that he or she has gone to some effort to find a job during the past four weeks. The final classification, "not in the labor force," includes people who are neither employed or unemployed as described above. Those who are not in the labor force include not only such obvious categories as young people under 16, students, and homemakers, but also people who might be employed but who have given up seeking em- ployment. This means that the unemployment statistics under- count unemployment; discouraged workers who have given up looking for a job because there do not seem to be any jobs around are not included among the unemployed. On the other hand, the statistics may also be off in the opposite direction since many of the people working in the underground economy are not recorded as working.

One of the striking positives about the U.S. economy in re- cent years has been its ability to absorb a rapidly expanding la- bor force and to achieve significant declines in unemployment from recession peaks. This contrasts sharply with the European experience where unemployment has remained at recession— one could even say depression—highs in many countries.

Business economists match up this employment-unemploy- ment data, the so-called household data, with another source

"It says here that things have turned the corner."

from *Herblock Through the Looking Glass* (W.W. Norton, 1984)

of labor market statistics. Each month, the Bureau of Labor Statistics (BLS) collects data on employment, hours, and pay from a sampling of business establishments throughout the country. The "establishment series" derived from this survey are usually considered a more accurate indication of employment trends than the household survey data. Some of the more sensitive indicators of labor market conditions also arise from this survey of establishments. The primary one of interest to us here is the "Average Workweek of Manufacturing Production Workers." As the economy begins to accelerate or decelerate, one of the first sectors to feel the change is likely to be manufacturing. And businesses are likely to increase or to decrease the number of hours worked by production workers in order to accommodate the shifting demand for their products before actually hiring or laying off workers. Accordingly, the change in the hours worked represents a sensitive monitor of the fortunes of the economy.

Measuring Inflation

The forecast of inflation plays a crucial role in many aspects of business decision making. The price indexes—Consumer Price Index (CPI), Producer Price Index (PPI), and the broadest of them all, the GNP deflator—are the most used measures of inflation. None of them is perfectly adapted to its purpose since price indexes by their very nature establish a generalization under the average change in price. Prices increased at a double digit rate in the early 1980s. More recently, the good news has been that inflation has come down to a 3 to 4% range but, of course, there is no certainty about the future.

Consumer Prices

The Consumer Price Index affects the economy since it serves as a basis for indexing wage contracts and Social Security benefits. The CPI is a weighted average of price changes, with the weights based on the importance of each consumption category in the consumer's market basket according to data gathered by the Survey of Consumer Expenditures. Such a survey is carried out only every ten years and, as a consequence, the expenditure weights are usually way out of date.

The CPI is not a cost-of-living index. It does not attempt the difficult, if not impossible, task of seeing what it would take to maintain a certain standard of living. It does measure the movement of prices for a specific basket of commodities. Consumers, however, adapt their spending to relative prices of different products, and this accounts for one of the deficiencies of the CPI. It is a fixed weight index. Consumers traditionally spend less on those products that have risen most in price. Consequently, the index tends to weight the products that have risen in price too heavily, and thus to overstate inflation.

Producer Prices

The *Producer Price Index* (PPI) is of particular importance to the business forecaster. It focuses specifically on goods rather than services and it catches products at various stages of transactions before they are sold to final consumers. Three major price series comprise the PPI: for raw materials, for intermediate goods, and for finished goods. The producer price index for raw materials is the most volatile and its movements tend to foreshadow the other price movements. There is also some small lead of the index for intermediate goods in advance of the index for finished products.

One of the most valuable aspects of the PPIs is that they are available in a fine breakdown applicable to narrow product categories. Such detailed price data go into computations of costs for business planning and contract relationships. But the detail stretches the underlying statistics quite far. In most cases, the narrower the product category, the less reliable the data.

The GNP Deflator

The CPI or the PPI cannot be used, however, to measure changes in prices of all goods and services in the economy. The CPI draws a price picture for consumer purchases, not what government or businesses buy, and the PPI deals only with merchandise. For an overall measure of inflation for all goods and services making up the nation's product the GNP deflator is more comprehensive.

The procedure for computing the GNP deflator is different from that used for the consumer and producer price indexes. Each of the flows of products and services that goes into the GNP is restated in terms of prices in the base year. The base year is 1982. Real GNP (in 1982 dollars) is the sum of all goods and services purchased in any given year, valued at their prices in 1982. The GNP deflator is simply the ratio of GNP in current prices and GNP measured in prices of the base year, that is,

$$\text{GNP deflator} = \frac{\text{GNP in current dollars}}{\text{GNP in 1982 dollars}}$$

The importance of the various prices in the GNP deflator is according to the current quantities of various products in GNP (whereas in the CPI the weights of various products are those of the base year). Because of the differences in construction and coverage, there is no reason for the two indexes to show exactly the same rates of inflation. Between 1974 and 1981, the GNP deflator rose 69% as compared to an increase of 84% in the CPI. Fortunately in recent years *both* measures have moderated to around 4%. And as pressures on wages and primary commodity and petroleum prices have eased so have concerns with forecasting inflation. Nevertheless, it is premature to assume that inflation is dead. Inflation forecasting, particularly prediction of early warning signs, remains an important task for the business forecaster.

Financial Statistics for Business Forecasting

With the turn of public policy and of many economists toward a more monetarist view of the world has come increasing focus on the monetary aggregates as a way of analyzing the path of the economy. Interest rates are still the dominant concern for business economists or corporate financial officers since they are seeking either to raise funds on the most favorable terms or to place liquid balances with maximum return. Monetary aggregates are important insofar as (1) they can be seen as factors impacting on the economy in general or (2) they affect financial markets.

The growth rate of money supply is more important in a world where the Federal Reserve is known to focus strongly on the monetary aggregates than under conditions as in the 1950s and 1960s when the primary concern of the Federal Reserve was interest rates. As we noted in Chapter 2, an interesting example of the power of business expectations in this regard is the sharp response of financial markets when the Federal Reserve switched to somewhat less strict monetarist focus in the latter half of 1982. The switch recognized the easing of inflation and the difficulties of measuring the monetary aggregates at that time. Financial markets, which had been concerned about budget deficits and strict adherence to monetarism, greeted the change with enthusiasm. Interest rates fell precipitously and the stock market rose. However, large budget deficits quickly caused many business executives to worry again about possible Fed efforts to tighten money and raise interest rates.

Measuring Money Supply

There are problems associated with measurement of the money supply. The initial question is definitional. The distinctions between the monetary aggregates and their behavior as compared to the Fed's targets during the second half of 1984 and early 1985 are shown in Figure 3-1. The cone-shaped areas are the target growth zones established by the Fed. It is apparent that in March 1985, money supply growth was above target but not beyond a somewhat broader growth path determined by the dotted lines.

Traditional monetary policy has focused on M1 and M2 as, respectively, a narrow and a broad measure of the economy's money supply. But it is difficult to measure these statistics, particularly since they are affected by seasonal movements, by the timing of government payments such as Social Security, and

M1 Private checking deposits and cash. Monthly average, seasonally adjusted. The Fed's 1985 target calls for 4% to 7% growth, shown in the usual way by the large cone and, more flexibly, by the dotted lines. The 1984 goal was 4% to 8% growth. The inset shows the latest period.

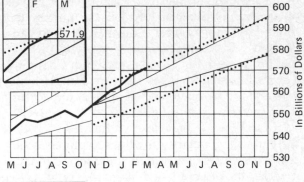

M2 Adds to M1 most types of personal savings including money market funds and money market deposit accounts. Monthly averages, seasonally adjusted. The 1985 target, depicted by the large cone and dotted lines, is for 6% to 9% growth, unchanged from last year.

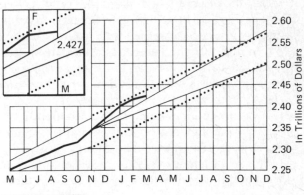

M3 Includes M2 plus some investments such as large certificates of deposit and money market funds sold to institutions. Monthly average, seasonally adjusted. The Fed is seeking 6% to 9.5% growth this year, compared with 6% to 9% last year.

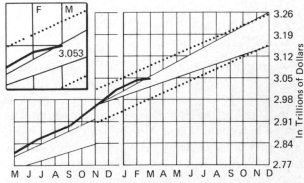

Figure 3-1. Money growth versus the Fed's targets. (*Source: Wall Street Journal*, April 12, 1985.)

61

by institutional changes. For example, the very sharp rise in M1 during the first half of 1983 has been attributed to the shift of funds from money market mutual funds to bank money funds. The latter are included in M1 whereas the money market mutual funds were not. This, as noted in Chapter 2, is only one of the institutional changes that are transforming financial markets and which may have significant impact on the meaning of the monetary growth figures.

In fact, the Federal Reserve has found it difficult to control the rate of monetary growth, sometimes seeing it shoot way above the target and being unable for extended periods to bring it within the desired target range. As a result, some experts have accused the Fed of fostering monetary instability, that is, of pursuing pro-cyclical rather than counter-cyclical policies. But it is doubtful that the Fed could do an improved job. Monetary growth rates are unstable in the short run. Looking at the monetary aggregates alone, the Fed never knows precisely where it is. This is a measurement problem that has been greatly aggravated by institutional changes. Consequently, it has been suggested that monetarist policies be implemented by controlling monetary reserves rather than money or alternatively by using a proxy for outstanding bank credit or total nonfinancial debt as the central measure used by the Fed to guide monetary policy.

Interest Rates

A number of interest rates are watched by business executives and economists with particular care since they serve as effective guides to conditions in financial markets. The Federal Funds rate is the most sensitive short-term rate, for overnight loans between banks. The interest rate on the three-month Treasury bills (Table 3-1) is representative of short-term interest rates on government securities, whereas the rate on commercial paper is for short-term financial instruments that are subject to commercial risks. The long-term interest rate shown here is a representative rate for Moody AAA-rated corporate bonds. Numerous other interest rates for mortgages, CD's, passbook accounts, other ratings of corporate and municipal bonds tend to fluctuate along with the principal long-term (or, if appropriate, short-term) rates. These rates are the bread and butter of banks, stock brokers, pension funds, and other financial institutions. Corporate financial staffs concerned with meeting funding requirements and cash management also follow and project interest rate data in great detail.

Financial markets and monetary growth are at the heart of recent debates about the impact of deficits on the economic outlook. In the mid-1980s federal deficits have been very large indeed, approaching $200 billion—some 6% of GNP. The deficit is a figure to watch, and one for which projections prepared by agencies like the Office of Management and Budget and the Congressional Budget Office and various Congressional committees differ widely. Nevertheless, there was agreement on one point: federal budget deficits would remain large unless the Administration and the Congress agreed on massive expenditure cuts and tax increases. The Gramm-Rudman-Hollings budget-balancing bill was a step in that direction.

Anticipations Data and Economic Indicators

The business forecaster takes advantage of the numerous variables that foreshadow the movement of economic activity over the business cycle. This type of information supplements the econometric model forecast. The anticipations variables have been integrated directly into the Wharton model.

The available information on anticipations varies considerably. Some variables report broadly on expectations, that is, the sentiment of consumers or business executives. Other variables measure business plans. And still others are records of new orders, construction starts, or other early stages in the production process. The so-called economic indicators are a collection of many different variables that are sensitive to diverse aspects of the cyclical movement of economic activity.

Consumer Expectations

Expectations are at the heart of economic decision making and have become the center of the rational expectations controversy, as noted previously. But these anticipations are seldom measured and, for that matter, they are often not even measurable. Some important expectations variables are obtained with surveys of businesses and consumers. To give a specific example, the Survey of Consumer Sentiment of the University of Michigan Survey Research Center measures how households "feel" about the economy and their personal economic situation. The survey compiles responses to questions like:

- "Are you better (worse) off today than you were a year ago?"
- "Do you expect to be better (worse) off a year from now than you are today?"
- "Is this a good (bad) time to buy durable goods or cars?"

The answers do not measure specific decisions, but they can provide important insights on how consumers view the future, and they relate closely to consumer purchases. The extremely high levels of consumer sentiment recorded in 1983 and 1984 reflected the improvement in the employment and inflation picture and foreshadowed the boom in sales of automobiles and durables in that period.

An interesting contrast is the response of consumer sentiment to inflation. When inflation rates are modest, consumers are reasonably satisfied with their prospects. If, on the other hand, the inflation rate rose suddenly in the 1970s, consumers might be expected to "buy ahead," that is, to purchase goods before prices went up. But this has not generally been the American experience. Consumers have generally reacted to double-digit inflation with fear for the future. They have pulled in their tentacles by cutting back on durable expenditures and increasing their savings.

Investment Plans

Most economic decision-making requires some advance planning. The information embodied in these plans is another important ingredient in the forecast. For example, the Bureau of Economic Analysis (BEA) carries out a survey of business plant and equipment spending plans. This survey, which is also the basis for national statistics on investment, provides important advance information. Early in 1984, it gave a significant signal of the strength of business investment plans in the face of high interest rates.

Even more closely tied to the economic process are the variables that record new orders or the actual start of production activity. The new orders for durable goods data are a closely watched indicator of demand for durables. The user should be aware, however, of some of the complications of these data (the treatment of automobiles on the basis of current production rather than orders, for example). The user should also be aware of the considerable variability of the statistics from one month to the next, tending to give frequent false signals.

Housing starts are another anticipatory measure that has been fully integrated in most econometric models. Residential construction takes place over a period of six to nine months after construction has started so that the housing starts statistics offer a significant forward view for this sector.

The Leading Economic Indicators

The anticipation variables have been listed above in inverse order to their closeness to the actual working of the economy, that is, consumer sentiment is purely expectational whereas new orders or housing starts actually record the beginning of activity. Where on this scale are the "economic indicators"?

Some comments on the old National Bureau of Economic Research (NBER) approach to business cycle measurement are appropriate here. The classic work of the NBER during the prewar years involved the search for consistent patterns of movement or regularities in many cyclical variables. "Measurement without Theory" one critic called it.[3] Out of this work has grown a systematic way of dating the timing of business cycles, establishing the dates when business cycle turning points have occurred. Many statistical series have been analyzed to see if their turns lead or lag the cycle. From these studies have come regularly revised lists of the so-called *leading* indicators.

Figure 3-2 shows the historical patterns of the most recent leading indicators list. The vertical lines establish the timing of the national turning points, peaks, and troughs. The leading

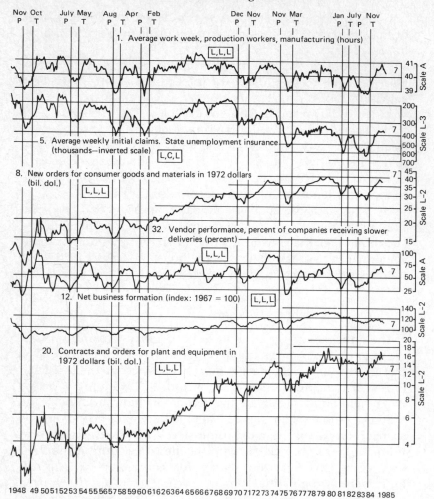

Figure 3-2. The leading indicators.

series are only a small part of the many that could have been chosen. These are selected as the most reliable from the perspective of cyclical lead. The leading indicators include:

- Average work week, manufacturing
- Layoff rate, manufacturing

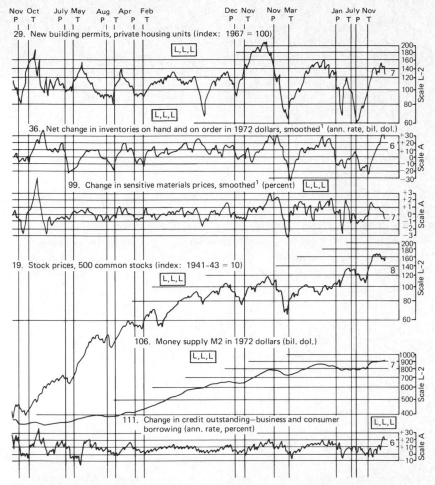

- New orders for consumer goods and materials in 1972 dollars
- Vendor performance
- Net business formation
- Contracts and orders for plant and equipment in 1972 dollars
- New building permits, private housing units, number
- Net change in inventories on hand and on order in 1972 dollars

- Change in sensitive materials prices
- Standard and Poor's index of 500 common stock prices
- Percent change in liquid assets
- Money supply (M2) in 1972 dollars

The leading indicators are combined by the Department of Commerce into an index whose movement from month to month gets considerable publicity in the press. The resulting series is quite variable. No doubt the index of leading indicators gives some forewarning of impending cyclical turns (a considerably longer lead for peaks than for troughs), but there have been occasional problems of false signals.

The questions that arise around the use of the index of leading indicators in a formal forecasting environment relate specifically to its varied content. Some of the underlying indicator variables are indeed closely tied to real changes in economic conditions, for example, the work week and change in inventories. Others measure altogether different dimensions such as price change, stock market, and money supply. Each of these measures is valuable in its own right and can be fitted into a structural view of the economy. Merged together into one indicator their common element is principally empirical; e.g., their performance relative to other time series during past business cycle turning points.

Trade and Exchange Rate Statistics

The increasing internationalization of the U.S. economy makes international information more important for business planning than it once was. Many U.S. firms are affected by import competition. Many also sell, produce, raise funds, or invest in foreign markets and require analyses and forecasts for these areas abroad.

Statistical materials on foreign trade and exchange rates present special problems. The complex figures on imports and exports are a good example. Trade statistics are assembled in the United States in nominal terms on the basis of customs data. These figures, which are closely watched, are available monthly and in current dollars. Deficits for the U.S. commodity trade mounted to almost $150 billion in the mid-1980s. This deficit is a serious matter. It represented a leakage of demand out of the U.S. economy toward foreign producers and accounted for the slow growth of industrial activity.

From the perspective of financial flows, the current account balance is more meaningful. (This figure is shown in Table 3-1.) In the recent past the current account balance on goods and services has also turned sharply negative—but not quite as much as commodity trade since there is still a surplus in U.S. services trade.

The exchange rate represents another important dimension for business forecasting. Exchange rates are notably variable and have turned out to be difficult to predict. Expectational and speculative factors play a large role in determining short-term exchange rate movement. International money flows are not, as one might suppose, so much determined by the needs of trade as by financial institutions that seek to maximize safety and the return on their portfolios by taking advantage of interest rate differentials, differences in economic-political climate, and expected exchange rate movements. There has been a flight of capital to the safe haven of the United States from Latin America, Socialist countries in Europe, and the uncertainties of the war in the Middle East. In the mid-1980s the United States has been "the only game in town for the international investor" and this caused the dollar to be greatly overvalued despite the unprecedented trade deficit. Whether the capital inflows would continue in large enough volume to offset burgeoning trade deficits was the $64,000 question. The headlong slide of the dollar from its March 1985 peak answered this question decisively.

European and Japanese statistics are often as good and sometimes more detailed as figures on the United States. Much data, originally produced by national sources, are collected by international organizations such as the Organization for Economic Cooperation and Development (OECD) in Paris and EUROSTAT, the statistical arm of the European Community, in Brussels.

Statistical information is far less abundant and less reliable on less developed countries than on the advanced world. The United Nations, the International Monetary Fund, and the World

Bank assemble statistical information covering many developing countries as well as the industrial world. This information is distributed in their publications and on computer tapes. Much of this statistical material is available in the data banks of the major forecast vendors. These also offer forecasts for many of the international statistics from their world econometric model systems.

Business Perspectives on Economic Statistics

Business economists and planners supplement the national statistics with industry and firm statistics. The Departments of Commerce, Energy, and Agriculture publish many industry and product specific data. The Census of Manufactures and the Annual Survey of Manufactures provide detailed data disaggregated by industry and region.

Most of the nation's industries have trade associations, which serve as the primary collection agencies for industry data. The American Petroleum Institute and the American Iron and Steel Institute are excellent examples. These organizations maintain elaborate statistical series on their respective industries available to their members and published regularly for public use. These data, which often include information on sales, market shares, profitability, stocks, employment, and so on, are valuable supplements to more aggregate statistical information. Private data firms, such as Standard and Poors and Dun and Bradstreet, also assemble and sell many important industry-specific statistics.

Industry economists, and particularly accountants and company planners, are loaded with information about their own firm: its sales volume, its output, costs, profit margins in various product lines, investment costs, and so forth.

Each of these levels of data should not be seen separately. There is much to be learned at each level. A broad and useful perspective is to recognize the interrelationships between the prospects for the economy as a whole and for the business enterprise that operates within it. Some firms rightly may think of themselves as relatively isolated from the vagaries of the business cycle, though recent experience suggests that few of even these are insulated from the shocks of higher energy costs or skyhigh interest rates. But most business activity is interrelated and greatly dependent on the condition of the economy at large. The problem for the business economist or planner, is twofold: (1) how best to go from the aggregate to the industry-specific and (2) how best to link the statistics that describe the performance of the national or regional economy and the industry to the critical variables that affect the performance or profitability of the business venture. These questions will be considered in further detail below.

Computer Distribution of Economic Statistics

Along with the increasing use of economic statistics have come improved systems of data distribution. With the development of computer-based data banks in the late 1960s, the typical business economist no longer searches directly through the pages of the *Survey of Current Business,* and *Monthly Labor Review,* or similar publications. Almost all regularly-produced statistical data for the United States and many thousands of series on foreign countries are kept up to date on the data banks operated by Wharton Econometrics, DRI, Citicorp, and some other data vendors. The advantages are phenomenal. Any data series can be called to the computer screen, and adjustments for seasonality, price change, and trend can be made immediately as required. Numerous alternative graphic presentation forms are available, many of which can be drawn directly or transferred to color slides. Regression relationships between variables can be computed almost instantaneously and these can be quickly put together into model systems. It is not surprising that the old-fashioned chartroom and data library has gone the way of the buggy whip.

And we are now on the threshold of still another data supplying revolution. The increasing use of microcomputers means that new links will be forged between data banks and users. In many cases, this may simply mean a downloading of data series from the central data bank to the user's microcomputer—

not much different from the use of the computer terminal until now. But distribution of data on diskettes or similar distribution tools now cheaply provides a large quantity of information to many users without requiring the time-shared connection with the central mainframe computers. This greatly reduces costs and makes data series and other current information available in a user friendly format. The implications of the changes in data distribution will be discussed at greater length later.

It is perhaps important to note that some of the advantages of widespread data availability in the computer have come at a cost. Few of the footnotes and data descriptions that used to accompany the printed presentations of the data from the original source appear on the secondary distribution of the national time share data banks. Fewer still of the users of the statistical material seek out in the original source the limitations of the statistical material being utilized. The result is much greater ease of use, but the consequence is also much more indiscriminate use of statistical material.

Further Readings

Much of the information on current economic statistics is summarized in the official publications (and the relevant handbooks) where this material originally appears. Thus, the reader is referred to the *Survey of Current Business*, the *Monthly Labor Review*, *Business Conditions Digest*, and the United Nations *Monthly Statistical Bulletin*, the *Monthly Economic Indicators* of the OECD, and the *International Financial Statistics* of the International Monetary Fund. As we have noted, most of these data are contained in the data banks of the forecast vendors, but the original tabular presentations, footnotes, and descriptive comments are frequently lost when the material is put on a computerized data bank.

Economic measurement is a much neglected subject in the literature. On the national accounts, see John W. Kendrick, *Economic Accounts and Their Use* (New York: McGraw-Hill, 1972) and Murray F. Foss, ed., *The U.S. National Income and Product Accounts* (Chicago: University of Chicago Press, 1982). Albert T. Sommers, *The U.S. Economy Demystified* (Lexington, Mass.: D.C. Heath, 1985), is a layperson's guide to major economic statistics and their importance to business. For "The Underground Economy: An Introduction," see *Survey of Current Business* (May 1984). The literature on the economic indicators is well summarized in Geoffrey H. Moore, *Business Cycles, Inflation, and Forecasting*, 2nd edition (Cambridge, Mass.: Ballinger, 1983).

Notes

1. Drawn from various pages of the *Wall Street Journal* during the periods indicated.
2. Statement of Andrew F. Brimmer, in *Impact of Budget Cuts on Federal Statistical Programs*, Hearing before the Subcommittee on Census and Population of the Committee on Post Office and Civil Service, U.S. House of Representatives (May 16, 1982), p. 34.
3. The title of a critique by T. Koopmans (*Review of Economics and Statistics* [1947]) of Burns and Mitchell's pathbreaking book, *Measuring Business Cycles*.

❖ 4 ❖

Forecasting—
The Econometric Approach

Econometrics has throughly invaded, if not captured, the world of business. Most large corporations and banks use econometric forecasts. Many major firms have hired their own econometricians and some are even building their own models. But few use econometric forecasts exclusively. Judgmental considerations, recent trends, and evaluations of likely policy developments remain important inputs into the forecast—as well they should! In the final analysis, corporate management must be persuaded that the forecast is reasonable and realistic. That is not a matter of econometric model mechanics. The evaluation of the outlook which will be factored into corporate decision making must be grounded in facts and logic that can be readily related to real world developments as they are reported in the day's *Wall Street Journal.*

The words econometrics and models sometimes inspire in people a mystique tinged with an element of distrust. Some economists say: "It must be so because my model says it's so!" At the opposite extreme, others claim that models are unreliable and have little to do with the real world. The truth probably lies somewhere in between. In so elusive a field as economics, econometrics represents about as close an approach to the scientific method as can be achieved. The information produced by the models is useful. Indeed, that is why business executives buy it. But it would be foolish to build unrealistic expectations about the reliability or automaticity of the econometric crystal ball.

This chapter considers the nature of econometric models. It looks closely at the structure of one of the big macromodels, the Wharton Quarterly model of the U.S. economy. Chapters 5 and 6 show how models are used for forecasting and policy simulation and evaluate their forecasting performance.

Some Historical Perspective

Applied econometrics dates back only to the decade just before World War II when the groundwork of national accounts and aggregate Gross National Product (GNP) measures had been laid and when Keynesian theory was developed. The first experimental macroeconometric models were built in the 1930s by Jan Tinbergen for the League of Nations. But the real impetus to this field is owed to Lawrence Klein, who served as the father of econometric modeling worldwide during the postwar period. Out of his pioneering work, for which Klein was awarded the Nobel Prize in 1980, has sprung not simply an academic discipline, but also a tradition of applied econmetric forecasting and analysis in business and in government. Out of it has grown an entire new industry, the forecasting and econometric service firms.

Beginning in the early 1950s, the results of econometric model forecasts were presented to business outlook conferences at the University of Michigan. These meetings were important since they first contrasted simple academic models with the complex facts of the business world. But the forecasts were on an annual basis and the data were only the broadest national aggregates. Business executives wanted to relate the forecasts to current data in a quarterly or even monthly time frame; they were concerned with information on their particular sectors (e.g., automobiles, steel, chemicals, or finance), and they wanted to look ahead for several years. It was not until 1963 that quarterly econometric forecasts were being discussed regularly by Klein and his associates with practicing economic forecasters from business and government in the framework of the Wharton Econometric Forecasting Unit at the University of Pennsylvania. This was the beginning of the Wharton forecasting service. It established a pattern of interaction, a dialogue between observers of the real-world business scene and econometric model forecasters that continues to this day. (See the discussion of Wharton Econometrics forecasting procedures in Chapter 5).

The usefulness of the new approach was soon recognized. The 1960s were a period of active development. The forecast horizon was stretched to 8 quarters for the short-term outlook and to 10 to 20 years for long-term forecasts. The models grew rapidly in size and complexity from 20 to 30 equations for early versions of the Wharton Model to 1500 equations for the current version of the Wharton long-term forecast model. In part, this reflects a broadening of the scope of the models and improvement of their structure, but largely it means increased disaggregation. The most recent version of the Wharton Quarterly Model contains 12 consumption categories, 24 investment variables, 96 prices, and 35 interest rates. Technical refinements also expanded the models. Input-output relationships were entered into the model system to break down the forecasts to the level of individual industries. Regional disaggregation was introduced. Flows of funds models helped to explain the financial sector. Anticipations variables were integrated into models to improve short-term forecasting. Agricultural sector models produced price and farm income forecasts. Better linkages to the outside world, now modeled with a comprehensive World Model, recognized the growing internationalization of the U.S. economy.

Modern computer equipment came just at the right time for the econometricians. Computers hold the large-scale data banks. They do the calculations involved in estimating the values of the behavioral coefficients and in solving the models under alternative assumptions about external developments. Were it not for the computer, econometric models could not be anywhere near as large and useful as they are today.

Toward the end of the 1960s, the development of time-share computer networks further changed the perspectives of the industry. Models located on a central computer could be operated through computer terminal telephone links from anywhere in the country or even the world. The forecast consulting firms—Wharton Econometrics, DRI and Chase Econometrics—were a logical consequence. Along with forecasts, they offer their huge data banks, statistical programs, econometric models, even news services, all accessed from the clients' own offices by way of terminals and telephone lines.

It was once suggested that the President should have the econometric forecasts appear on the TV in the Oval office. This was easily feasible but it was probably not a good idea because that would get in the way of the TV broadcasts during baseball season and, more seriously, because the technical details of the forecasts should be left to the technicians.

The 1970s saw an explosion of business econometrics. Almost all large and many medium-sized businesses now are tied in to some aspect of the econometric services, often drawing on the models and forecasts of more than one econometric consulting service. The name of the game is no longer just the macro forecast. Models have been stretched to provide information on industries, regions, commodity markets, exchange rates, and the entire world economic environment. At the same time, business economists have been hard at work creating the links from the macromodels to the newly developed model systems that describe their industries and firms and relate directly to business decision making. (These models are discussed in Chapters 7, 8, and 9.)

The 1980s, the age of the microcomputer on every desk—perhaps ultimately in every briefcase—are bringing another revolution. Delivery of forecasts and econometric services is changing, dramatically reducing the cost and vastly expanding the scope of business applications of econometrics.

Essentials of Econometric Models

Models are simplified descriptions of the real world. They may take many forms, from physical mock-ups to sets of mathematical equations. A model airplane in a wind tunnel is a classic example of a useful model. In much the same way, econometric models are useful because they represent the enormously large and complex economy in simple form and allow us to simulate its behavior. Econometric models generally are sets of simultaneous equations mounted on the computer for ease of solution and manipulation.

It is important to note at this point that we are concerned with structural models. Trend forecasting and time series analysis methods are frequently advanced as useful forecasting methods. And, for certain purposes, they are indeed useful. Their forecasts cannot be explained in terms of the underlying forces, however, because they lack structural underpinnings. Nor can they be used for simulation of alternative situations. The econometric approach focuses on identifying and quantifying the essential structural relationships of the economy.

The national income and product accounts provide the data and structure for models of the economy. But there is a critical difference between an accounting summary and a model. The difference that "makes" an economic model is that it describes behavior. The behavioral relations of a model show how the participants of the economy—consumers, business firms, and government units—respond to internal and external developments.

Theory is the dominant consideration guiding how the model should be structured. The theorist explains how and why households and businesses act as they do. The theory of consumption determines the formulation of the consumption equations; the theory of the firm determines the output relations and investment; the theory of the labor market determines how the model treats labor force participation and wage determination, and so on.

A model of an industrialized economy like that of the United States emphasizes demand, employment, and price determination, focusing on the business cycle fluctuations that are a dominant concern of public policy in the United States. On the other hand, models for less developed countries are more concerned with long-run production or supply aspects since these set the limit for the developing economy's growth and well-being. The purpose for which a model is used is an important factor influencing its design. Monetary models emphasize money, financial institutions, and interest rates. Industry sector models present the input-output relations between sectors. Forecasting models maximize the use of current indicators and anticipatory information. Policy models elaborate the fiscal and monetary policy mechanisms that policy makers use to influence economic activity. And industry and firm models elaborate the behavioral and technical characteristics of particular sectors.

A Simple Demand Model Example

Our basic view of models is structural. Models should describe the principal elements of how the economy operates. These include the accounting identities that tie together the system of national accounts and the behavioral relations that describe behavior in the economy.

The essentials of model structure can be illustrated in simple terms in relation to the basic Keynesian model. The simplest formulation recognizes the demand aspects of the economy only. The flow diagram in Figure 4-1 describes such a model. GNP is determined by the purchasing of consumers (C), investors (I), and government (G). The central horizontal line in the diagram corresponds to the national income and product accounts identity for GNP. Government purchases and investment are *exogenous;* government purchases are determined by government budget decisions; and investment, which takes some time to put in place, is set by business decisions, a year or two earlier.

Consumption is *endogenous,* that is, it is determined internally by the working of the model. Consumption depends on the current income stream generated by GNP. The model is simultaneous since in turn GNP depends on consumption. Note that the line leads without interruption from GNP to consumption and from consumption to GNP. This illustrates feedback, a characteristic of simultaneous models.

The same system can be described as a set of two equations:

$$C = \alpha_0 + \alpha_1 GNP \tag{1}$$

$$GNP = C + I + G \tag{2}$$

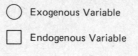

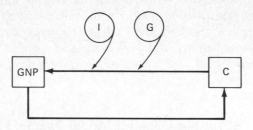

Figure 4-1. Diagram of a simple economic model.

Equation (1), a behavioral relationship, is a simple consumption function explaining consumption in terms of GNP. Equation (2) is the basic definition of GNP.

The variables to be explained by the system, the endogenous variables, are GNP and C. The exogenous or predetermined variables are G and I. The α's are the coefficients that qualify the behavior of consumers. For example, α_1, the marginal propensity to consume, measures how much consumers will spend out of each added dollar of income. We can solve the two equations for the two unknowns by substitution to obtain:

$$C = \frac{\alpha_0 + \alpha_1(I + G)}{1 - \alpha_1} \tag{3}$$

$$GNP = \frac{\alpha_0 + I + G}{1 - \alpha_1} \tag{4}$$

These are what are known as reduced form equations, showing the endogenous variables of the system in terms of the exogenous variables and the constant.

The difference between a theoretical economic model, such as the one discussed so far, and an econometric model is that in an econometric model the values of the behavioral coefficients have been estimated from observed statistical information. To illustrate, some years ago this author asked a graduate student to run a regression to calculate values for the behavioral coefficients of the consumption equation. The data chosen from the national accounts were for 1952–72. The equation fit well. This gives us a model as follows:

$$C = -6.8 + .67 \text{ GNP} \qquad (5)$$

$$\text{GNP} = C + I + G \qquad (6)$$

While this appears simplistic, it is in fact a true econometric model.

Our little model taught us an interesting lesson. Up until 1972, the model fit the real-world data surprisingly well, producing a fairly accurate estimate of the observed GNPs. But, using the model for forecasting from 1972 on, the graduate student reported with some dismay that it forecast very badly. This should not have been a surprise. The 1973–74 oil crisis influenced the economy in ways the little model was simply not equipped to handle.

The model is simple enough so that it can be solved by direct analytic solution as above, but we will illustrate here the iterative solution procedure that is actually employed by the computer in solving large complex models. This procedure is quite similar to that used by many economists for "back of the envelope" forecasts. Begin with values for all the variables for year 1 and propose to make a forecast for year 2. First, values for the exogenous variables must be established, assuming that real investment will rise only very little—here, the increase is $1 billion. Government spending is assumed to increase by $2 billion (a total increase in the exogenous variables of only $3 billion). The value for the left-hand variable of each equation is computed using the last known values of the variables on the right-hand side. The iterative procedure is summarized in Table 4-1.

The first column shows the year 1 values that will be used as

Table 4-1   Iterative Solution of Simple Model
(Billions of 1972$)

	Year 1	Year 2				
		Iterations				
		(1)	(2)	(3)	...	(n)
C	554	554	556	557.3		560
I	138	139	139	139		139
G	145	147	147	147		147
GNP	837	840	842	843.3		846

a starting point. Equation (5) computes a value for consumption using the previous estimate of GNP as a base value. [In iteration (1), $-6.8 + .67 * 837 = 554$]. Then, equation (6) is used to sum up to GNP on the basis of the just estimated preliminary value of C. ($554 + 139 + 147 = 840$). The second iteration round goes through the two equations and uses the latest available values for GNP and C in each case. This process is repeated until successive calculation rounds yield the same values. Iteration (n) is the equilibrium solution, and the forecast for year 2 GNP is $846 billion. Note that the multiplier $[\Delta GNP/\Delta(I + G)]$ is approximately 3 as we would expect it to be on the basis of equations (5) and (6). A forecast for year 3 would go through the same process using the estimated values for year 2 as a starting point.

The computer is ideally suited for rapidly going through a solution process on many equations over and over again. This iterative approach to model solution that is available in numerous computer programs and imposes almost no restrictions on the structure of the model is widely used by practicing econometric forecasters. On a mainframe computer, model solutions are practically instantaneous and on today's sophisticated microcomputers, even solutions of full size macromodels are a matter of a few seconds.

Extrapolation and Time Series: A Digression

The emphasis in this volume is frankly on structural econometric approaches, on estimating the behavioral and structural relationships that lie behind economic phenomena. This is the soundest forecasting approach. It is based on logic, structure, and data. Disregarding nonstructural forecasting methods, noting that they do not "explain" and consequently lack a basis for the forecast, is a temptation. But the facts are that time series methods, which are strictly nonstructural, have become increasingly popular—they are a growth industry, and they appear, in some limited cases, to forecast as well or better than traditional econometric approaches. This section briefly contrasts the structural econometric approach with nonstructural methods of extrapolation and time series analysis.

Table 4-2 lists the qualities of various types of forecasting methods. Structural econometric models, single equation reduced form forecasting equations, and trend and time series methodologies are compared. Of these approaches, only the first is, strictly speaking, structural. Direct use of reduced form equations, like equations (3) and (4) above, also bring causative factors to bear on the forecast but in an unstructured way. The trend and time series methodologies are nonstructural; they do not pretend to consider causation or structural description of the underlying economic process.

The structural econometric approach can be termed either a paradigm or a caricature of the scientific method: a paradigm because, as in science, econometric techniques serve to challenge theory with empirical information; a caricature because economists, unlike scientists, cannot make experimental tests of causation. Formal econometrics is the attempt to verify theoretical concepts in real-world data. The theory comes first and the empirical tests follow. Often they suggest the need to return to the theoretical drawing board.

Econometric forecasters begin with an effort to explain, to find the causative basis (if causation can be inferred from association) of the underlying behavior. They then proceed to statistically estimate the values of the relationships and to structure them into an integrated model.

Finally, the forecasters insert the values of the exogenous variables into the model to produce a forecast, one that is entirely conditional on the assumptions about the structure of the model and the exogenous variables. A different model or a dif-

Table 4-2 Evaluation of Alternative Approaches to Forecasting

Characteristic	Multi Equation Structural Model	Reduced Form Equation Regression	Trend Projection	Time Series Methods
Data requirements	Dependent and independent variables for structural relations	Predicted variable Appropriate independent variables	Long time series Predicted variable only	Long time series Predicted variable only
Computation	Several regressions and model simulation	Regression	Various forms of regression on time variable only	Box Jenkins or other time series methods
Nature of forecast	Conditional	Conditional	Unconditional	Unconditional
Forecasting ability	Satisfactory	Satisfactory in most cases	Useful for long-term prediction	Good for very short run
Simulation ability	Good, coefficients represent structural relations	Does not show structure	Not possible	Not possible No causative variables

ferent set of exogenous assumptions would produce a different forecast.

> Hence, the term GIGO (garbage in, garbage out).

That it might be possible to forecast without a knowledge of the structure has been known for a long time. Trend projections rely only on the passage of time to forecast a future path, and for some variable like population or technological trends that is all one might want or be able to do. Only in recent years has this approach gone beyond simple trend projections to methods that rely on the dynamic properties of the data for a forecast. These techniques take advantage of the *Auto Regressive Moving Average* (ARMA) properties of the data series itself. The forecast is entirely a result of the past behavior of the forecasted variable—no information on other factors that might influence the forecast enters at all. The forecast is unconditional. Of course, the forecast has a band of uncertainty. There are always random variations, which the information scientist calls "white noise." This approach has been found useful mainly for short-term forecasting when the momentum of the data series often seems to explain better than an analysis of the underlying factors. An example is in projecting retail sales one to three months into the future. Of course, such an approach will not capture the impact of external influences nor will it allow for changes in the time series process itself.

Models of the Real World—The Wharton Quarterly Model

Of necessity, applied models are considerably more complicated than the simple econometric model discussed above. The real world is so complex that any model, even a large model like Wharton Mark 7, the seventh generation of Wharton Quarterly Models, is a drastic simplification. Simpler econometric models, similar to textbook models, have been built. Some of these models have done surprisingly well as forecasting tools, but they cannot give a truly detailed and structured description of the economy.

Detail is important information in its own right. It is also a means to check whether the model is operating consistently and on track. For example, do the predictions of consumer demand correspond to the flow of wages and other income? Do changes in wage or energy costs feed through properly to prices of final products? Do changes in tax rates yield appropriate impacts on government revenues and the deficit? The model needs to be sufficiently detailed so that policy changes can be fitted in properly and their effects throughout the economy evaluated. The applied model has "policy handles" so that fiscal and monetary policy can be introduced and policy simulations can be carried out.

Many of the essentials of Keynesian macro theory can be recognized in real-world models like the Wharton Quarterly Model. New theoretical developments and empirical considerations, however, result in significant modifications. The following special aspects are particularly noteworthy in the Wharton Quarterly Model:

1. Considerable elaboration of the model, showing breakdowns into the principal demand categories and many details for production, employment, wages, and prices. The detail of the data available in the quarterly national accounts and other principal current statistical sources is a guideline for the breakdowns used in the model.
2. Elaborate dynamic specification of the principal behavioral relationships. Time lags reflect time delays of the real world.
3. Introduction of the mechanism that links new orders, output, and inventory determination.
4. Elaboration of labor demand to explain manhours, as well as number of workers employed.
5. Disequilibrium formulation of the labor market, linking wage changes to the level of unemployment. This is the well-known Phillips curve relationship, augumented by adjustment of wages to inflation.
6. Detailed price determination, linking prices in the principal producing sectors to labor cost per unit of output and to capacity utilization. Deflators are estimated for the principal final demand categories.
7. Elaboration of the income side of the model to yield informa-

tion on profits and dividends and on personal disposable income.

8. Detailed description of the revenue and expenditures side of federal and state and local budgets. This detail is particularly useful for fiscal policy studies.

9. A monetary sector that explains the most important short-term and long-term interest rates, and permits analysis of the impact of alternative Federal Reserve monetary policy actions.

10. An international sector that provides endogenous estimates of imports and exports and of the balance on current account.

The problems of operating and solving a model skyrocket as the model becomes more complex. The sheer number of data series that must be recorded and tracked is a serious challenge. Indeed, the data may not be available in sufficient detail and with sufficient accuracy to permit the desired elaboration of the model. With highly complex models, it is not always possible to figure out, by analytic reasoning, the channels through which the behavior of the model operates. The Wharton model consequently has been planned as a compromise: between the advantages of still more detail, and the disadvantages of operating a still larger model. Fortunately, with the use of computers, even a fairly large complex system like the Wharton model can be solved in a few seconds of computer time to become a flexible tool for forecasting and analysis.

The original Wharton model has undergone numerous revisions to keep it abreast of the latest developments in state-of-the-art macroeconomic theory and practice, and up to date with major revisions in economic data. The structure of the most recent version, Wharton Mark 7, is shown in Figure 4-2.

A simplified discussion of the most important equations and identities follows. It will give the reader a feel for the complex interrelationships in this model. A high degree of disaggregation typifies the model throughout so that discussion must of necessity be somewhat simplified.

Final Demand

The Wharton quarterly model, like most business cycle models, places great emphasis on demand (shown on the left side of the diagram). Economic theory suggests that different forces lie

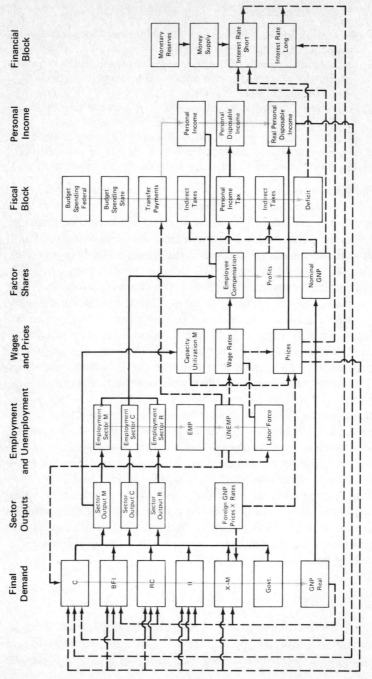

Figure 4-2. Simplified flow diagram of Wharton model.

behind each of the demand components that sum together to make GNP. There are consequently separate equations (shown by the boxes in Figure 4-2) to explain each demand component: consumption functions, investment functions, inventory functions, and import and export functions. Government spending for goods and services is exogenous in the model.

Consumption The model disaggregates consumer expenditures into 12 categories, including automobiles, appliances, food and beverages, clothing and shoes, and household operation. Following traditional consumption theory, consumer spending is a function of consumer spending power measured in the model by real after tax income. (Note the arrow connecting disposable income with consumption). The model allows for the fact that consumption does not adjust immediately to changes in income; consumers establish their spending patterns gradually in relation to their expectations of income. The consumption functions also take a variety of other endogenously and exogenously determined factors into account. For example, the inflation rate, changes in unemployment, and interest rates and installment credit terms affect consumer spending particularly on cars and other durables. The consumer sentiment index plays an important anticipatory role here.

Investment Investment spending includes several significantly different categories: business purchases of plant and equipment, residential construction, and inventory accumulation. Each category poses its own special challenges and is represented by different equations in the model.

The equations for plant and equipment spending see business executives building their capital stock of machines and buildings in light of needs for production capacity and the so called user cost of capital. The latter represents the long-term interest rate adjusted for tax treatment of interest and for other tax incentives such as tax credits and accelerated depreciation under the Accelerated Cost Recovery System (ACRS) of the 1981 tax act. (Figure 4-2 shows links from production activity in the principal sectors and from the interest rate to the business fixed investment box.)

Residential construction is influenced by different forces. The equations for residential construction recognize the importance, on one hand, of needs for new housing in the economy and, on the other, of the cost of financing and the availability of funds for mortgages. The availability of funds is captured here by introducing the differential between the long- and short-term interest rates. As noted earlier, the differential between these rates determines whether funds go into mortgages or whether they are "disintermediated," that is, drawn into short-term financial instruments. But changes in the organization of financial markets may significantly affect the continued validity of this equation.

Finally, inventory accumulation is also an ingredient of investment demand—a highly volatile one at that. In the postwar years, business cycle dynamics were dominated by inventory swings. The inventory equations adjust inventories in relationship to current sales, the inventory-to-sales ratio, and the interest rate, which represents the carrying cost of inventories. (The arrows point to inventory investment from GNP and from the financial sector.)

Imports and Exports   Import equations respond to the sensitivity of imports to domestic economic activity and to foreign prices compared to domestic prices. Exports, in turn, are a function of economic activity abroad and of U.S. export prices relative to prices in foreign markets. The exchange rate (exogenous in the Wharton Quarterly model but modeled in its own right in Wharton's exchange rate system) is a major determinant of the competitiveness between American and foreign products. The demand component that enters the domestic GNP identity is the net difference between exports and imports.

Government Purchasing   Government purchases of goods and services are a unique part of the model's demand identity. Government purchases are determined by budget decisions made by federal, state, and local governments. However, the federal budget has been as difficult to predict as to control. The model does not deal with this problem. Government spending is an exogenously determined policy input; consequently, the model operators have to deal with it directly. The impact of government spending assumptions for forecasting is developed at greater length in Chapter 5.

Output and Employment

Output and employment (shown in the center of the diagram) are determined in this model primarily, but not entirely, from the demand side.

Output   Final demands are translated into value-added in each of 13 industrial sectors (only three, manufacturing, commerce, and regulated industries, are shown in Figure 4-2) through an input-output framework embedded within the model. (Note the lines linking final demand to sector output.)

While value-added by sector is the principal measure of industrial production in the Wharton Quarterly Model, a satellite industrial production model calculates the Federal Reserve's industrial production indexes for many specialized industrial categories.

Employment   Since output is determined from the demand side, production functions in this model serve to establish employment and labor-hour requirements. A production function would explain output in terms of inputs of labor and capital. In the model, the production functions have been inverted. Given output and capital stock, the equations explain the amount of labor that is required, both in terms of hours worked and of employment for each sector. Here, it is important to remember that it takes time to hire new workers. When a firm wants to satisfy increased demand with greater production, at first there may be little, if any, change in employment. The existing workforce may simply work harder—a gain in productivity—or may work overtime—an increase in labor-hours. After some time, more people will be hired to adjust the workforce to the new production schedule. These phenomena have been built into the employment functions. (The arrows go from sector output to employment.)

Unemployment To determine unemployment, the model compares total employment requirements to the total available labor force. The latter represents all people who are working or actively seeking employment. Labor force participation depends on wage rates, reflecting the incentive effect of income. The function also recognizes the impact of unemployment on people's efforts to seek jobs, the so-called discouraged workers. Unemployment is computed as a difference between total labor force and total employment. (Note the arrows from employment and labor force to unemployment.)

Supply

The supply side of the model is embedded in the wage and price mechanism. Supply constraints—unemployment and capacity utilization—influence wage and price increase. As a result, increases in demand are translated into real output or alternatively into higher prices depending on whether sufficient supply capacity is available. That capacity is itself explained endogenously in the model. The economy's production potential depends on its accumulated capital stock, the result of investment, and on labor productivity. Thus, supply side policies that encourage business investment in plant and equipment can fundamentally alter the path of economic growth.

Wage Rates Wage rates depend on demand and supply on labor markets. The wage equations follow the familiar pattern of the Phillips curve. This is a nonlinear relationship: the lower the rate of unemployment, the greater the upward pressure on wages. Inflationary expectations operate in the wage equation since workers seek, sometimes successfully, to maintain their purchasing power when prices are rising. This is the point where rational expectations would make a big difference. We are taking expectations into account but we have not gone all the way in the direction of assuming that expectations are "rational."

Prices The notion of price as a markup over costs underlies the mechanisms of price determination. But, as practicing business executives know, competitive conditions in the marketplace limit the extent to which costs can be marked up into prices. The price level is explained for each of the principal producing sectors of the economy as functions of costs—that is, labor costs, reflecting the wage rate and productivity, and capital and material costs. Capacity utilization and import prices represent the competitive forces operating in the sectoral price equations. When union wage demands cause labor costs to rise more rapidly than productivity or when material costs go up, manufacturing prices can be expected to increase. On the other hand, underutilized capacity or low-cost foreign competition tend to hold down prices. Fortunately, cost and capacity pressures have eased in recent years, so that the model projects the wage price spiral turning less rapidly.

The prices of each of the various demand categories are then linked to the prices prevailing in the main producing sectors. (The disaggregated prices are not shown in Figure 4-2.) As we noted above, prices times real output determines the GNP in current prices.

The Income Side

Next, we turn to the income flows that have been generated by production activity. Compensation of employees is calculated from the estimates of employment and wage rates. Disposable personal income includes some additional income flows, such as dividends and interest, plus transfer payments, less personal taxes. The disposable personal income deflated by the deflator for personal consumption expenditures, is an important feedback channel in the model and appears in all the consumption equations. (Note the dashed line from Real Personal Disposable Income to Consumption Demand.) The calculation of corporate profits in the model is as a residual by subtracting from GNP, depreciation, indirect business taxes, compensation of employees, and various other income flows. (Note the arrows from Employee Compensation and Nominal GNP.) This is a rather simple way to handle corporate profits and one that leads, occasionally, to substantial forecast errors. In the real business world, profits are highly variable over the cycle precisely because they are a residual claim on the economy's product. It has so far been difficult, however, to capture in the econometric model the concept of profit targeting that lies behind many business decisions.

Tax Equations

Tax payments are closely linked to the income flows. (The flow diagram of Figure 4-2 does not show the complexity of the tax equations.) Personal income tax receipts are modeled by income bracket. This means that the model endogenizes an aspect of the income distribution and that it is responsive to changes in the bracket structure of the income tax, an important factor when various forms of flat taxes are being considered. Some other aspects of income tax regulations, such as personal exemptions and standard and itemized deductions, are also modeled. Paradoxically, the model cannot easily accommodate the closing of tax loopholes such as some of the changes being considered in current efforts to simplify the tax system. The corporate income tax is linked to corporate profits. There are also equations for other components of federal, state, and local tax revenues.

An important point here is that revenues are endogenous in the model. Given tax rates and other tax regulations, the model estimates government revenues on the basis of taxable income, corporate profits, sales, and so on. The spending side of the government budget also has some endogenous aspects—for example, the impact of interest rates on the interest paid on the government debt. But spending depends much more directly on current decision making by the administration and Congress. The federal budget deficit (shown at the bottom of the Fiscal Block in Figure 4-2) is thus estimated within the model system. Not only is it very sensitive to economic environment, but it feeds back on the economy. To assure consistency, budget projections must be made in a macroeconomic framework.

Monetary Sector

The monetary sector (shown on the bottom of Figure 4-2) is a summary of the determinants of money supply and interest rates. A broad range of interest rates are determined in the financial sector. The key interest rate is the Federal Funds rate; it serves in the model as a central interest rate and determines, directly or indirectly, all other rates. To it are linked the Treasury bill rate, which influences all other government interest rates, and the commercial paper rate, which swings business and private financial market interest rates. This market is directly affected by fiscal and monetary policy developments, since both changes in the national debt and open-market operations are accomplished largely through purchases and sales of Treasury bills.

The Federal Funds rate is derived from demand for money equations, given available monetary reserves. The supply of money originates with monetary reserves that are linked to money supply through the Fed's reserve requirements. Fiscal deficits enter into interest rate determination as the supply of new government debt instruments. Monetary policy affects interest rates through nonborrowed reserves of commercial banks, the key exogenous monetary policy variable. While it cannot be said that the model is monetarist, money makes a big difference. A significant monetarist influence, moreover, is in the way Federal Reserve policy is entered into the model system, with careful monitoring by the model operators of money supply growth.

Numerous interest rates are forecast within the financial sector, such as: rates for Treasury obligations with maturities ranging from six months to 30 years; market-specific short-term rates, such as the Federal funds rate, the prime, rates on large certificates of deposit, commercial paper, and three-month Eurodollar deposits; mortgage rates for both new and existing homes; Moody's AAA for newly issued and seasoned corporate bonds; and Moody's AAA utility rate.

Foreign Sector

The foreign sector (shown in Figure 4-2 as the *X-M* demand component) plays an increasingly important role in the mounting U.S. trade deficit. Imports and exports are broken down by major product category. Import demand relates closely to the expansion of the domestic economy and to the competitiveness of imported goods with respect to the domestic price level. Here is where the extraordinarily high foreign exchange value of the U.S. dollar in recent years had a big effect. Exports depend most directly on economic conditions abroad and, as with imports, on foreign competitiveness. This is a place where forces outside the model of the domestic U.S. economy play an important role in the outcome of the forecast.

Summary

Some of the principal feedback interrelationships of the Wharton model may be summarized briefly as follows:

1. *Consumption; Income.* Consumption depends on the flow of disposable income and that in turn depends on production and demand.
2. *Investment accelerator.* Investment depends on the capital requirements for production, and production in turn is influenced by demand.
3. *Labor, wages, and prices.* Labor requirements, which depend on real output, determine unemployment. The Phillips curve relationship influences wages and unit labor costs and prices, which in turn influence GNP.
4. *Capacity utilization and prices.* Real output determines capacity utilization, which influences prices and then affects GNP in current prices.
5. *Monetary and real sectors.* Current dollar GNP influences interest rates and money supply, and these in turn affect real expenditures and economic activity. As a consequence, both interest rates and money supply are endogenous variables in the model system.
6. *Federal budget.* Expenditures and revenues in the federal budget influence the demand side of the economy by way of federal spending and their impact on other spending components in the system, state and local spending, consumption, investment. At the same time the deficit affects financial markets and interest rates and, in turn, these feed back on the real sector.
7. *Foreign sector.* The trade balance effect on demand and output is apparent in the depressed mass production industries that are encountering a flood of imports. In turn, reduced pressures

in industrial and labor markets ultimately help to improve productivity and international competitiveness. The so-called "adjustment process" to balance of payments disequilibrium is an illustration of the feedbacks from the foreign sector.

These are only some of the most important interrelationships in the Wharton model. Now we turn to a discussion of (1) how the internal linkages operate and (2) how and through what channels the model responds to changes in external forces.

Multiplier Responses

Careful analysis of what happens as one changes policy assumptions in simulations is one way to observe the model's response characteristics. Numerous aspects of the economy are affected directly and indirectly. Multiplier calculations are so called because they measure the multiplied effect on the economy of a unit change in an exogenous variable (e.g., the change in GNP for each one dollar of the change in exogenous spending). For our purpose, the essential lies in the size of the multiplier, the dynamics over time, and the channels of impact of exogenous policy changes.

The simplest type of multiplier simulation compares a fixed base simulation with an alternative simulation where only one exogenous variable has been changed. Table 4-3 presents multiplier simulation values for some important exogenous policy changes. The simulations were computed for the third quarter of 1984 to the second quarter of 1986. In each case, the exogenous change was made in 1984 and then maintained at a constant level (in current dollars) above what had been assumed in the base solution for the remainder of the simulation period. Three alternative simulations were made:

1. *$10 billion Government Purchasing Increase*—An increase in federal government nondefense purchases of goods and services amounting to $10 billion.
2. *$10 Billion Tax Cut*—An across-the-board personal income tax rate cut worth approximately $10 billion.
3. *$1 Billion Increase in Monetary Reserves*—Federal Reserve open

Table 4-3   Multiplier Simulation Effects of Alternative Policy Changes

Policy		Number of Quarters Following Policy Change				
		1	2	3	4	8
$10 Billion Increase in Govt. Purchases						
GNP Nominal	$ billion	12.4	15.7	21.4	21.1	23.5
GNP Real	1972$ billion	5.6	6.7	8.3	7.6	6.4
GNP Deflator	% change	0	0	0.1	0.1	0.2
Unemployment	%	−0.1	−0.12	−0.15	−0.17	−0.18
Pers. Disp. Income	$ billion	2.7	3.8	5.3	6.3	10.9
Cons. Expenditure	$ billion	1.2	2.1	3.3	6.3	10.9
Deficit	$ billion	6.4	5.1	4.5	4.7	−5.3
$10 Billion Cut in Personal Income Taxes						
GNP Nominal	$ billion	1.7	4.2	7.3	10.1	22.4
GNP Real	1972$ billion	1	2.1	3.3	4.1	6.9
GNP Deflator	% change	0	0	0	0	0.1
Unemployment	%	−0.01	−0.02	−0.05	−0.08	−0.21
Deficit	$ billion	8.4	7.7	7.6	7.6	8.8
$2 Billion Increase in Nonborrowed Reserves						
GNP Nominal	$ billion	16	32.4	51.5	67.8	98.3
GNP Real	1972$ billion	6.4	12	17.2	20.2	14.5
GNP Deflator	% change	0	0.1	0.3	0.5	1.5
Unemployment	%	−0.08	−0.21	−0.37	−0.54	−0.8
Interest Rate—short-term	%	−1.74	−2.12	−1.98	−1.81	−1.21
Interest Rate—long-term	%	−0.27	−0.26	−0.37	−0.46	−0.14

market operations resulting in an exogenous increase in reserves of $1 billion.

Table 4-3 records the impact on the economy, measured as a
deviation of the alternative solution from the base solution, for
each of these alternatives. We are going to look under the sur-
face of the model, so to speak, to examine the structure and
timing of the adjustments that occur as a result of the exogenous changes.

These simulation results apply to an economy in the middle of a cyclical upswing. They are fairly representative of typical model behavior, although similar computations carried at the peak of the cycle when unemployment rates are very low and capacity utilization is very high would yield different results. In such a case increases in demand would translate more into increases of the prices rather than into higher levels of real GNP.

Impact of $10 Billion Increase in Government Purchases

The increase in government purchases of $10 billion current dollars translates into a considerably smaller amount ($4.6 to $3.4 billion) in terms of 1972 prices. This standard of comparison is used in the real (i.e., constant purchasing power) parts of the model and it will be used here. Note that the immediate impact of the increase in government purchases is an increase of $5.6 in GNP (1972$). The impact in real terms rises during the first year (up to $7.6 billion) but declines somewhat thereafter. As a result of the increase in government purchases, personal disposable income increases and that in turn provokes an increase in real consumption expenditures. As a consequence of greater economic activity, unemployment is somewhat reduced by approximately .2%. The impact on inflation is small but perceptible. Thus, the inflation rate rises gradually and the price level at the end of 8 quarters is 0.2% higher than in the base solution. A striking and important result is that the $10 billion (current dollars) increase in government spending does not cause a $10 billion deficit but only one of approximately $4 or $5 billion. Clearly, the higher level of wages and profits brings in tax revenues that offset some of the expenditure increase.

Impact of $10 Billion Cut in Personal Income Taxes

The tax cut has much smaller impacts than a spending increase throughout the economy since an increase in disposable income is not all translated into a direct increase in demand for product as was the increase in government purchases. The impact is through the increase in personal income after tax, which then translates into an increase of consumption. The tax cut simulation has considerably less impact on the deficit than the spending increase simulation because there is not nearly so much stimulus on economic activity.

Impact of $2 Billion Increase in Monetary Reserves

The management of bank reserves, so-called "open market operations," is the principal instrument of monetary policy used by the Federal Reserve. A $2 billion increase in monetary reserves is considerable amounting to a sudden addition of 5% to the reserve base. The immediate impact is to increase the money supply and to reduce the short-term interest rate. Impacts on GNP build up gradually but there is significant impact some quarters after the policy change. The sharpest increases come between the fourth and the eight quarter. At this point, increases in business fixed investment and residential construction begin to mount. There is quite a perceptible impact on inflation. After eight quarters the price level is higher by 1.5%. The slow but large impact of greater financial availabilities and lower interest rates is the striking aspect of monetary policy effects throughout the model.

A Family of Interrelated Models

The above discussion noted numerous places where external forces impinge on the Wharton model. The model of the domestic economy is obviously influenced by (1) forces from the outside world and (2) domestic developments that are not fully integrated into the model. There are, after all, limits to how much of the world one might want to encompass in a single model. On the other hand, external inputs must be forecast as well as possible and they must be consistent not only among themselves but also with respect to the domestic macromodel simulation.

The international context is a good example of the need for consistency. For example, the estimates of imports in the U.S. forecast must match the exports to the United States projected

The need for consistency in a world system is easily apparent from the experience of the OECD in Paris. At its regular forecasting conferences, OECD staff used to tabulate the import and export projections of the experts from each participating country. Invariably, the sum of the exports exceeded the total projected imports.

for other countries. The rapid expansion of the U.S. economy during the 1983–84 period and the overvaluation of the dollar fueled a flood of imports into the United States. The result was that the U.S. economy served as a "locomotive" pulling along the rest of the world, particularly our trading partners in the Pacific Basin, and, to a much smaller extent, those in Europe. In turn, the expansion of economic activity in the rest of the world influences the export possibilities of U.S. industry. This information must be fed back into the U.S. model.

Similar interactions operate through financial and foreign exchange markets. The high level of interest rates in the United States has been one factor attracting foreign capital flow. And, as a result, the U.S. dollar has been overvalued and American goods lack competitiveness in foreign markets. A picture of foreign developments that is consistent with what is happening in the U.S. economy and which recognizes the massive impact of the U.S. economy on the world economy is required.

Sectors of the domestic economy and primary commodity markets raise similar needs for interactive linkages. The macromodel requires inputs of data from agriculture, for example, the prices of major agricultural products and the incomes earned from farming. These variables are affected by the general economic environment and, in turn, they influence it.

The need for consistency with respect to external developments is one factor that has led the econometric forecasting services to extend their reach by building new econometric models. (Obviously, another reason is the possibility of providing improved forecasting and simulation studies for a wide range of new users.)

An entire family of model systems is being operated. In some cases these are formally linked to the U.S. macromodel. In others, their results are used informally as exogenous inputs introduced into the U.S. macromodel. The results of the U.S. model, in turn, go into the other models.

In addition to the U.S. macromodels, the principal models serving as inputs into a coordinated forecasting operation at Wharton Econometrics are:

Global Model of the World Economy—Following the patterns originally developed in Lawrence Klein's academic world model project at the University of Pennsylvania, Project LINK, a World Model system (Figure 4-3) integrates domestic models for 24 countries and 6 regions of less developed and centrally planned economies through trade flow linkages and price linkages.

This is a massive undertaking. Even with moderate scale models for each separate country (37 behavioral equations and 140 idenities), the world model comprises several thousand equations. Yet, it is readily operational and used for forecasting and simulation on a current basis. It provides much of the international information going into the U.S. model.

International Regional Forecasting—Detailed information is frequently required on countries in various parts of the world. The regional international forecasters, in many cases using special country models, study the major countries in various regions— Latin America, the Middle East, the Pacific Basin, and the Socialist Economies. Each forecast embodies not only economic information, but, importantly, it introduces political and social developments that often dominate economic forces. The regional international forecasts provide an important check on the forecasts of the world model.

International Debt Simulators—International debts, which have become such an important source of concern, are modeled in detail in microcomputerbased *country monitors*. The latter are systems to track the outstanding country debts and to analyze the debt burden under alternative assumptions about exports, imports, interest rates, and debt rescheduling.

Foreign Exchange Model—A comprehensive global exchange rate model, now providing exchange rate forecasts on a monthly basis for 31 currencies, is closely linked to the world model and to the individual country studies. Exchange rate forecasts, a critical matter for financial firms and corporations in international markets,

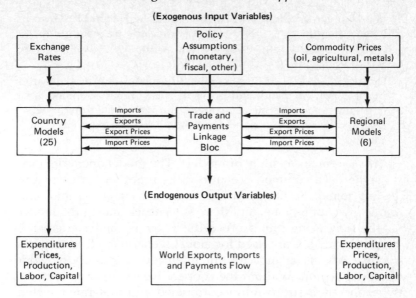

Figure 4-3. Wharton world model system.

feed into the world model and into the United States macro models, as we note above.

Petroleum Supply and Demand Models—A global petroleum supply and demand balance system provides a basis for appraising petroleum markets and probable developments in the price of oil.

Industry Model—An industrial production and pricing model provides industrial breakdowns for industrial activity and prices. Besides its usefulness on the industry level, this material provides a valuable check on the reasonableness of the macro forecast. More detailed models for individual industries are also available.

Domestic Regional Model—A model breaking down the results of the national model to the nation's principal regions provides information valuable to firms operating in regional market areas and to state and local governments. Models are also available for individual states and metropolitan areas (e.g., New York and Philadelphia).

Agricultural Model—An international agricultural model system appraises developments in agriculture, in the US and elsewhere, as a basis for forecasting agricultural prices, agricultural trade, and income from farming. The focus is particularly on food and feed grains, wheat and corn, soybeans, and on the closely related meat sector: beef, pork, and chickens.

Commodity Models—Primary commodity models are used to appraise supply, demand, and prices of other primary commodities (e.g., the nonferrous metals, copper, tin, nickel; the tropical beverages, coffee and cocoa; and agricultural materials like rubber and cotton.)

This is seen as a family of models. The model operators meet to settle on a common scenario of assumptions in each forecasting round. Results from one model are integrated into other models, as appropriate, and there is feedback among the models as the forecasting round proceeds. There is similar interaction when the models are used for global scenario studies, as in the recent study of the impact of the international debt on the world financial system. Without the cooperative efforts of economists who operate a structurally coordinated and integrated system of models of the domestic and international economy, such a major study would not be possible.

Further Readings

There are a number of excellent econometrics textbooks, for example, G. G. Judge, W. E. Griffiths, R. C. Hill, T. S. Lee, *The Theory and Practice of Econometrics* (New York: Wiley, 1980), and J. Johnston, *Econometric Methods*, 3rd edition (New York: McGraw-Hill, 1984). Most of these books, however, emphasize estimation of the structural equations rather than the structure and application of econometric models. Robert S. Pindyck and Daniel L. Rubinfeld, *Econometric Models and Economic Forecasts*, 2nd edition (New York: McGraw-Hill 1983), and Edwin Kuh and Richard I. Schmalensee, *An Introduction to Applied Macroeconomics* (Amsterdam: North-Holland, 1973), give a useful overview as does, on a somewhat more applied level, Lawrence R. Klein, and R. M. Young, *An Introduction to Econometric Forecasting and Forecasting Models* (Lexington, Mass.: D. C. Heath, 1980). The latter is the closest presently available to the "Care and Feeding of Econometric Models."

To learn about the models themselves, see: Michael J. McCarthy, *The Wharton Quarterly Econometric Forecasting Model, Mark III* (Philadelphia:

University of Pennsylvania, Economics Research Unit, 1974), unfortunately now somewhat outdated. A recent book is Otto Eckstein, *The DRI Model of the U.S. Economy* (New York: McGraw-Hill, 1983). An older classic is still J. S. Duesenberry, G. Fromm, L. R. Klein, and E. Kuh, eds., *The Brookings Quarterly Econometric Model of the United States* (Chicago: Rand McNally, 1965). For a survey of the multiplier properties of many different econometric models of the U.S. economy, see L. R. Klein and E. Burmeister, eds., *Econometric Model Performance* (Philadelphia: University of Pennsylvania Press, 1976).

The basic volumes on World models from Project LINK are R. J. Ball, ed., *The International Linkage of National Economic Models* (Amsterdam: North-Holland, 1973) and J. A. Sawyer, ed., *Modeling the International Transmission Mechanism* (Amsterdam: North-Holland, 1979).

❖ 5 ❖

Forecasting and Policy Analysis with Macroeconometric Models

Despite the fact that computer simulation is both automatic and easy, econometric models are not "magic black boxes" for forecasting. Much hard work and tender loving care go into an econometric forecast. The process of forecasting is eminently practical; it is essential to be in touch with the real world. The human expert makes a vital contribution. He must check and tune the model. He must introduce the latest information—on what is happening in the economy, on policy, and on outside developments that are likely to influence the course of economic activity over the forecast period. The expert must also evaluate all aspects of the forecast and correct them, if necessary, to assure a coherent and logically consistent "outlook." He must work out alternative scenarios to present optimistic and pessimistic forecasts and to measure the potential impact of possible new policies.

Econometric Forecasting Procedures

A good example of the process of forecasting with a large-scale econometric model is the procedure followed each quarter at Wharton Econometrics with the Wharton Quarterly Forecasting Model.

Wharton's Professional Board, consisting of the forecast-ing group directors and academic advisers, meets once a week to review current economic trends, evaluate fore-cast performance, and resolve questions connected to model structure and behavior. A meeting is generally planned for the day when new quarterly data come in. The following is a brief summary of the agenda at a meeting (Thursday, April 18, 1985).

1. Review of the new data. GNP in the first quarter had grown only 1.3%, less than the Commerce Depart-ment's "flash" forecast a month earlier of 2.1% and sig-nificantly less than Wharton's forecast of 3.3%. What accounted for the difference? Some of the shortfall re-lated to a delay in the IRS's processing of income tax refunds. That had cut into consumer spending as was apparent from the sharp decline in retail sales during March. The Quarterly Model manager felt that some of this would be made up when checks reached consum-ers the following month. But the group recognized that the underlying softness of the economy resulting from the sharply rising imports and the poorer than expected export performance would drop the forecast for 1985 below earlier estimates.

2. Implications for policy. It was concluded that the Fed might further ease monetary policy even though mea-sures of M1 growth were above the policy target. This could be expected to further ease interest rates over the course of the summer. With respect to budget policy, recent developments in Congress provided support for only modest expenditure cuts, like those already in the forecast, with little expectation of significant tax reform until the following year.

3. Trade. The most recent figures for U.S. trade partners in Europe were coming in higher than earlier, but the European specialist felt that this would mean only very little for U.S. exports.

4. Exchange rate. The exchange rate expert indicated that the decline of the exchange rate from its peak in Feb-ruary had been much more rapid than had earlier been anticipated. There was no good explanation for the pre-

cipitous drop, except that the increase earlier had been very rapid. He suggested that the exchange rate model was showing a forecast of only moderate further decline of the dollar until the end of 1985 and then some additional drop thereafter. While the fall of the dollar would help U.S. trade, it was agreed that the full effect would be delayed and would not greatly affect trade for 1985. Similarly, it was agreed that the immediate impact on the inflation rate would be modest though, ultimately, a lower dollar could be expected to produce somewhat higher prices.

5. After some further discussion of model adjustments and exogenous assumptions, arrangements were made to review the new forecast the following Monday.

Step 1: Tuning the Model

Approximately 20 days after the end of each quarter—in mid-January, mid-April, mid-July, and mid-September—the Bureau of Economic Analysis in Washington releases preliminary Gross National Product (GNP) statistics for the quarter just passed. This is the signal for a new forecasting round to begin. Other new data on personal income, employment, wage rates, prices, retail sales, housing starts, capacity utilization, and money and interest rates are also available about this time. This is the occasion for a general review of the economic situation and the model's performance.

First the model must be adjusted. The new data (and revised data for earlier time periods) are entered into the data bank and the computer is instructed to produce a "residual check." For each separate behavioral equation the left-hand value is computed using the most recent actual values of the right-hand side variables. (This is not a model solution or a forecast. It is simply a test, on a one equation at a time basis, of how the equations would have performed had the actual information been available for the right-hand side variables.) The pattern of the (differences) residuals between the observed values of the dependent (left-hand side) variables and the estimated values tells us whether the equation is tracking properly.

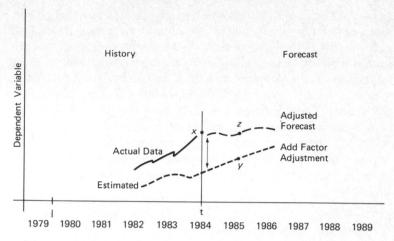

Figure 5-1. Illustration of equation adjustment.

Often, as one might expect, the residuals take a random pattern with only moderately greater errors than were seen over the time period over which the parameters of the equation were estimated. But sometimes errors are not random. An unusually large error or systematically positive or negative residual may be found. This means that the equation has slipped. Such a situation is shown in Figure 5-1. The solid line represents the observed values and the dotted line shows the estimated values using the appropriate model equation and known values of the right side variables. Note how the dotted line (estimated) has slipped below the solid line (actual) during the recent historical period. This slippage could be expected to continue into the forecast. Without an adjustment the forecast would go from an actual value x in 1984 to a forecast value y in 1985, a decline.

The adjustment shown on the chart brings the forecast to point z well in line with past history. For each behavioral equation, we must decide whether to make an adjustment and, if so, how much of an adjustment to make. Perhaps the error can be explained as the result of an extraordinary event—a hurricane or a strike and in that case the slippage would be a one-time occurrence and no adjustment may be necessary. But, in many cases, residuals are systematic because the data have been revised or—rarely—the behavior itself may have changed. In these cases, error is likely to persist. It would be foolish to use the model without making allowances for such deviations. Without adjustments, the problem variables would be badly predicted, and that, in turn, would affect the results for other variables of the model. The adjustment usually take the form of additions or subtractions from the constant of the equations, called constant adjustments or add factors, sufficient to bring the estimated value of the dependent variable approximately into line with the corresponding observed values in the last two or three quarters.

Step 2: Exogenous Assumptions

Econometric model forecasts are conditional forecasts. They can be no more realistic than the assumptions that have gone into them.

The first task is to put together the forward values of the exogenous variables. Numerous important figures remain outside the model. It is the forecaster's job to obtain "best guess" values for them. Sometimes the forecaster can draw on official forecasts; sometimes other specialized econometric models can be used. Still other times the exogenous variables are projected "by guess or by gum."

Federal Budget Estimates

This discussion begins with an analysis of the federal budget. The President's budget proposal is the starting point for our appraisal of probable federal purchases, transfer payments, grants-in-aid, and other outlays. But we must keep in mind that even the most responsible government cannot always accurately control its spending. Congress frequently authorizes additional expenditures. Military expenditures frequently exceed what had originally been authorized. It takes expertise and judgment to derive a realistic picture of government expenditure trends and to translate them into appropriate inputs for the model.

Drawings by Redinger

On the revenue side of the budget, federal tax rates must be predicted. This, too, is tricky because it is necessary to second-guess whether the President will ask for, and the Congress pass, changes in tax laws. Frequently, tax changes take the form of specific reforms such as loophole closing, instead of across-the-board rate changes. Such revisions must be carefully accommodated in the model. Estimates of the revenue implications of alternative tax regulations prepared by the Congressional Budget Office are very useful in this task.

The 1985 Budget experience posed a particular challenge in this regard. The President's budget proposal with its huge continued budget deficit lacked political support. At the same time, the President put forward an ambitious plan for tax reform that simultaneously (1) eliminated many loopholes and (2) simplified and somewhat reduced the progressiveness of the income tax rate schedule (i.e., a modified flat tax). Congress, however, had its own agenda: a reluctance to make massive civilian expenditure cuts, priority on reducing the deficit if necessary through tax increases, and a bipartisan interest in tax simplification. The forecaster was faced with the questions: What is the likely outcome? What should fiscal policy assumptions for the baseline forecast be? The Wharton forecasters assumed that (1) Congressional deliberations would delay a comprehensive tax reform program until mid-1986 and (2) it would be toned down considerably at that point. For 1985, the forecasters assumed a compromise of spending cuts and loophole closing. Fortunately, numerous alternative model simulations could be carried out to test the implications of alternative fiscal policy scenarios. (See the discussion of policy simulation later in this chapter.) But, even so, much uncertainty remained about the appropriate budget assumptions.

Government policy depends on the outcome of elections: a Democratic administration might handle spending quite differently from a Republican one. What is an econometric forecaster to do? One election year, Wharton produced two forecasts, one for a Democratic victory and the other for a Republican win. Distribution of the forecast to clients was delayed long enough for the election to be held, and the appropriate forecast was sent out. Perhaps it is more a reflection of our political system than of econometric forecasting that the two forecasts were quite similar.

State and Local Governments

The discussion now turns to state and local expenditures and revenues. Purchasing by state and local governments reflects needs for schools, police and fire protection, social welfare services, and the like. In the aggregate, these expenditures expand gradually and are predictable from recent trends. But these expenditures also depend greatly on federal grants-in-aid—and these have been cut back sharply. State tax rates must be adjusted (as much as voters are likely to approve) and revisions in spending must be projected in order to keep state and local budgets on an even keel.

Monetary Policy

Monetary policy is the other important macro policy input. As discussed in Chapter 1, in 1979, the Federal Reserve (the Fed) redirected its immediate policy objective from interest rates to direct management of the growth of the money supply. But the Fed found it difficult to control money. There are no direct "handles" on money supply. The Fed can only influence the volume of reserves available to the banking system through open market operations, changes in reserve requirements, and the discount rate. The main monetary policy variable in the model is nonborrowed reserves, that is, reserves held by the banking system that have not been borrowed from the Federal Reserve.

In preparing the forecast, forward estimates of the available nonborrowed reserves of the banking system must be made. Implicitly, this involves appraisal of the entire monetary policy posture of the Federal Reserve. In 1982, with the economy in recession and the inflation rate reduced, the Fed shifted toward easier monetary policy, a policy that had been introduced into the Wharton forecast well in advance. In 1983 and 1984, rapid growth of money supply and prospects of large deficits raised fears that the Fed might once again tighten credit. For a time there was the added uncertainty of whether Fed Chairman Volcker would be reappointed to a second four-year term. Fortunately, easing of inflation eventually allowed a gradual expansion of money supply and reduction in interest rates.

In dealing with such a situation, the forecasters must think of themselves in Chairman Volcker's chair at the head of the Federal Reserve Open Market Committee table. What is the situation of financial markets and of the economy in general? What are the policy tools at the Fed's disposal? How might the Fed use them to achieve its declared objectives? In the model, reserves must be adjusted in accord with expected Federal Reserve open market operations and in line with what is required to come close to targets for growth of money and credit and for interest rates. The discount rate must also be adjusted, but these days that tends to be an adjustment to the prevailing short-term interest rates rather than an exogenous policy variable.

Policy responds to economic developments. Consequently, policy steps cannot always be predicted long in advance. When the economic environment changes, Federal Reserve policy takes a turn. As our exogenous monetary policy variables are developed, similar adjustments are made. If the economy is seen to be in need of additional stimulus, additional borrowed reserves must be pumped in to ease monetary markets, reduce interest rates, and stimulate demand. This requires careful judgment in formulating a realistic set of policy assumptions. Often, it calls for repeated forecast runs until a most probable combination of policy and economic prospects is obtained.

Other Exogenous Variables

There are numerous other exogenous variables for which forecast values must be determined. Even in a large model, many parts of the economic world remain exogenous. Among the most important of these are the exogenous variables for foreign trade. Exports depend on the volume of world trade. A reasonable path for world trade is thus projected using available forecasts for other major countries. The Wharton world model and international regional service forecasts are essential for this purpose. A price variable for foreign trade—that is, the prices of imported goods into the United States and the prices of goods competing with American exports in world markets—must also be provided. The competitiveness of American and foreign prices has been greatly influenced in recent years by the volatile exchange rate for the dollar which is projected on the basis of the monthly forecasts of the Wharton exchange rate service.

The agricultural sector remains largely exogenous in the model. The Wharton agricultural models and the work of the Department of Agriculture are heavily relied on for estimates of agricultural production and probable trends of agricultural prices.

A word about consistency is appropriate here. The assumptions of the forecast must be consistent. Assumptions about the exchange rate must fit with the view of U.S. and foreign monetary policy, interest rates, and capital inflows; assumptions about energy prices must be consistent with what is happening in energy markets in the United States and abroad; and so on. The interrelated system of models at Wharton has been invaluable to maintain a high degree of consistency between model inputs. The model operators meet regularly to assure a common and consistent assumption scenario. The results of each model are fed into the other relevant models. Thus, for example, the trends in world economic activity projected by the world model enter as an assumption into the quarterly U.S. model. If necessary, the results of the quarterly forecast would then be used to modify the world forecast. Such a procedure calls for a high degree of interaction, but the payoff in terms of a consistent—and thus persuasive—picture of the economy is considerable.

These, in turn, determine farm income and purchasing of the agricultural sector.

Numerous "special events" disturb the movement of the economy. In the short run, strikes in major industries and on the docks may disrupt production, inventories, and foreign trade. Hurricane and flood damage interrupt output and call for sudden investment expenditures for rebuilding and repair. To obtain a realistic forecast, these special developments must be factored into the model.

There are various other exogenous variables. The labor force, much affected by the increasing participation of women, has been hard to track in recent years and an exogenous adjustment of the labor force figures is required. Population, employment in agriculture, self-employment, the number of men in military service, rental income, and business transfer payments are among the exogenous variables in the model. Many of these variables can be projected by recent trends. The forecaster must develop a "feel" for the movement of these variables. If the forecast is to be relevant and accurate, the exogenous assumptions must be realistic.

Paradoxically, the demand for econometric forecasts is greatest just when extraordinary developments modify the behavioral relations built into the model. Careful adjustment to build in the new developments can make the model a valuable instrument for appraising the new situation. When the Arab countries imposed an oil embargo on the United States in October 1973, many authorities feared that our economy would come to a sudden catastrophic halt. An analysis of the model was done in a three-step process:

1. Evaluating how serious the oil shortage would be and how long it would last was the first step. The estimate of between 2 and 3 million barrels per day over a period of three to six months was correct.
2. The shortfall of petroleum was allocated among various users. Most of it was directed to consumers in order to minimize the impact on industrial production and employment.
3. Numerous adjustments were made so that the forecast would reflect the fuel crisis—that is, reducing consumption of oil and gas and purchases of cars, cutting back inventories, lowering imports, and raising prices.

The results of these calculations proved, in retrospect, to have been quite accurate. The prediction of a relatively mild economic slowdown that would develop immediately as a result of a brief oil embargo was right. Later forecasts projected the large recession that was associated with the increase of oil prices in 1974–75. More recently, questions about the issue of oil prices have been in the other direction: How far will oil prices come down? How will the economy be affected?

Step 3: The Preliminary Forecast

Once these exogenous inputs have been set, a preliminary forecast is computed. This forecast must be examined carefully in light of the following:

- There should not be any anomalies.
- The predicted values should not be unreasonable.

- There should not be unaccountably large jumps in some of the variables.
- The various parts of the forecast should be broadly consistent. For example, price movements should not be out of line with wages and profits, movements of unemployment must be consistent with changes in employment, and the latter must be consistent with changes in output and productivity, and government tax receipts must reflect movements in taxable incomes.

A number of preliminary solutions are usually required until all problems have been cleared up. Sometimes the problem is just a clerical error in the exogenous data inputs, such as a misplaced decimal point. At other times, the assumed constant adjustment may not have been sufficient to put a variable in line with known recent information. However, the economist must be sure that any prior intuitions about economic conditions have not influenced the overall forecast. It is all too easy to adjust the model to one's preconceived notions of the economic outlook. The model must be adjusted and repeated forecasts must be made until a "good" forecast is obtained—but the adjustments must not reflect the forecaster's bias. As much as possible, the model must be allowed to "speak for itself." This represents a difficult challenge.

There is a saying among business economists: "If you must forecast, forecast often!" Some wags would have it: "If you can't forecast, forecast often!"

Step 4: The Forecast Meeting

The forecast meeting is the occasion for practicing forecasters from business, government, and the academic world to evaluate the forecast and its underlying assumptions. The preliminary forecast, in full detail, is sent out to the subscribers one or two weeks in advance of the meeting. When these meetings were originally started, now about twenty years ago, they were held around a big table with perhaps 10 or 12 economists participating. These sessions have grown to between 100 and 150 people, usually economists and planners from subscribing business and government organizations. The dialogue format between the Wharton forecasters and the economists from business and government is still maintained. Microphones are scattered throughout the audience and the subscribers participate actively in the discussion. (Many of them are warned in advance that they will be called on and they will have prepared remarks on their industry.)

Each part of the forecast is examined systematically: the adjustments and policy assumptions, the aggregate forecast, each of the demand components, the forecast for wage and prices, the monetary sector, and so forth. In the meeting, the federal budget expert's appraisal of budget prospects is presented; economists from major banks consider the assumptions about monetary policy and evaluate whether the interest rate forecasts are in accord with recent trends; the expert from the auto industry discusses inventory levels and model changeovers, the steel industry representative discusses prospects for a steel strike and likely wage settlements; experts from the Agriculture Department contribute crop and price forecasts for the agricultural sector.

As a result of the discussions, the exogenous assumptions are refined; the remaining anomalies of the forecast are ferreted out; the latest current information (frequently "inside information") is introduced. The Wharton meetings are off the record, and participants frequently provide candid comments about all but the most confidential data.

The meeting serves the Wharton forecasters as an invaluable check on the realism of their work. For the consumers of the forecast, the meeting provides a detailed overview of what is going on in the economy, what other business economists are thinking, and what lies behind the Wharton forecast.

At the close of the forecast meeting, a consensus is reached on the appropriate adjustments and exogenous assumptions for a revised base forecast. This also serves as the occasion to consider alternative simulations using different sets of assumptions. Business economists generally prefer a point forecast to a range forecast because they need a particular figure to use in their business planning—even if that figure is subject to error.

However, they frequently also call for an optimistic and a pessimistic forecast. Since the model only produces one forecast for each set of exogenous assumptions, it is necessary to develop a scenario of optimistic assumptions (e.g., faster growth for the world economy and easier monetary policy) and a set of pessimistic assumptions (e.g., a tighter monetary policy scenario). Alternative scenarios about prospective fiscal policy changes, for example, alternative proposed tax plans, or about labor negotiations, a potential strike, for example, are also considered. As many as a half-dozen alternative forecasts are often proposed. Subscribers to the time-share service can at all times run their own alternative scenarios on the computer, as can those with a personal computer version of the Wharton model.

Step 5: Base Forecast and Alternatives

On the basis of the discussions of the meetings, new forecasts are prepared. A month has now passed since the preliminary forecast was made, and the new forecasts embody revised data that have become available in the meantime. Again, several tries may be necessary until the new assumptions have been properly put into the model and until all anomalies have been eliminated. The base solution remains the standard forecast for the Wharton model until the next month's forecasting round when an updated forecast is distributed. Intervening policy changes or crises call for an intermediate revision. Thus, keeping the forecast updated is practically a continuous process.

The alternate forecasts are all variants of the base forecast. All adjustments and assumptions are the same except the ones describing the special attributes of the alternative scenarios.

Step 6: "What If" Forecasts

Frequently the meeting reveals differences of opinion about the most probable policy scenario. The possibility of a tax increase, tight money, or various tax changes must be examined. In 1985, the impacts of various tax and spending alternatives to reduce the budget deficit—cuts in various spending programs, deferral of a Social Security cost-of-living adjustment, elimination of certain personal income tax deductions, and even some more far out proposals—were being looked at. Alternative policy simulations are useful not only from the point of view of prediction, but also as tests of the effect of policy on the economy. The policy maker should not manage the economy without fairly clear notions of in what way, by how much, and with what time lags policy moves affect the economy.

The multiplier solutions shown in Chapter 4 are simple examples of tests of policy alternatives. In practice, however, complex policy packages are often required. When the economy faces a problem—for example, a huge budget deficit, a foreign exchange crisis, or runaway inflation—a mixture of policies is appropriate. The policy response must be tailored to the situation. *What if* alternatives often focus on particular problem situations. A recent Wharton scenario study considered "crunch, crisis, or crash"[1] in relation to international debt and the world economy. The study also examined the policy prescription appropriate to bring the economy back on target. Policy simulations and special studies are an important ingredient of the continuing forecast and simulation process.

The Time Horizon of the Forecast

The above discussion was concerned with a short-term forecast, one focused in the coming year but usually extended over eight to ten quarters. There are important differences between such a short-term forecast and medium-term and long-term forecasting. The short-term forecast is primarily concerned with the short-term prospects and the business cycle. The medium-term forecast looks ahead two to four years. The long-term forecast is focused on projection of the economy's growth potentials over many years.

The Short-Term Forecast

Much of the forecasting effort in the business world focuses on the short-term outlook. Business economists follow closely

"I foresee an upturn within the next six to eight million years."
Drawing by Stevenson; Copyright © 1983, The New Yorker Magazine, Inc.

the indicators of current economic activity in the economy and in their industry. Much of the discussion in Wharton's quarterly forecast meetings concerns a very short-term time perspective—production plans, the status of inventories, the probable effect of impending tax cuts or budget plans, the current situation of financial markets and the movement of interest rates over a six- to twelve-month time horizon. While a focus on the immediately impending twists and turns of the business cycle is understandable, it is not clear how much of the short-term economic intelligence is actionable from the point of view of business. There is only limited scope for modifying production schedules or financing plans over a short time horizon. Insofar as the short-term forecast projects further, say 12 to 24 months, the information becomes more directly relevant to many business decisions but over that time span the forecast also becomes considerably more uncertain.

The Medium-Term Forecast

A medium term (three to five years) forecast must show both the ups and down of the business cycle. Preferably, it will depict a typical business downturn or a recession somewhere in the "out years" of the forecast period. It is important for capital planning to recognize the possibility of a recession and to consider its implications for business decisions. The timing of the recession may remain uncertain, but it is easier to adjust to changes in the timing of a recession than to plan on a trend projection that is not likely to materialize.

The Long-Term Forecast

While econometric models have been most widely used for business cycle forecasting, businesses have important needs for long-run projections over a five- to seven-year time perspective on which to base corporate plans and investment evaluations and even over longer spans to the year 2000 or beyond for strategic planning purposes.

It is not a good idea to forecast long-term trends with a short-term business cycle model. Specialized long-term forecasting models have been developed. These emphasize the supply side, particularly the characteristics of the production functions, technological change, the accumulation of capital stock, and the growth of labor force. While a short-term model may focus mainly on cyclical movements, a long-term model must tend to some equilibrium path, or else it can get badly thrown off track as it is projected far into the future. Finally, a long-term model need not be concerned with quarterly movements and can be built in an annual time frame, making use of much data that are not available on a quarterly basis.

For a simple "back of the envelope" long-term forecast, labor force and the trend of productivity can be used to get a long-term GNP projection on the basis of the identity:

$$\% \text{ change GNP} = \% \text{ change labor force} + \% \text{ change productivity}.$$

While this quick and dirty method is sometimes helpful, it clearly is not sufficient. Both labor force and productivity are endogenous variables in the system. Labor force participation depends on wage rates and on the availability of employment opportunities. Productivity is difficult to predict since many of the factors that lie behind productivity trends are not well known. But productivity also must be treated as an endogenous variable dependent on the accumulation of capital stock and on its utilization. This means that long-term models cannot only treat the supply side without recognizing demand. Both supply and demand sides must be represented.

For long-term forecasting, Wharton operates the mammoth (2500 equations) Wharton Annual and Industry Model. This system has the special features of long-term models noted above. In addition, it incorporates an input output system—an essential ingredient if long-term growth is to be related to industrial structure. The latter is flexible adjusting to relative prices of inputs and technical change and serves to draw a complete picture of industry activity (a breakdown of some 50 industries) for the economy throughout the entire long-run forecast period.

Some forecasters would argue that the long run is easier to forecast than the short run. "It is just a matter of putting a ruler to a piece of semilog paper." But that is far from the truth. Outright trend projections lacking a structural basis sometimes go badly wrong. And they are not likely to be persuasive to the business decision maker. Our understanding of long-run growth processes is imperfect. There have been numerous attempts to explain the secular slowdown in productivity growth that has affected most of the Western economies during the past decade, but most of them end up with a large unexplained component. Econometric models catch long-run developments only broadly. After all, even the fairly long postwar data series only contain one or two examples of long-term developments as compared to six or seven or eight business cycles. This means that the statistically estimated coefficients in the models that deal with long-term relationships are not likely to be reliable. This is all the more true since many variables follow a common long-run trend making it extremely difficult, if not impossible, to disentangle their separate effects in the statistical estimation process.

The long-run forecast is fundamentally different from its

shorter run cousins. Whereas the latter predict what is likely to happen—good or bad—the long-run forecast is a projection with substantial normative content. In the long run, if an initial policy assumption produces undesirable results (e.g., if the assumption of tight money turns the economy into recession and high unemployment), there is time for public authorities to change their policies. It would make little sense to project economic scenarios that are politically unacceptable. Consequently, the long-term forecaster begins with some notion of the macroeconomic targets of the economy. The forecaster uses policy mixes that will come close to achieving these targets. If employment falls short of target or if inflation is too high, the policy assumptions are adjusted to bring the economy (as simulated in the model) back to the desired target range. Consequently, long-term forecasts are sometimes projections of targets rather than realistic appraisals of where the economy may actually end up.

But this poses a further problem. Should there be business cycle fluctuations in a long-run forecast? Surely, if macro policies are effective, there should no longer be a business cycle, or so we used to think. But even if they are not, we would be hard put today to predict the dating and magnitude of business cycles out in the far distant future. Consequently, even though long-term forecasts may show the impact of existing cyclical forces at the beginning of the forecast period, they generally forecast smooth trends.

On seeing a long-term trend projection, an inexperienced young business economist returned to the home office and reported to management: "I have good news. Wharton says there will be no more recession between now and the year 2000!" Klein on the other hand, writes "a forecast of several years running without a business cycle correction defies the law of economics and documented history."[2]

Business forecasters are frequently dissatisfied with this approach. They fear that long-term targets will not be achieved

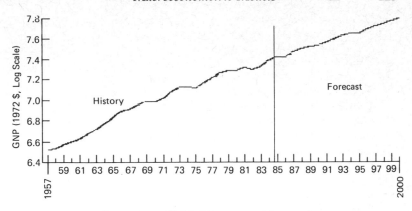

Figure 5-2. GNP: History and forecast.

and, if past history is any guide, that a smooth trend is likely to be interrupted by business cycles and other "shocks." Consequently, in order to give a realistic picture of the risk, a typical recession pattern is included in our long-term forecast. (See for example, Figure 5-2, a recent Wharton Econometric long-term forecast.) Business forecasters must recognize that the future is uncertain, and, consequently the further out one projects, the more uncertain it is. What appears in Figure 5-2 as a clear, fairly narrow forecast line should really be an increasingly broad haze that can encompass a variety of possible outcomes. The business decision maker can then ask how to accommodate to some of the "worst case" outcomes.

All in all, long-run forecasts are essential in many applications. They project the long-run growth trend of demand, the effect of demographic shifts, the likely impact of technological changes, the shifts in the structure of industry, and so forth. The long run is the appropriate time perspective in which to study both supply side policies and industrial policies to improve productivity and competitiveness.

Short- and Long-run Forecasts Compared

In summary, then, the distinguishing characteristics between short- and long-term forecasts are:

- Short-term and medium-term forecasts are dominated by business cycle swings; long-term forecasts focus on the evolving trend and on compositional and structural change.
- Short-term forecasts embody numerous elements of current information—for example, investment plans, inventory levels, and consumer and business sentiment. Long-run forecasts are considerably more independent of current developments, but they must still take into account long-term changes in technology, social organization, demographic structure, and even behavior.
- Short-term forecasts can often treat policy as an exogenous element. Known budget plans and policy postures can be integrated into the forecast. The long-run forecast must treat government policy as a quasi-endogenous factor adapting it toward the attainment of economic objectives.

Policy Simulation

Strictly speaking, to the extent that *what if* forecasts represent consideration of alternative policies, they are simulating policy. In actual practice, such policy simulation is in its own right an important application of econometric models in the academic world, business, and government. An example of this is the recent interest by business leaders, concerned by the large projected government budget deficits, in devising an acceptable strategy to balance the budget.

Numerous policy alternatives have been proposed: some involving tax increases, others expenditure cuts or changes in monetary policy, and still others calling for a mixture of policies. The macroeconometric model is an excellent tool for evaluating the effects of alternative policies on an economy-wide, consistent basis, particularly since the proposed policies have consequences not only for the deficit but also for numerous dimensions of the aggregate economy. Indeed, the effect on the deficit depends greatly on the impact of the proposed measures on economic activity, inflation, unemployment, interest rates, and similar variables.

One of the most interesting possibilities for raising additional revenues is the value added tax (VAT), a principal source of government revenue in European countries. In Figures 5-3A to 5-3C, a model solution imposing a value added tax is compared

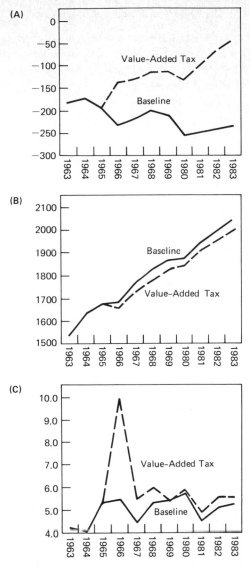

Figure 5-3A. Federal deficit—baseline and value-added-tax
alternative (in billions of current dollars).

Figure 5-3B. Real GNP—baseline and value-added tax alternative (in
billions of 1972 dollars).

Figure 5-3C. GNP implicit price deflator—baseline and value-added-
tax alternative (percent change).

127

to a baseline forecast. The tax is imposed at all stages of the production process on the value added—that is, the value of the product sold less the producer's purchases of materials and supplies. Typically, such a tax is passed on to the final purchaser and, consequently, it is often considered similar in its impact to a sales tax.

A 5% VAT is assumed to go into effect in 1986. The impact on federal revenues and on the federal deficit (Figure 5-3A) is immediate and dramatic. The deficit is reduced by approximately $90 billion from its baseline solution values in 1986, and there is further steady improvement thereafter. As most analysts fear, imposition of a VAT is inflationary with an inflation rate of almost 10%, up some 4½% in 1986 (see Figure 5-3B). But the effect on inflation is temporary and inflation gradually returns to its baseline simulation path. The simulation assumes only partial accomodation by the Federal Reserve so that the imposition of the tax causes a rise of some 3% in short-term interest rates in 1986. The restrictive effect of the tax increase plus the impact of the higher interest rates result in a somewhat lower level of real GNP throughout the forecast period (Figure 5-3C).

This simulation is an example of a typical model application. Similar policy simulations were being made by government agencies like the Office of Management and Budget (OMB) and the Congressional Budget Office (CBO) and are being used in decision making by the Administration and the Congress.

Policy simulation calls for careful econometric craftsmanship and even model building. For tax and expenditure simulations, the model already contains many policy "handles," variables that describe tax rates and expenditures and can be altered according to the desired policy scenario. Even in this case, care is needed to assure that the policy change is carried through by the model to the appropriate impact points in the economy and with reasonably sized effects. But many policies involve complex changes affecting the economy in ways that are not easily integrated into the model structure.

An example is an econometric study of national industrial policy.[3] Such a policy has often been proposed as a remedy to the problems of slow growth and international competitiveness of the U.S. economy. As past experience in the United States and, particularly, abroad shows, such policies can take a vast variety of forms:

- Broadly general incentives or narrowly industry- or project-specific policies
- Tax incentives, preferential capital flows, or direct public investment
- Tariffs or import quotas
- Broad aid to research and development and education

The University of Pennsylvania industrial policy study was designed to investigate the impact of alternative types of tax incentives for investment and to examine the impact of general versus targeted industry-specific policies. The large-scale Wharton Long-Term Model is ideally suited to this kind of work since it includes a fully endogenized interindustry structure that is sensitive to the relative prices of inputs into production. But, even so, extensive model modifications had to be made to assure that the adjustment of industrial capital stock was fully responsive to the relative cost of capital—to be affected by the tax incentives—relative to that of labor. Once appropriate tests and a base solution had been completed, the simulations involved introducing alternative industrial policy tax incentive schemes into the model and comparing the results.

As shown in Figures 5-4 and 5-5, the impact on the economy of the various schemes differs but follows a time path of gradual upward adjustment and then decline in all cases. It is clear that the impact of the investment tax credit is greater, for the same general cost to the U.S. Treasury, than other schemes of investment stimulus (for example, a general reduction in corporate income taxes).

With regard to the question of targeting policy to benefit particular industries, only fairly broad schemes were considered (a narrowly targeted scheme would have been hard to accommodate in the model). Consequently, general, nontargeted incentives were compared with incentives targeted on broad industrial categories—the high technology industries, the basic industries, and the metals using industries. The results show that, not surprisingly, a targeted policy, particularly in the high technology industries has more impact dollar for dollar than do

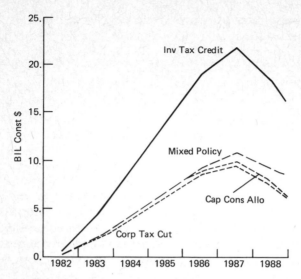

Figure 5-4. Impact on real GNP—industrial policy scenarios.

Figure 5-5. General versus industry-specific incentives.

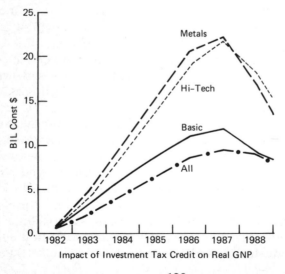

Impact of Investment Tax Credit on Real GNP

130

the general incentives (Figure 5-5). But it is important to note that the general industrial policy, which is supposedly not targeted on any particular industry, also had more impact on certain industries than others, a fact that is probably not lost on the supporters of such programs. The results of these simulations provide a first rough level of empirical information on industrial policy. They represent a challenging application of policy simulation.

On the other hand, these simulations also illustrate some of the limitations of econometric modeling for policy analysis. Many aspects of an industrial policy that one might like to test empirically are difficult, if not impossible, to build into an econometric model. An example is more narrowly targeted policies that affect a narrow industrial category, such as large-scale integrated electronic circuits, and do not show up separately in the model. Also, it is difficult to appraise the potential impact of aid to research and development. Such policies are likely to have important outcomes, but their results are poorly measured in econometric models. For that matter, most macromodels do not even have a category for research and development expenditures. Finally, industrial policies are more than the sum of their parts. They frequently consist of broad strategies intended to turn around entire industrial structures and to shift the production functions of major industries. Analysis of these phenomena is challenging. While the model simulations may be helpful, they may not provide a complete picture of the impacts of industrial policy scenarios.

The Business Perspective

Where then does the macroeconomic forecast fit from the perspective of potential users in business and in government?

The Forecast Users

One indication is in the makeup of the economists who attend Wharton's quarterly forecasting meetings. These economists represent a cross section of major American industries, retail companies, transportation, and banks. State and federal government agencies including such important departments as the Office of Management and Budget, the Department of Defense, and Congressional Committees are also represented.

What jobs do they hold in their organizations? Again, the range is wide, particularly since some companies send their senior forecasters while others send more junior personnel. Generally though, the attendees fall into two categories: (1) those who are the "company economist" or in the economics department; and (2) those who are part of a planning department or company financial office. In the first case, they see their job as fairly strictly economics, though with an orientation to the industry or the company. They advise the company on the economic environment and its implications. The functions of the planning and financial staff, on the other hand, are with internal planning or company financial matters. Their concern with the macro economy is considerably different, seeing the macro forecast largely as an external input. They are likely to be less interested in the general outlook and more in the specific variables affecting their industry and firm.

The Applications of the Forecast

What are the principal uses for the macro forecast? The uses vary from the most general background information to the most specific inputs closely tied to the company's operations.

As a Measure of the Economic Environment at Present and into the Future   The traditional role of the business economist has been to evaluate the current economic environment and economic prospects for management, the corporate chief executive, and the board. Often, the information needed is broadly comprehensive but not numerically precise. Management wants to know when the turnaround in the economy will occur, approximately how rapid economic growth will be, what the impediments to faster growth or the forces that cause a more rapid expansion will be, what the likely impact on inflation rate will be, what activity in major industries will be, and what interest rates will be. Such information, sometimes provided by the economist's office or an outside consultant, is now frequently taken from the forecasts of the econometric forecasting services. With the greater availability of economic forecast data and with greater understanding of what the statistics mean, even this broad background calls for more precision and more detailed information than it used to. As we have noted, economic literacy has increased in general and many business executives have been exposed to advanced economics in their MBA training. The forecast meetings described above are clearly useful to provide the desired economic background.

How is this information used by the corporation? Often, it is factored into business decisions in an informal nonempirical way. It serves as a basis for business planning. It relates to the company's public position on current policy issues. This information deals only broadly with the company's specific business or product lines for which typically the marketing and planning departments have primary responsibility.

As a Basis for the Company's Planning Assumptions   Companies differ greatly in the degree to which the planning process is formalized and the degree to which detailed planning assumptions are factored into corporate decision making. But in almost all cases a set of planning assumptions represents a compromise view of exogenous economic variables (and sometimes targets) that are to be used throughout the corporation for planning. Such planning assumptions avoid the inevitable problems that would arise if one division projects the economy in one way and another makes different assumptions. The economic forecast frequently serves as the basis of the economy's planning assumptions. These assumptions may be quite general—for example, the growth rate of real GNP, inflation, and interest rates—or they may be more narrowly focused on the variables relevant to the particular industry—for example, the growth of consumer disposable real income and purchasing for a retail or consumer goods company, the cost of raw material and fuel inputs for a manufacturing company, the growth of construction and the sales of durables and capital goods for a steel company, the movement of Eurodollar interest rates and exchange rates for the company operating in the world market.

Details of the forecast provided by the forecasting services and their consistency are important ingredients. Thus, the firm can be sure that the assumptions it has made about interest rates are consistent with the assumptions about money supply, real growth, and inflation. It can also obtain detailed figures for other variables appearing in the forecast. Often the planning assumptions serve as background for the planning process. Some companies, however, link the planning assumptions formally into simulation systems and models.

As an Input into the Company's Models and Product Line Forecasts   This represents the furthest integration of forecast data and the company's operating system. Again, various degrees of integration are possible. In some cases, only a few macro variables are fed into a company's product line forecasting equations. In others, the macro inputs are directed into industry models and these in turn may be linked to simulation systems of the company's operations and financial system. (For a discussion of this, see Chapter 9.)

The most advanced and most efficient approach is direct linkage of macro variables to company models. Typically, this has meant storing the company model on the time-share system of the forecast vendor. This meant keeping company data on a central computer and keeping the company's models on that system as well. Every time the macro forecast changes, the new forecast is fed into the company model. The result is a proprietary company simulation consistent with the changed forecast of the national environment.

As will be discussed further below, this approach is rapidly changing. Forecast data are being downloaded from the central mainframe computer to the client's computers, often directly to microcomputers in the planner's office. The considerable potentials for introducing current and forecast information into microcomputer model systems used for capital budgeting, market development, cash management, inventory and production decisions, and so forth need no elaboration. The significant advantages of using the microcomputer with respect to cost and convenience of operation suggest that this will be the basis for a great expansion of the use of econometric models and forecast data.

Further Readings

Blue Chip Economic Indicators, a newsletter published by Eggert Enterprises of Sedona, Arizona, regularly reports the macroeconomic forecasts of many business and academic forecasters. A $5000 prize is awarded annually to the best forecaster, based on the forecasts reported in the newsletter.

To have the full detail of the forecasts, as many as 2000 variables, it is necessary to subscribe to one of the forecast services: Wharton Econometrics, Chase Econometrics, or DRI. Other smaller forecast vendors are found in academia and in business. Some of these are the University of Michigan and UCLA, for example; often they have a strong local following. Others specialize in regional forecasts or in narrow aspects of the economy. Georgia State's forecasting group has made a specialty of forecasting producer prices, for example.

C. W. J. Granger, *Forecasting in Business and Economics* (New York: Academic Press, 1980), is a straightforward book on forecasting. It contains numerous examples. Scott Armstrong, *Long Range Forecasting,* 2nd ed. (New York: Wiley, 1985), is a survey volume.

Policy simulation is an ongoing activity in government (e.g., at the Congressional Budget Office). Many of the budget studies published by the CBO are based on macromodel simulations.

For more detail on econometric studies of industrial policy, see F. G. Adams, ed., *Industrial Policies for Growth and Competitiveness,* Vol. II (Lexington, Mass.: D. C. Heath, 1985).

Notes

1. Wharton Econometric Forecasting Associates, *The World at the Crossroads: International Financial Crunch, Crisis, or Crash?* (Philadelphia: Wharton Econometrics, 1983).
2. *Journal of Forecasting* (March 1984).
3. Adams, F. G. and V. G. Duggal, "General versus Industry-Specific Industrial Policies: Quantifying the National and Sectoral Impacts," in F. G. Adams, ed., *Industrial Policies for Growth and Competitiveness, Volume II* (Lexington, Mass.: D. C. Heath, 1985).

✻ 6 ✻

The Track Record of
Econometric Macro Forecasting

Almost invariably, presentation of a forecast to a new group is followed by the question "How accurate are your forecasts?" That is a tough question to answer! How accurate in comparison to what? Over what time span? With respect to what dimension: GNP, prices, or interest rates? On the basis of what underlying assumptions?

Forecast Accuracy

Forecast accuracy depends greatly on the specifics of the forecast being made and varies with the particular variable being predicted. An aggregate like GNP moves relatively smoothly, allowing room for some offsetting errors in the various sectors. On the other hand, forecasts for particular industries, or for volatile magnitudes like inventory change or investment, are subject to both a great deal of uncertainty and a relatively wide range of error.

There is evidence that forecast accuracy deteriorates as the distance into the future increases. However, this is not a simple relationship. Forecasts for the current quarter are often relatively inaccurate also, depending greatly on the amount of current information available. For this reason, forecasts made later in the quarter are likely to be more accurate than forecasts made early in the quarter. But—if the underlying trends prevailing in the economy have a chance to operate—forecasts stretching out over a year or more may be closer to the mark than nearer-term forecasts. Finally, much depends on exogenous assumptions. Are the assumptions about external conditions and policy made by forecaster accurate descriptions of future developments? Sometimes the underlying uncertainty is great, for example, when the policy of public agencies remains uncertain or when there are external shocks that cannot be predicted. Consequently, it is not surprising that many forecasters went wrong during the period of the oil shocks.

The ambivalence of many economists on the subject of econometric models is well illustrated by some passages that appear in the *same* chapter of Lester Thurow's *Dangerous Currents*[1]

Page 104

In the 1950s, when econometrics first emerged, the discipline was seen in America as an icebreaker that would lead the economics profession through the ice pack of conflicting theories. Econometric techniques would, it was presumed, conclusively prove or disprove economic hypotheses, accurately quantify economic relationships, and successfully predict the economic future.

Page 105

But whatever the problems, mathematical models and their empirical analogue—econometric models—have now become the standard tools of economics. From their beginning in macroeconomic modeling, they have spread out to encompass everything. No branch of economics, including economic history, is now free of their use.

Page 110

The failings of the [econometric] macromodels are also often exaggerated. Better than any other forecasting technique— certainly better than what we had before—the models have consistently predicted some variables and have often produced good overall results.

The question about forecast accuracy is usually answered by pointing out the difficulty of giving a simple answer. In any case, properly analyzing the economic situation is often just as important as forecast accuracy. The conclusion is that our forecasts are "pretty good"!

Forecast accuracy is not the only thing business economists are after. Their objective is to help management reduce uncertainty. In this respect accuracy of the forecast is certainly an important consideration. But for the business economist a black box forecast alone is not sufficient, no matter how accurate it is. It must be possible to support the forecast persuasively to the corporate executives who will be using it as a basis for making potentially costly decisions. It must be possible to appraise the risks of alternative outcomes: Might the forecast be off? By how much? At what time? Gaining acceptance for the forecast is often an educational process showing management that a realistic and consistent picture lies behind the forecast. In this regard econometric model based forecasts offer important advan-

---

Some business forecasters seek safety in numbers. There is a good reason for this. A forecast similar to what others are predicting may be better accepted by management and may have more influence than a contrarian forecast. Moreover, to be out on a limb and to be wrong as well is an unpardonable sin.

The forecast may be affected in other ways. For example, moderate changes in forecast assumptions are more acceptable than wide swings. And, predicted economic changes are often attenuated when compared to the amplitude of observed business cycle fluctuations. Similarly, it is often easier to project a continuation of existing trends than to forecast a turning point. In fact, forecasts are notably inaccurate at turning points.

But one of the professional forecasters claims to have operated differently—with a "going out on a limb" approach. If he was right, he would be noticed; if his forecast was wrong, it would be quickly forgotten!

tages as compared to time series methods or judgmental techniques.

By what standard can forecast accuracy be measured? McNees writes:[2]

> To adopt perfection as the appropriate standard for forecast evaluation would not only be naive, but counterproductive—naive because we *know* that the future cannot be foretold perfectly, and counterproductive because experience has shown that even less than perfect forecasts provide valuable information about the future.

The 1980 Nobel laureate Lawrence Klein has proposed that there may be an underlying "uncertainty principle" to economic forecasts beyond which accuracy cannot be carried, since the data themselves can only be measured with error. In addition to that are the facts that the parameters of the model are estimated subject to statistical error, that the specification of the model is at best an approximation and simplification of the real world, and last, but surely not least, that the exogenous variable assumptions that underlie the forecast may be in error.

For econometric models, but not for nonstatistical forecast methods, it is possible to establish a statistical estimate of error. But statistical error computations for econometric models give only a partial view of the likely error bands around forecasts since they can only be done on the basis of hindsight. In effect, the experimenter does a series of simulations asking how well would the model have worked in the past using known values of the exogenous variables and introducing random error terms to allow for the statistical errors in the structural equations. Such calculations suggest that error bands around the typical one-year GNP forecast might be in the range of plus or minus 1%. Even such an incomplete error band is considerably bigger than most business forecasters would like to see. Error bands around forecasts of some other variables (e.g., fixed investment or inventory change) are a good deal larger. And, as the forecast is projected into the future, beyond the period on which the model has been estimated, error bands widen.

If absolute measures of performance are difficult to establish and evaluate, then forecast accuracy must be a relative concept: relative to extrapolations, relative to conventional noneconometric forecasting procedures, or relative to other econometric model forecasters. Trend extrapolations, or more sophisticated time series methods, have often served as a standard. Comparisons relative to trend extrapolation or time series methods point out one of the difficulties of making these comparisons. For the very short term, it has been found that econometric forecasts do not do as well as time series extrapolation. Is that not a serious indictment of econometrics? Can we say that time series analysis could provide a target that econometric modeling should strive to better over time. Surely there is an element of truth to that notion, if time series forecasts do systematically better than econometric approaches, and if time series provide acceptably accurate forecasts. But the point is not valid, for example, when time series do not produce good forecasts, as happens when underlying conditions are changing over the business cycle, or when a true conditional *what if* analysis of economic prospects is required.

> One economist finds that the accuracy of econometric models represents "folklore" as compared to the "fact" that econometric models are no better than trend extrapolation. But his survey fails to recognize the nature of the economic forecasting process and the dependence of forecast performance on the time span and on the variable being predicted.

When the economy is following a smooth upward trend, extrapolation methods will give a good result. But if the forecaster is concerned with catching the turning points, or with responses to changing policy, a comparison with the results of extrapolation is not helpful. Time series methods miss turning points. These are the most difficult and uncertain times for forecasting; paradoxically, they are also the ones where the forecast is most important.

That leaves comparison relative to other forecasters, noneconometric and econometric. Objective comparisons between econometric and noneconometric methods, independent of the individual forecast practitioners, have not been possible. Noneconometric techniques are not separable from the forecaster. Some use one method, others another. Some document their assumptions, others throw in a large dose of judgment. Some draw heavily on the econometric model forecasts available from the forecast services, others stress the independence of their forecast from all others.

Contrary to what one might think, some of this *ad hominem* aspect of forecasting also applies to most econometric model forecasts. Forecasters using econometric models adjust their equations, as we have noted. Moreover, most of them admit to imposing a judgment factor of between 30 and 50% (Table 6-1). Klein and Young[3] argue that the shifts in the personnel of the Wharton forecasting group and even the changes in the structure of the model do not seem to have affected its forecast error performance on average over a period of 16 years. But, if the varying judgment of different forecasters played a significant role, that result may simply reflect the insensitivity of the measures of accuracy. It is hard to believe that the skill of the model operator, the structure of the model, and even the economic uncertainty of the times being forecast does not affect the accuracy of the predictions.

> Students of model error properties often ask us for our first forecast, that is, the result of the model solution without any adjustments. But that is simply not a meaningful forecast, not only because of lack of realistic adjustments, but more often because the first solution still contains data input errors that may throw the results off widely.

The Forecast Record

Stephen McNees, an economist at the Federal Reserve Bank of Boston, has established himself as the unofficial scorekeeper

Table 6-1 Major Forecasters and Their Techniques

Forecasting Organization (Abbreviated Title) contact for further information	Number of Macroeconomic Variables Forecasted	Typical Forecast Horizon, Quarters	Frequency of Release, Per Year	Date Forecast First Issued Regularly	Forecasting Technique(s) (Approximate Weights)	Published Reference(s)
American Statistical Association and National Bureau of Economic Research Survey of regular forecasts, median, (ASA), Victor Zarnowitz	17	5	4	1968	Most participants rely primarily on an "informal" GNP model; the majority also consider econometric model results.	V. Zarnowitz chapter in Butler, Kavesh, and Platt, eds., *Methods and Techniques of Business Forecasting*, Prentice-Hall, 1974 and NBER *Reporter*, Summer, 1982
Bureau of Economic Analysis, U.S. Commerce Department, (BEA), Michael McKelvey	About 900	10 to 12	8	1967	Econometric model (70%), judgment (20%), current data analysis (5%), interaction with others (5%)	A. Hirsch, et al., ch. 10 in Klein & Burmeister, *Econometric Model Performance*, U. of Penna. Press, 1976
Charles R. Nelson Associates, Inc., Benchmark forecast, (BMARK), Charles R. Nelson	3	4	4	1976	Time-series methods (100%)	C. Nelson, *Applied Time Series Analysis*, Basic Books, 1973
Chase Econometrics, (Chase), Lawrence Chimerine	About 700	10 to 12	12	1970	Econometric model (70%), judgment (20%), time-series methods (5%), current data analysis (5%)	None

Organization				Methods	Reference
Data Resources, Inc., (DRI), Roger Brinner	About 1,000	10 to 12	12	1969	Econometric model (55%), judgment (30%), time-series methods (10%), current data analysis (5%)	O. Eckstein, *The DRI Model of the U.S. Economy*, McGraw-Hill, Inc., 1983
Economic Forecasting Project, Georgia State University, (GSU), Donald Ratajczak	300	8	12	1973	Econometric model (60%), judgment (30%), current data analysis (10%)	None
Kent Economic and Development Institute, (KEDI), Vladimir Simunek	1,699	10	12	1974	Econometric model (60%), judgment (20%), time-series methods (10%), interaction with others (10%)	V. Simunek, *Kent Model of the U.S. Economy*, Kent Econometric Associates, Inc., Kent, Ohio, 1974
Manufacturers Hanover Trust, (MHT), Irwin Kellner	37	4 to 5	3	1970	Econometric model (50%), judgment (50%)	None
Research Seminar in Quantitative Economics, University of Michigan, (RSQE), Saul Hymans	About 100	8	9	1969	Econometric model (80%), judgment (20%)	Harold T. Shapiro and George A. Fulton, Appendix in *A Regional Econometric Forecasting System: Major Economic Areas of Michigan*. University of Michigan Press, 1983
Townsend-Greenspan & Co., Inc., (TG), Alan Greenspan	About 1,400	6 to 10	4	1965	Econometric model (30%), judgment (50%), current data analysis (20%)	None

Table 6-1 *(Continued)*

Forecasting Organization (Abbreviated Title) contact for further information	Number of Macroeconomic Variables Forecasted	Typical Forecast Horizon, Quarters	Frequency of Release, Per Year	Date Forecast First Issued Regularly	Forecasting Technique(s) (Approximate Weights)	Published Reference(s)
University of California at Los Angeles, School of Business, (UCLA), Larry J. Kimbell	About 1,000	8 to 12	4	1968	Econometric model (70%), judgment (20%), interaction with others (10%)	None
Wharton Econometric Forecasting Associates, Inc., (WEFA), Lawrence R. Klein	About 1,200	12	12	1963	Econometric model (60%), judgment (30%), current data analysis (10%)	Lawrence R. Klein and Richard M. Young, *An Introduction to Econometric Forecasting and Forecasting Models*, Lexington, Mass., D.C. Heath & Co., 1980

Source: New England Economic Review (November/December 1983).

144

of the forecasting industry, with frequent reports of the track record of the major forecasters. In his latest compilation (November/December 1983) McNees compares the forecasts of 11 econometric forecast groups (Table 6-2) to the median forecast of a survey carried on by the American Statistical Association (ASA). The ASA survey brings together results from a fairly large number of forecasters but specifies nothing about the methods used. However, according to McNees, most participants (1) rely on an informal GNP model and (2) consider econometric model results.

The compilation of forecasts is based on the notion of the average absolute error (AAE). In verbal terms, AAE represents an unweighted average of the forecast errors disregarding sign, over the forecast horizon considered.*

The McNees compilation covers the seven-year period between the second quarter of 1976 to the second quarter of 1983. This was a span of great cyclical variation. It was first a period of upswing, the later phases of the recovery from the first oil shock. In 1979 and 1980 came an unexpected Federal Reserve policy shift toward tight money and the second oil shock. The result was first a one-quarter mini-recession in 1980 and then the most severe postwar recession in 1981–82. By mid-1983, the U.S. economy was on the way to recovery. This was not an easy time in which to forecast and many excuses have been made

---

*The error is defined as:
$$e_{t+n} = P_{t+n} - A_{t+n}$$
where
P is the forecast value
A is the actual value
n is the forecast horizon beyond the starting point period time t
AAE over m forecasts takes the following form:

$$\text{AAE} = \frac{1}{m} \sum_{t=1}^{m} \left| e_{t+n} \right|$$

An often used alternative measure, root mean square error (RMSE), puts greatest weight on large errors:

$$\text{RMSE} = \sqrt{\frac{\sum_{t=1}^{m} e_{t+n}^2}{m}}$$

for the failure of many forecasters to track the economy well during this period.

A headline in *Barron's* (March 22, 1982) read: "Econometricians Prosper Despite Bum Forecasts!" And the *Philadelphia Inquirer* wrote in bold type "In hindsight, '84 stumped the economic forecasters." Curiously, the same *Philadelphia Inquirer* article (December 30, 1984) reports that Wharton's economists came within a couple of tenths of a percent in predicting the rate of inflation and the growth of real GNP.

McNees shows a range of short-term forecast horizons from one-quarter forecasts to those extending over an eight-quarter forecast period. Since forecasts are prepared at various times during the quarter, McNees seeks to standardize by comparing forecasts prepared at approximately the same time. Table 6-2 shows the error records of the "early quarter forecasts" of the major forecast groups (Chase, DRI, and Wharton). The forecasts were prepared between the third and seventh weeks of each quarter and consequently are benchmarked on the preliminary data for previous quarter's GNP. In each case, the winner of the "horserace" among the three firms is shown in boldface type. We also show for the major aggregates the comparable figure for the American Statistical Association (ASA) survey of forecasts. This is the median of a group of forecasters reporting. The statistics shown in Table 6-2 are based on the concept of average absolute error. They are the percentage difference between the forecast value and the actual value observed (after adjustment for data revision). The following generalities can be drawn from the forecast horserace shown in Table 6-2:

- The errors have been relatively large.
- The errors increase as the forecast horizon is extended into the future.
- The accuracy of the forecasts varies considerably among the various dimensions being forecast.
- Forecast performance varies among the different forecasting

Table 6-2 A Horserace—Forecast Record of Major Forecasters
Average Absolute Errors*
(Annual Rates of Growth)

	Forecast Horizon (quarters)				
	1	2	3	4	8
Real GNP					
Billions of 1972$					
Chase	0.9	1.3	1.8	2.1	2.8
DRI	**0.8**	**1.1**	**1.4**	**1.6**	2.8
Wharton EFA	**0.8**	1.2	1.9	**1.6**	**2.4**
ASA (mid quarter)	0.8	1.2	1.6	1.6	2.4
Nominal GNP					
Billions of current $					
Chase	**1.0**	1.7	2.8	3.6	5.6
DRI	**1.0**	**1.5**	**2.1**	**2.7**	4.6
Wharton EFA	**1.0**	1.6	2.2	**2.7**	**4.0**
ASA (mid quarter)	0.9	1.0	2.1	2.6	—
Deflator for GNP					
1972 = 100					
Chase	**0.3**	**0.6**	1.0	1.4	3.8
DRI	**0.3**	**0.6**	**0.9**	**1.3**	3.6
Wharton EFA	**0.3**	**0.6**	1.0	**1.3**	**3.4**
ASA (mid quarter)	0.3	0.5	0.8	1.1	
Unemployment Rate					
Chase	0.3	0.6	0.8	1.0	1.6
DRI	**0.2**	**0.4**	0.6	0.7	1.1
Wharton EFA	**0.2**	**0.4**	0.5	0.6	**1.0**
ASA (mid quarter)	0.1	0.4	0.6	0.7	
Net Exports (real)					
Chase	**3.1**	**3.5**	**5.5**	6.8	12.3
DRI	3.5	4.1	**5.5**	7.0	12.2
Wharton EFA	3.5	4.3	5.6	**6.8**	**10.5**
90-day Treasury Bill Rate					
Chase	**0.7**	1.7	2.1	2.8	4.2
DRI	0.8	**1.5**	2.0	2.6	3.9
Wharton EFA	**0.7**	**1.5**	**2.0**	**2.4**	**3.5**
Nonresidential Fixed Investment (real)					
Chase	1.9	3.0	4.5	5.9	8.8
DRI	1.8	3.0	**3.6**	**4.6**	7.4
Wharton EFA	**1.6**	**2.7**	3.9	4.7	**5.6**

Table 6-2   (*Continued*)

	Forecast Horizon (quarters)				
	1	2	3	4	8
Personal Consumption Durables (real)					
Chase	2.5	3.2	4.2	4.5	8.8
DRI	2.4	3.1	3.6	4.1	6.4
Wharton EFA	**2.0**	**2.5**	**3.0**	**3.6**	**5.8**
Personal Consumption Nondurables and Services (real)					
Chase	**0.4**	**0.6**	**0.7**	0.8	1.6
DRI	**0.4**	**0.6**	**0.7**	0.7	1.0
Wharton EFA	**0.4**	**0.6**	**0.7**	**0.6**	**0.8**
Investment in Residential Studies (real)					
Chase	4.3	6.6	10.2	13.5	23.6
DRI	3.3	6.2	8.5	10.9	21.8
Wharton EFA	**2.9**	**6.0**	**8.4**	**10.5**	**16.8**
Change in Business Inventories (real)					
Chase	4.9	7.1	8.8	9.1	13.1
DRI	**4.6**	**6.3**	8.8	**8.6**	12.4
Wharton EFA	5.0	**6.3**	**8.7**	9.3	**10.7**
Consumer Price Index					
Chase	**0.4**	**1.0**	1.9	2.4	6.4
DRI	0.5	1.1	1.6	2.3	6.4
Wharton EFA	**0.4**	**1.0**	**1.4**	**1.8**	**5.4**

*Winners are noted in boldface type.
Source: Computed from McNees and Ries (1983).[4] Note that the original document shows errors in growth rates in annual rate terms. We have converted the figure to show difference between forecast and actual level in percent terms.

groups, with some better in one variable and others better on other variables.

• The record of the average of noneconometric forecasts, the ASA consensus, is often as good or better than the major forecasting groups.*

Since the Federal Reserve would hesitate to endorse any particular forecaster, it is fortunate for the economists of the Bos-

---

*This result may be deceiving. The survey is an average of the work of many forecasters, some better than the econometric models, others worse. The ASA forecast comes out later in the quarter than the other forecasts. Some of the forecasters in responding to the ASA survey may themselves be using econometric models or may have had the benefit of the earlier forecasts of the model services.

ton Fed that no forecasting group comes out unequivocally better in all dimensions of the forecast than any others. McNees and Ries (1983) say that "no single forecaster has been most accurate for all or even most macroeconomic variables." A most important point is their conclusion that "the difference between the best and second best performance—and even between the best and worst performances—is typically fairly small, too small to place much confidence in the assumption that it will persist in the future."

Looking at the components of the forecast record, we make the following observations:

Real Gross National Product
- Errors over the first year (four quarters) amount to 1.6%. To give an example, at times when GNP rises by 4% from one year to the next, the forecast could typically be as much as 5.6% as little as 2.4%. That's the difference between a healthy boom and very poor growth.
- But note that the error in the first quarter, the current quarter during which the forecasts are made, is almost 1%, a problem of uncertainty about current developments and forecasting for the ongoing quarter which we consider below.
- Over the longer two-year period, forecasts deteriorate somewhat further with errors of almost 2½%.

GNP Deflator
- Price forecasts are fairly good at the beginning but deteriorate substantially. By the end of the two-year period, the GNP deflator is on average underestimated by 3.4% and the Consumer Price Index (CPI) forecast error is 5.4%.

Nominal Gross National Product
- Forecasts for nominal GNP combine errors in the forecast of prices and real economic activity. There appears to be some offset in the errors of these two components since the errors in nominal GNP are a little less than the sum of the errors in inflation and real activity.

Unemployment
- Forecasts of the unemployment rate are substantial with errors of 0.6% for the best forecaster over a one-year period.

Interest Rates
- The abrupt changes in monetary policy and the instability of interest rates associated with the emphasis on controlling money

supply, particularly in the period 1979 to 1982, made forecasting of interest rates particularly difficult.
- Errors in the forecast of interest rates (Treasury bill rate) are substantial.

GNP Demand Components
- Personal consumption of nondurables and service, which traditionally shows a fairly smooth path, is predicted with relative accuracy.
- Not surprisingly, consumer purchases of durables and investment show much larger percentage forecast errors than for GNP as a whole. One is tempted to stress that these components represent relatively smaller magnitudes in absolute terms than nondurables and services. But, along with business inventory changes, they do represent the dynamic elements in the business cycle. Misses in forecasting of these variables can account for misses in forecasting business cycle turning points.

Forecasting Cyclical Movements

Another way to look at forecast performance is to concentrate on the cyclical movements. Many business executives say that the precision of the forecast is of less concern to them than the need for early warnings of changes in growth trend, the topping out of the business cycle, or the bottoming out at the end of the recession. It is useful to evaluate models from this perspective, though there is not a systematic analysis like that of McNees for this purpose.

It is difficult to make an evaluation of forecasting performance simply in terms of whether the forecast hit the peaks and troughs. A comparison of growth rates—forecast against actual—gives a view of the forecast performance of the model over the cycle. Such a comparison is shown for the Wharton Econometrics forecasts in Figures 6-1 and 6-2 for the annual growth rate of real GNP over recent cyclical periods. (Note that these rate of change graphs would reflect a turning point in the level of GNP data when the rate of change is zero—i.e., when the movement of the economy flattens at the peaks and troughs of the cycle.) In many cases, forecasts may be helpful even when

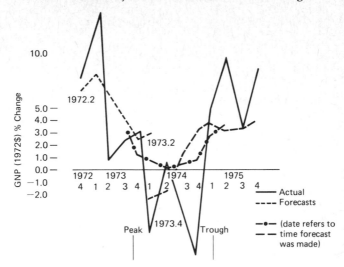

Figure 6-1. Comparison of forecasts with actuals, 1972–76. (*Source:* Compiled by the author from past forecasts of Wharton Econometrics.)

they do not track actual turning points. For example, if the forecast indicates only a slowdown, this is important information even if ultimately the slowdown presages a turning point. Similarly, if the predicted turning point occurs a quarter earlier or a quarter later than the actual turning point, the information may still be valuable. It is important that the forecast not signal false turning points or other false movements.

A graph for the difficult period around the first oil shock 1973–75 is shown in Figure 6-1. The wide swings of the growth of real economic activity, the high growth rate in the first quarter of 1973, and the drop during the recession are notable. No model would hope to catch these jagged movements and it has been suggested that the growth rates on a quarterly basis should be averaged to semi-annual growth rates to give a somewhat smoother and perhaps more accurate picture. Seen with that notion in mind, the forecasts give a rather good picture of the downward and upward movement of the rate of growth of the economy during this volatile period. The forecast during the

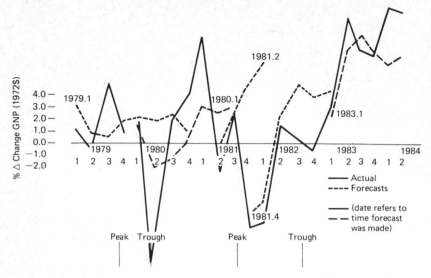

Figure 6-2. Comparison of forecasts with actuals, 1979–82.
(*Source:* Compiled by the author from past forecasts
of Wharton Econometrics.)

second quarter of 1973 followed the timing of the recession closely but it predicted only a growth slowdown not a recession! The fourth quarter forecast predicted the upswing, but too early.

Figure 6-2, for the period 1979 to 1982, includes two dips of recession: (1) a sharp decline in part associated with the Carter Administration's sudden turn toward credit restrictions during 1980 and (2) the more extended dip in 1981-82. This has been a period of difficulty. Institutional changes and a new policy approach affected the forecast. The 1980 dip was underestimated—not surprisingly since there was no way to gauge consumers' responses to the threat of restricted credit. More seriously, with the economy in a high interest rate situation for so long, the forecast failed to catch the full impact of high interest rates when it finally came in 1981. The serious dip of 1981 was not forecast until the slowdown was well under way. The forecast of economic recovery, in late 1982 was successful though it first overestimated and later underestimated the dynamic of the 1982–84 economic recovery.

Can the Forecasting Record Be Improved?

Two important, indeed controversial, issues are (1) whether the record of econometric forecasting is sufficiently good for the forecasts to be useful, and/or (2) whether the forecasts can be improved. Despite the occasional complaints that econometric forecasting does not work, business and government forecasters are using econometric approaches today more than ever in the past. Judged by success in the competitive marketplace, econometric forecasting must be useful, even if econometric forecasts are imperfect. So long as they reduce the uncertainty facing the decision maker, they appear to be helpful.

Nevertheless, there is clearly room for improvement. We cannot hold out much hope for large sudden improvements attached to some new wonder forecasting method. Improvements are likely to come in small steps focused on particular parts of the forecasting horizon and on particular dimensions of the forecast. It should be kept in mind that econometricians have been using models for forecasting for more than 30 years, and during the last 15 years on a regular monthly forecast cycle. A good deal has been learned in the process, but there is still room for improvement.

The major areas for improvement lie in the following directions:

1. Improvement of the underlying data. Chapter 3 noted the contradiction between increased data use and limited, even declining, real budgetary support for federal data gathering efforts. Additional resources put into data development could pay off in significant ways. Improved current data would provide better signals on the current situation of the economy and on its prospects. For example, a more detailed inventory survey would go a long way toward remedying the problems of forecasting the turns of the inventory cycle. Regionally detailed data on retail sales would be helpful to improve the modeling efforts and forecasting of retail marketing organizations. Data on business and consumer anticipations and plans are a particularly fruitful area for further development. Currently available surveys are based on relatively small samples. Frequently, they do not gather sufficiently detailed information. Improved surveys of manufacturers as a basis for regular and timely updating of input-output matrices and systematic accounting systems for major industries would be useful for industrial modeling and forecasting.

2. *Better current GNP accounts.* Currently, national accounts statistics are prepared with a minimum of time lag. The first figures are tabled by the Department of Commerce only three weeks after the end of the quarter. But even this is not sufficient to give the forecaster a sound basis for starting the forecast. Several forecasting services have built "current quarter models." These are not really structural models. They are calculator systems using all the latest information available in order to compute the current quarter's national accounts. The data on retail sales, automobile sales, employment, shipments, and so forth, are projected forward, often with time series methods. The current quarter model uses this material to imitate the GNP computation ordinarily carried out by the Department of Commerce. These systems are in need of further refinement but they promise to provide some help with the problems of forecasting the jump off quarter.

3. *Improved estimation methods.* While much work is going on in developing more advanced statistical methods to estimate the coefficients of econometric models, it is unlikely that a new method offering a quantum improvement in forecasting performances will come along. More advanced methods offer unbiased efficient estimates, but often at the cost of more computation and loss of flexibility in controlling the model's coefficients.

Nevertheless, there is some hope to improve model performance through new estimation procedures. Methods that allow the model builder to constrain the coefficients in the models in line with theoretical preconceptions are promising since they make better use of the available information than blind regression procedures. Constraints may be imposed on the coefficients themselves—for example, theoretically determined values may be introduced or limits imposed. The lag distributions may also be constrained. This means that (1) the model's properties can be better controlled and (2) its forecasting performance can be improved. Other new approaches for estimation in continuous time, for example, are also worth investigating.

4. *Restructuring the model.* Undoubtedly, there are still important ways in which the structure of the models can be improved. But it is not likely that replacing the standard model with either a simpler or a greatly more complex alternative will be helpful. The proposal to build simple supply side models foundered on the fact that models must have both supply and demand sides. The ideas of rational expectations may well have a place in models, though not in the crystal pure form in which they have been proposed. Economic decision makers simply do not have the informed and objective evaluation of the future which the rational expectations approach requires. Similarly, it is unlikely that simple monetarist models will replace the current standard even though aspects of monetarism must be integrated into the model, particularly if the Federal Reserve takes a monetarist policy posture.

On the other hand, the evidence does not support the notion that forecast accuracy can be improved by making models still larger and more complex. All in all, as the economy changes and as economists have an improved grasp of how the economy operates, it is necessary to update the econometric models. The Wharton model is currently in its eighth major revision. As equations are updated or as structure is changed, careful track is kept of the behavioral characteristics of the system since what appear to be minor equation changes may occasionally greatly alter model performance. Model revision is a continuous process. But it is hardly likely that such changes will suddenly improve the forecasting effectiveness of the models.

5. *Improved model adjustment.* We have noted that the alignment of the model to the latest data is an important part of the forecast process. Optimal adjustment methodologies, sometimes based on time series methods, have been suggested as a means of improving model accuracy. This proposal appears to have some modest value, but care must be taken not to do the adjustments too automatically. In some cases, where the equa-

tion is "slipping," adjustment is appropriate, but in others where the current forecast value is off because of a temporary happening (a strike, for instance) automatic adjustment, even if mathematically optimal, would bias the forecast.

6. *Averaging of forecasts.* The evident success of the ASA survey (Table 6-2) suggests that there may be some advantage to averaging forecasts made by a number of forecasters. Some experiments have shown that there may indeed be some advantages to averaging, particularly if the forecasts that underlie the average bring to bear different perspectives or different methodologies. But what about the exogenous assumptions that lie behind the averaged forecast? And what about the consistency between the different variables? Does it make sense to have a forecast that assumes an average, often an unknown or even inconsistent average, of policy assumptions? Can we live with a forecast of GNP that is not consistent with the sum of the forecasts of its parts? We may be willing to overlook these problems when there is a broad consensus on the forecast. Perhaps it conveys something about expectations out there in the real world that the econometric model does not know.

Even in this age of computerization it turns out that one or two individual forecasters have exceptional forecast records. Some claim to use models, others not. Paul Samuelson has suggested that someone should study how *good* forecasters do their jobs. Perhaps the best advice to a young man or woman who wants to become a business forecaster is to become an apprentice with a top quality forecasting team.

---

7. *Substitution of other forecasting methods.* Other forecasting approaches have been proposed. In particular, as we have noted in Chapters 4 and 5, time series analysis has been suggested as a way of improving the forecast. The time series approach makes use of the serial correlation properties of the data, but does not use the other information available about the economy. Time series methods are useful applications, particularly for short-term predictions. But they are at a disadvantage for business cycle

forecasting. This is not only a matter of accuracy, which deteriorates over time. It is also a matter of lacking structural justification. When a tax cut is anticipated, time series forecasters must explain to their managers that the forecast is the way it is because of the dynamics of the time series. They cannot, like the econometrician, explain that the forecast outlook is favorable because the income tax cut will stimulate consumer spending nor can they say that a weaker forecast would result if the tax cut were not enacted.

Another alternative might be survey methods. Some survey organizations simply ask business executives whether they expect business conditions to improve or to deteriorate. Whether this type of opinion survey, which is popular in Europe, is useful remains a matter of controversy. But, as we noted in Chapter 3, there is important forecast information in surveys of consumer sentiment like these of the University of Michigan's Survey Reasearch Center, evaluating consumers' perceptions of their well-being and willingness to spend, and in surveys of investment plans like the Bureau of Economic Analysis's Plant and Equipment Anticipations.

Forecasts of the very distant future may sometimes call for trend projections. But we have noted above the risks attached to long-term trend projections when underlying conditions are undergoing change. Sometimes, when the forecast crystal ball is particularly hazy, businesses rely on the so-called Delphi method. That is simply a systematic approach to assembling and evaluating a number of expert speculations about the future. This method may have some value in reporting what decision makers think, or in gaining some perspective on possible structural or technological changes. Its use may be more appropriate to obtain a qualitative rather than a quantitative judgment about the future, but in some circumstances that may be safer than a simple extrapolation of past trends.

From the perspective of business forecasters, what does all this mean? Can they continue to rely on the econometric model forecasts? Should they turn other forecasting methods? There are a number of possible approaches to forecasting. Business forecasters should use what best suits their purpose. For the short run, time series methods have advantages, certainly with respect to simplicity and in some cases also with respect to accuracy. But this may only be true for a period short enough so that exogenous changes and policies do not have time to greatly affect the outcome. When there is uncertainty about the structure of the economy, and hence about the model, other forecast methods may also be advisable. Over the business cycle and for *what if* studies, the econometric model appears to be the forecasting tool of choice even though econometric models do not forecast as accurately or reliably as we had once hoped they would. The model considers exogenous developments and policy; it takes account of the economy's structural and behavioral characteristics, it considers the dynamics of movement over time, and it provides detailed, yet structurally consistent, forecasts.

However, forecasts should not be taken without evaluation or judgment. Just because the forecast was made with a model does not make it correct. What was the model that was used? What were the exogenous assumptions and the adjustments that were made? What is the degree of confidence that can be attached to the forecast and how sensitive is the result to changes in the underlying assumptions? Used with understanding and caution, the modern econometric forecast offers a forward view of the economy that is not available with other means. That is why econometric forecasts have become so popular.

Further Readings

The standard articles reporting on the forecasting performance of econometric models are published every few years by Stephen McNees in the *New England Economic Review* of the Federal Reserve Bank of Boston. The most recent is Stephen K. McNees and John Ries, "The Track Record of Macroeconomic Forecasts," *New England Economic Review* (November/December 1983).

The *Journal of Forecasting*, and the *International Journal of Forecasting* frequently publish articles about forecasting, for example, Lawrence R. Klein, "The Importance of the Forecast" *Journal of Forecasting* (January–March 1984) and comparisons between forecasts produced with econometric models and by alternative methods, for example, J. A. Longbottom and S. Holly, "The Role of Time Series Analysis in the

Evaluation of Econometric Models" (January–March 1985). The editors of the *International Journal of Forecasting* sponsor a worldwide International Symposium on Forecasting on an annual basis.

Some classic papers on forecasting performance are in Bert G. Hickman, ed., *Econometric Models of Cyclical Behavior* (New York: Columbia University Press, 1972). Some recent papers are "Are Economic Forecasters Worth Listening To?" by Peter L. Bernstein and Theodore H. Silbert, *Harvard Business Review* (September–October 1984) and Leonard Silk "How To Win At Forecasting," *New York Times*, July 27, 1983.

Notes

1. Thurow, Lester, *Dangerous Currents: The State of Economics* (New York: Random House, 1983).
2. McNees, Stephen K., "The Recent Record of Thirteen Forecasters," *New England Economic Review* (September/October 1981), p. 10.
3. Klein, Lawrence, and R. M. Young, *An Introduction to Econometric Forecasting and Forecasting Models* (Lexington, Mass.: D. C. Heath, 1980).
4. McNees, Stephen K., and John Ries, "The Track Record of Macroeconomic Forecasts," *New England Economic Review*, (November/December 1983), p. 166.

❖ 7 ❖

Linking the Industry
to the National Model

Today, it is no longer enough to restrict econometrics to macromodels focused on the operation of the economy as a whole
and on the aggregate measures of economic activity. Business
requires forecasts for the industry and the firm—product line
forecasts, sales forecasts, predictions of product prices, costs of
materials, and labor, measures of industry investment, and capacity utilization and profits. One of the principal functions of
the business economist has always been to translate general
economic statistics into numbers that are directly relevant to
business decisions. Judgmental methods, developed over years
of experience, often provide these linkages. Many firms have
constructed formal linkage models that tie important industry
variables to broad measures of aggregate economic activity. True
industry and company models have also been developed. Such
models offer a dynamic description on the computer of the industry or the firm and its relationship to the macro economy.
This chapter examines the links between the national model and
models of industries and firms.

Forecast Information for the Business Firm

What are the variables of interest to the business manager?
The business operates in an economic environment and its activities depend to a significant extent on developments in that

environment over which the business has little or no control. The decision maker must take these external forces into account in order to (1) make wise decisions and (2) continue to operate profitably. Thus, for example, sales are greatly influenced by the real purchasing power of the consumers in the relevant market area, employment prospects, interest rates, the prices of alternative products, and so on.

Business executives like to be informed on general developments, but they need narrowly specific information to back up management decisions. If they produce cars, their production schedule depends critically on the market for cars in the next three to six months: Will the outgoing models sell so that new models can be sent to the dealers' showrooms? How much of a rebate may be necessary? What mix of models is the market likely to accept? In what regions will sales be strong?

Sales of automobiles are sufficiently important in the scale of the entire economy so that automobile sales are explicitly included as a variables in many macromodels. But the automobile sales variables in the models (e.g., number of units, dollars of sales) are national aggregates without information about the regional distribution of sales, their breakdown by make, size or price class, and so on. A good deal of supplemental information is necessary in order to make the figure useful for business decisions.

An automobile distributor asked for a model of automobile sales. Aggregates would not be enough. The distributor wanted sales by sales region, model, and color, if possible, and the forecast must be accurate. How to respond to such a query?

Many products are far less important on a national scale than cars. These products represent only an undisaggregated component of a much larger aggregate shown in the model solution. In the highly detailed Wharton Long-Term Model, for example, beer is simply one of many components in the large category "consumer purchases of food and beverages." Machine tools are part of the broad category "business fixed investment—equipment." Even the largest macromodel does not come close to providing detail for such a relatively small sub-category. From the perspective of the beer producer or machine tool builder, this is a serious omission. Similar problems arise with respect to other important informational elements. The national macromodels may provide data on price aggregates at the consumer and wholesale levels and they may give information on value added deflators for final demand categories, but they often do not provide detailed information on the prices of particular inputs—for example, copper, steel tubing, or diesel fuel. The models do provide considerable breakdown for wage rates, but they do not show the wages for particular classes of workers in particular locations.

How can the desired disaggregation be obtained? On one extreme is the possibility of endogenizing additional detailed variables in the model. On the other is the option of using as proxy variables other information that is part of the output of the existing model. These proxies would serve as guides to the movement of more narrowly defined variables. Finally, there is the option of establishing linkages that translate the broader categories available in the model into the specific categories desired by the user. These approaches will be considered in this chapter.

Small versus Large

The more disaggregated the model, the more detailed the information it provides. But the more disaggregated the model, the larger, more complex, and difficult to manage the model becomes. The question of how large and detailed the model should be was one of the important issues during the development of econometric model building.

The earliest models, Klein's Model I[1] for example, were small (six to twelve equations) simply because it was too burdensome to deal with larger models on the primitive mechanical calculators being used in the 1940s and early 1950s. But as soon as modern electronic computers eased these tasks, larger more complex econometric models became feasible. At the time it seemed that "bigger is better" and ever more complex, larger, and more detailed systems were developed. There was continued interest in small models however, for their simplicity and ease of understanding. For example, Friend and Taubman[2] showed that a five-equation forecasting model making maximum use of the Bureau of Economic Analysis Plant and Equipment Investment Anticipations data could forecast GNP as well as the big models. And it could be solved on the "back of an envelope." The dispute between small models and large models also revived when the St. Louis Federal Reserve Bank forecast with a simple monetarist model[3] linking changes in nominal GNP to changes in aggregate money supply some quarters previously.

There was never a clear resolution of the dispute. The simple models have fallen into disuse because they have not been able to meet the needs of business users and to take into account some of the changes affecting the present economy. To begin with, the world is highly complex, perhaps more so today than in the past. Simple systems may forecast well for a while, but they are not able to recognize the complexities. This became most apparent after the oil embargo in 1973. New forces, which had not been important earlier, affected the economy. Economic forecasters faced a challenge: how to incorporate physical shortages of petroleum as well as huge price explosions into the models. The detailed structural representation of the economy found only in the largest models was extremely valuable. As we have noted, it was possible to adjust the demand side to recognize changes in inventory accumulation and to allow for probable changes in purchases of gasoline and automobiles. It was also necessary to adjust supply to recognize the impact of fuel shortages and price increases. The structure of the model needed to be checked to see whether the full effects of petroleum shortage on various industries had been properly captured. The complex models served to make realistic and comprehensive appraisals of the impact of the oil shortage and of the price surge in a way that would not have been possible with simpler systems.

The most important reason for large models is without doubt

the detail required by business forecasters and policy analysts. The issue of concern is no longer, as economists once thought, just the general economic situation. The disaggregation of the model outputs has proliferated to many detailed data series. It is no longer surprising when the computer produces 30 pages of fine print every time new a forecast is generated.

> Even though the computer produces neat, well-labeled tables, the detail of the data is sometimes overwhelming. One of the secrets to easy use and understanding is a well-structured summary table that presents the national dimensions of the forecast in one easy glance.

Analysts of economic policy, too, are coming with specialized questions such as: What is the effect on the economy of specific budget changes for example, an increase in expenditures on an antimissile defense system? What is the effect of specific tax changes—an investment tax credit, a change in the income tax rate structure? The large multi-purpose macromodels are designed for this kind of analysis.

On the other hand, a system of that magnitude becomes difficult to manage. The structure of the model is designed to assure that consistency requirements are met in a forecast. As the detail of the data increases, the model structure becomes increasingly important to assure consistency. Paradoxically, the data series themselves become more erratic the narrower the definition. If a particular figure appears to be out of line, the model operator may wish to overrule the model and make an appropriate adjustment. But if the model is highly simultaneously interactive, such an adjustment may turn out to be like keeping a bear under a rug. An adjustment in one variable may throw others out of kilter.

When models were in their infancy, it appeared difficult to handle large systems. As we have become familiar with the structure and behavioral characteristics of the systems, however, and as the computer has made model manipulation easier, we have grown accustomed to handling large models.

This raises an important question of model structure. Since highly detailed simultaneously interactive models are sometimes hard to manage, some model builders have "Christmas treed" their models. This means using a relatively simple and aggregated model structure and then linking the detail on it like so many ornaments hanging on a Christmas tree. When employed with moderation, this is a useful device, but one must not forget that the economy is indeed interactive. Feedback circuits must be allowed to operate if the model is to give a true description of the economy.

Industrial Disaggregation

There are a number of possibilities for achieving disaggregation short of restructuring the entire large-scale macromodel:

Proxy variables. The basic idea here is simply the substitution of broad aggregate variables for the more narrowly specific ones required. In many cases, it is reasonable to assume that one's business will follow the same path as some other variable, for example, the industrial production index. A similar method is useful with respect to price trends. Company X knows that its material costs are closely related to the movement of a broad index of inflation, the raw material component of the Producer Price Index (RMPPI), for example. Projections of input costs are then at the same percentage growth rates as those forecast for the RMPPI by the macromodel. Such a methodology is rough, indeed more approximate than it needs to be.

Linkage equations. Linkage equations are simply a formalization and quantification of the method above. The linkage equation bridges the gap between the available macro variables and the desired variable. A regression equation is estimated on historical data with the desired variable as a function of one or more variables produced by the macro model. We will consider below a number of methods for improving the linkage equation.

Input-output. The input-output system serves to translate demands in a consistent and comprehensive way to the sectoral output level. Final demands from the macromodel—ideally disaggregated as much as possible—are introduced into the input-output system to determine activity in the various industries.

Industrial sector models. Industrial sector models are models specifically constructed to provide additional detail on a particular industry or sector. The industry model is linked to the macromodel, as we will consider in greater detail in Chapter 8.

Linkage Equations: An Example

Linkage equations, sometimes called bridge equations, are a simple but flexible method to obtain forecasts of the specific highly disaggregated variables required by the business. The linkage equations is just what its name implies, a way of linking a specific desired variable to other variables for which forecast values are obtainable from the macromodel.

To give an example, suppose the business plan calls for a forecast of sales of color television sets, in millions of units. The standard version of the model does not contain this particular variable—it is part of a broader variable, "personal expenditures on durable goods" (CED) measured in 1972 dollars. Nor does the input-output system disaggregate to this level.

Sales of television sets are closely related to many other economic variables. It might be tempting simply to view this as a convenient empirical relationship, picking a variety of cyclically sensitive variables and running a series of regressions

$$S = f(X_1, X_2, X_3, \ldots)$$

to find the best combination of variables X_1 to X_n to explain sales of TV sets (S). While this may yield a well fitting equation, it is not good practice. It entirely ignores what we know about the structural determinants of consumer behavior in the purchase of TV sets. There are two possible ways to proceed:

1. One may draw on the forecast variable describing the broader category of which TV sets are a part, the durables category, CED, mentioned above. This approach, a sort of top down view, since

it draws on a broader category to get to a narrow component, might yield an equation as follows:

$$S = f(CED, \ldots)$$

The dots indicate that other variables might be added if there is reason to think that they affect the share of televisions in the total durables category.

2. Alternatively, one might take a more directly structural approach based on the theory of consumer durables purchasing. Such a view would produce an equation specification not altogether different from that underlying the explanation of the CED category itself, along the following lines:

$$S = f(P_{tv}/P_c, Y_d, \%, A, S_{-1}, \ldots)$$

where
P_{tv}/P_c = the price of color TVs relative to other consumer goods
Y_d = real consumer disposable income
$\%$ = an appropriate interest rate—here presumably that on installment debt
A = an index of consumer sentiment, the Michigan survey
S_{-1} = a lagged S variable allowing for gradual adjustment

The precise specification of the linkage or product line forecasting equation is open to many possibilities. Any or all the above variables (and numerous other possible ones) can appear. The equations should take account of time lags between changing consumer well-being and television set purchasing. Market experts will have a good feeling for the appropriate variables, and they can use their microcomputers very effectively to choose an appropriate equation. It is important, of course, to obtain a specification that explains the dependent variable well over the estimation period. But good fit is not the only relevant criterion. Only if the equation has a logical structural basis, and the coefficients have the right signs and are of reasonable magnitudes, can one have confidence that the equation will provide as good a linkage in the future as it has in the past.

For forecasting purposes, the values of the righthand side variables produced by the macromodel are fitted into the linkage equation to obtain a forecast for the lefthand side variable (sales of color TVs in this instance). It is important that reliable forecasts of the right-hand side variables be available on a timely basis. The process can readily be automated on the microcomputer, downloading the macromodel inputs so that the linkage equation can be used to forecast every time there is a modification in the forecast of the macromodel.

The forecast shown in Figure 7-1 shows two lines on the graph during the period on which the equation is based (1965, first quarter, to 1979, fourth quarter). (The variables and coefficients of the equation are shown in Table 7-1). The solid line shows actuals and the dashed line estimates. The fit over the 1970s is pretty good, and the values of the coefficients are reasonable. In practice, the forecaster would do well to see how the regression line operates during the period between the end of the statistical estimation and the present. If actual data for that period are far from the figures projected, it may be necessary to reestimate the equation to include recent data or it may be appropriate to use the discrepancy between the actual and projected figures to adjust the entire forecast. The forecast is shown over the 1980s with the dashed dotted line. Its ups and downs reflect the business cycle fluctuations contained in the macro forecast that was used on a source of the data inputs.

The above discussion was presented entirely in terms of a product going into final demand. In numerous cases the variable is not one going into final consumer or investor demand—it may be one that is absorbed as an intermediate input. An approach to an appropriate linkage equation, making use of information from the macromodel itself and from the input-output system is discussed below.

Industrial Disaggregation and Input-Output

The input-output model, pioneered by Nobel Prize winner Wassily Leontief, and the system of interindustry accounts that assembles the required statistics are among the most fruitful

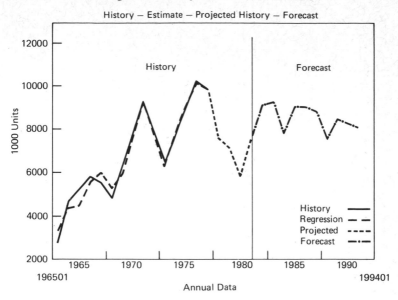

Figure 7-1. Sales of color TV sets.

developments in economics. They provide a valuable view of the industrial structure of the economy and of the interrelationships among the producing sectors. They are an important means of disaggregating the forecast to the level of the economy's producing sectors. The underlying theory will be discussed in simple terms here and then an application will be made.

Interindustry Flows

Instead of dealing with economic activity at a national aggregate basis as do the macromodels and the national income accounts, input-output focuses on the sectors that make up the economy and on the linkages between them. Intersectoral flows are an essential feature of modern production technology. They link the activity of all sectors—those producing primary products and intermediate products as well as those distributing final products—to the economy's final demand. For example, an

Table 7-1 Linkage Equation Variables and Estimated Coefficients—a Computer Output*

BANK U.P170037.TVADAMS.ANN

VARIABLE	FROM	TO	UNITS	SOURCE
COLSALES TOTAL SALES OF COLOR TELEVISION SETS	196501 -	197901	THOU UNITS	
CED PERS CON EXP, DUR, TOTAL	194701 -	198201	BILL CONSTANT $	NIA 2.3
NRUT CIVIL LABOR FORCE, UNEMPL RATE	192901 -	198201	PERCENT	EMPL & EARN
PDCED DEFL, PERS CON EXP, DUR, TOTAL	192901 -	198201	1972 = 100	NIA 7.12
NCH NUMBER OF US HSHLD, CENSUS DEFINITION	194601 -	198201	MILL	CENSUS P20 RPT

EQUATION NR 0043
****

PERIOD: 196501 197901   METHOD: OLS   DATE: 02/13/84

DEPENDENT VARIABLE: COLSALES   MEAN: 6870.00

VARIABLE	COEFFICIENT	T-STATISTIC	MEAN	ELASTICITY
CONSTANT	-5540.66	-1.12286	1.00000	
CED	111.261	3.80624	107.594	1.74250
NRUT	-324.011	-2.35705	5.41999	-.255624
PDCED	-88.3427	-3.33729	106.833	-1.37379
NCH	172.660	1.15001	67.3795	1.69342

R-SQUARED: 0.975   R-SQUARED: 0.964   SEE: 406.72   DW:1.586
(UNCORRECTED)   (CORRECTED)

F(4, 10):   95.944   RSS: .16542E+07

*This is a computer printout of an equation estimating session. On the top are listed the variables being drawn from the Wharton Econometrics annual data bank, ANN. Below is the equation, which can be written as follows:

COLSALES = -5540.66 + 111.26 CED - 324.01 NRUT - 88.34 PDCED + 172.66 NCH

The T statistic is a measure of statistical significance; statistically significant relationships show *t* values greater than 2. The elasticity shows the effect in percentage terms on the dependent variable, COLSALES, of a 1% change in each of the right-hand variables. The measure of correlation, R-squared, shows a good degree of fit, as does the standard error (SEE) and the measure of serial correlation of the errors (DW).

increase in the demand for cars is met with an increase in the production of automobiles. In order to make that possible, automobile industry requirements for steel must be met and, in turn, the steel industry requires coal, iron ore, and transportation services. The latter sectors are also interrelated in that they require services from each other.

A much simplified presentation of the interindustry accounts of an economy is shown in Figures 7–2A–7.2C. The accounts cover the outputs and interindustry flows of the entire economy. The sectors of the accounts are often referred to as industries but they include service activities as well. The economy consists of thousands of different activities, the most detailed account involves a good deal of aggregation. Figure 7–2A is a schematic diagram of the interindustry structure. Figure 7-2B shows some typical numerical entries. The table gives only three sectors for illustrative purposes—agriculture, manufacturing industries, and services. The reader should note that practical interindustry tables break the economy up into much finer detail. The 1977 input-output table for the U.S. economy is broken down to 537 sectors, thus going down to the detail of such varied categories such as:

Blast furnaces and steel mills
Cement, hydraulic
Pumps and compressors
Electronic computing equipment
Dolls
Carbon paper and inked ribbons
Burial caskets and vaults
Wholesale trade
Doctors and dentists
Owner-occupied dwellings
Elementary and secondary schools

The main block in Figure 7-2A shows interindustry flows, the flows of materials and supplies among sectors—from the sectors indicated on the left to the sectors listed across the top. Each flow is designated by X_{ij}, where i is the industry of origin and j is the destination.

The flows making up production are shown in the vertical direction. Each column says that output equals the sum of inputs of intermediate products and primary factors for each in-

(A) Schematic Diagram of Interindustry Flows

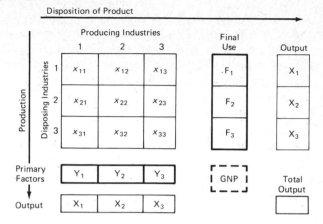

(B) Example of Interindustry Flows

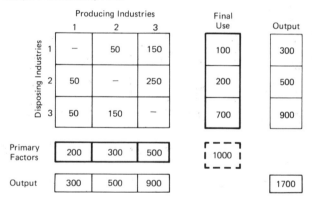

(C) Input-Output Coefficients

	Producing Industries		
Disposing Industries	1	2	3
1	—	.1	.17
2	.17	—	.28
3	.17	.3	—

Figure 7-2. Interindustry accounts and input-output.

173

dustry.* For example, in the first column of Figure 7-2A, the agricultural sector takes $50 of intermediate goods from basic industry (e.g., chemical fertilizers) and $50 from finished goods and services.† By far the largest input into agriculture is primary—that is, the labor of farmers and the services of their land and capital goods. Output of $300 counts not only the value added by primary factors but also the intermediate inputs.

Disposal of the product to intermediate use and final use is shown in the horizontal direction. The horizontal summation in each row says that total output of each industry is allocated between intermediate product, going into other industries, and final use.‡

For the agriculture row for example, out of total agricultural product of $300, the sum of $50 goes as intermediate inputs to basic industry and $150 to finished goods and services, leaving $100 of agricultural product to go directly into final use, which includes consumption, investment, and government purchases.

It should be clear that, for each industry, the same output being produced in the column is allocated in the rows. The output produced can be distributed—no more, no less.

The production process that is summarized in the columns of the table determines how much intermediate product is required and how much primary factors are necessary. As we have seen, agriculture requires relatively large inputs of primary factors such as land and labor. The nature of the product deter-

---

* Algebraically,

$$X_{1j} + X_{2j} + X_{3j} + Y_j = X_{.j}$$

where $X_{.j}$ is the output of industry j and Y_j represents the inputs of primary factors into industry $_j$

†Note that for simplicity intermediate shipments between establishments in the same industry (i.e., from agriculture to agriculture) have been omitted.

‡Algebraically,

$$X_{i1} + X_{i2} + X_{i3} + F_i = X_{i.}$$

where F_i represents output of industry i going to final use and X_i is total output of industry i.

This can also be written as

$$X_{i.} - X_{i1} - X_{i2} - X_{i3} = F_i$$

(i.e., the amount of i available for final use equals total production less what is required for intermediate uses).

mines whether it goes directly to final use or serves as an input into further processing. Demand for the products of some industries (such as steel) comes entirely from requirements of other industries. On the other hand, as we would expect, the finished goods and services industry sends most of its output directly to final use.

For the economy as a whole, production of $1000 of goods for final use involves total or gross output of $1700. The difference is double counting of intermediate products as they move from one sector into another. Production of $1000 of goods also involves inputs of primary factors worth $1000. The GNP of $1000 in the dashed-walled box (Figures 7-2A and 7.2B) adds up whether computed by summing up product going to final use or by summing up the value of primary factor inputs. This is the basic identity of the national income and product accounts.

Broken down to its full detail, the interindustry table provides a wealth of information useful for business analysis and planning. In the horizontal direction the perspective is on the market, the destination of the product. In addition to intermediate use, shown in the input-output table, detailed breakdowns of industrial flows into final demand categories are available. In the vertical direction, the breakdown in terms of the sources of materials is a matter on which firms are often better informed than on the market for their products. One serious problem in business applications is, as we have noted, that the preparation of input-output tables lags many years behind. For many industries, market patterns may have changed in important respects since 1977, the date of the most recent table.

The Input-Output Model

Input-output, a uniquely quantitative approach to the workings of the economy, supplements the interindustry accounts with a behavioral assumption about the production process. The basic assumption of input-output is that for each sector, inputs of intermediate products are proportional to the sector's output. For example, the amount of coal and iron ore needed by the steel industry is proportional to the output of steel. The requirements for steel depend in turn proportionately on the output of automobiles. The notion of inputs proportional to output—a recipe book approach—is a greatly simplified theory of production, but it makes it easy to compute the input coefficients from the interindustry accounts. The direct input coefficients measure the quantity of input needed to produce a unit of output for each sector. They are simply in each sector the ratios of inputs to total sector output. The input coefficients corresponding to our example are shown in Figure 7-2C. The coefficient of .17 for inputs from sector 2 into sector 1 means that for each dollar of agricultural output the agricultural sector needs $.17 of inputs from basic industry. For each dollar of output of sector 2, inputs of .1 are needed from sector 1 and .3 from sector 3, and so on. Production is interrelated. In order to supply final product from one sector it is necessary also to produce in the other sectors. Suppose, for example, that we want to meet the demand for agricultural product by final consumers of $100 in our example in Figure 7-2B. Agriculture will require direct inputs of $17 from sectors 2 and 3. To produce the input requirements of the agricultural sector, sectors 2 and 3, in turn, require inputs from other sectors and their production calls for still further inputs, and so on. These so-called indirect requirements may be successively traced in order to calculate the level of production necessary so that each industry can meet the direct and indirect input requirements of final demand. The input-output model can be described as an interrelated system of equations.*

---

*Using the input coefficients shown in Figure 7-2 C, we can write an equation for each sector:

$$X_1 - .1X_2 - .17X_3 = F_1$$
$$X_2 - .17X_1 - .28X_3 = F_2$$
$$X_3 - .17X_1 - .3X_2 = F_3$$

This system of three equations can also be solved simultaneously for the X's given the F's (i.e., for the industry outputs that satisfy the final demand requirements). In matrix algebra, which is typically used to represent input-output systems, this can be written

$$X = (I - A)^{-1}F$$

where

X = the vector of sector outputs
$(I - A)^{-1}$ = the inverse of the input output matrix
F = the vector of final demands disaggregated by sector.

In order to apply input-output for industry forecasting, one additional element is needed. The final demands entering into the input-output system are disaggregated by sector, but the final demands usually presented in a macroeconometric model are broken down by final demand category, for example consumption or investment. A so-called bridge matrix provides a way of translating the final demands. A bridge matrix is simply a table that disaggregates demand by final demand category into the underlying industrial classification. Assume that the market shares of each industry in each final demand category remain fixed. Now there is a means to go from the final demand categories as measured by most macromodels to industry sector outputs.

Thus, input-output is more than just an accounting statement. It is an economic model linking input requirements to output. It has important applications in industry economics. In an interdependent economy, projections of demand for one industry must recognize the implications for others. Typically, we begin on the side of demand. Given the final demand requirements of the economy—that is, the need for agricultural, industrial, and other products by consumers, investors, and so on—the required activity levels of the industries can be calculated. This information can then be utilized directly for business planning or, as shown below, the data can enter into linkage equations explaining other variables more closely relevant to business operations.

Input-Output and Macromodels

The input-output tables have been linked into macromodels. For example, the input-output system contained in the Wharton Long-Term Model, which comprises some 50 sectors, is fully linked into the demand, output, and price determination systems of the model. Most important, instead of the unrealistic assumption that input coefficients remain fixed, the coefficients are currently adjusted by assuming that input proportions respond to technological change and to the relative prices of the various material inputs. Another large macromodel system with input-output that provides a more detailed industrial breakdown but somewhat less detailed macro forecasting capability is the Inforum model of the University of Maryland.

Elements of the input-output framework can also serve as a basis for price forecasting. Remember that in the vertical direction the input-output system measures inputs in proportion to total output. Prices by industry can be built up on a cost basis depending on the cost of the inputs into production, and the cost of labor. This is the basis for Wharton's industry price forecasts.

Linkage Equations with Input-Output Data

The input-output system provides a considerably greater breakdown of production sectors than does the macroeconomic model. Therefore, forecasts for many intermediate products may be available from an input-output system that has been linked to the macromodel. Conversely, there are still many specific, narrow product categories that only appear as part of a larger category. How, for example, can a narrow category such as "manifold business forms" or "mechanical measuring and controlling instruments" be forecast? Two approaches are possible for obtaining a linked forecast for the narrow category:

1. The nearest broader category can be used as a starting point. In that case the growth of sales of the product S_i may be linked with a linking equation to the broader category S_I

$$S_i = f(S_I, \ldots)$$

   and some other variables, shown by the dots, may be introduced to allow for shifts in the share of i in the broader product class.

2. The other alternative is to turn to the input-output system to provide information about the market for product i. Assume, for example, that product i serves as an input into various product categories j in fixed proportions as known for a base year. Then we define a synthetic "market variable" S_{it} for product i and year t as:

$$\hat{S}_{it} = \sum_j a_{ijo} X_{jt}$$

where

$\hat{S}_{it}$ = the synthetic "market measuring" variable for product i in year t

a_{ijo} = the input coefficients of i into product j in base year o.

x_{jt} = the levels of activity of the industries j purchasing product i at time t.

The fundamental idea here is that the $\hat{S}_{it}$ variable represents a weighted average of the activities of the industries to which industry i sells its product where the weights are input coefficients from industry i to the various purchasing sectors. Another way to visualize $\hat{S}_{it}$ is as the shipments of industry i if its market share of total inputs into each industry j remained at base year levels.

It is entirely possible, however, that the base year relationships would no longer hold precisely perhaps because of technological changes or because product i has changed in price relative relative to other inputs. To handle such slippage, another linkage equation is introduced which regresses sales of product i (S_i) on the synthetic variable $\hat{S}_{it}$ and on other variables such as relative price (P_i/P_s) and on technological trends (T). That is,

$$S_{it} = f\left(\hat{S}_{it},\ P_i/P_s,\ T\right)$$

A similar procedure can be used when the product goes both into intermediate and final use. In that case a similar synthetic market variable can be computed with respect to the major components of final demand.

In developing linkage equations, it is important not to lose sight of the fact that products or industries are affected by specific events. For example, the engineer or planner in the steel industry is aware of what is happening to costs and production technology in that industry and in the steel-consuming industries: The demand for steel is affected by the downsizing of automobiles, the shift away from steel cans, the availability of steel from foreign sources, the cost and price implications of new production technology like the minimill, and continuous casting. These developments are frequently not captured by history-based econometric and input-output studies. The type of analysis discussed above must, consequently, be modified (or supported) by detailed industrial intelligence.

An Input-Output Based Linkage Equation Illustration

An illustration of an input-output based linkage procedure for Standard Industrial Classification (SIC) category 2761 "manifold business forms" is shown below.[4] The estimating equation is:

$$\text{Log } Q2761 = -3.473 + 1.417 \text{ Log } \hat{S}2761 + 0.025 \text{ TIME}$$

S2761 = shipments of Manifold Business Forms (deflated by the appropriate sector deflator)
$\hat{S}$2761 = intermediate requirements for products of industry 2761, assuming base year input coefficients.
TIME = time, 1967 = 1.0

The coefficient of the equation shows growth more than proportional with the market, that is, the coefficient of $\hat{S}$ is greater than 1. There is also a positive time trend. As is apparent in Figure 7-3, the sample period fit of the equation is satisfactory. Similarly reasonable results have been obtained with equations for other narrow product categories.

Prediction with this equation is based on outputs of the Wharton Long Term Model, specifically the production index of each sector and the appropriate deflators. An example of a projection is shown in Figure 7-3. To the right of the vertical line, the forecast reflecting the cyclical ups and down projected by the Wharton Long Term Model looks reasonable. But it is best to view such a projection cautiously. Suppose, for example, that the paperless society finally arrives. The best laid forecast for business forms based on linkage equations and macro predictions could be thrown off.

Business Applications of Linkage Equations

Linkage equations are receiving ever wider use in business applications. This section considers how and for what purposes such relationships are most suitable and how they are used operationally.

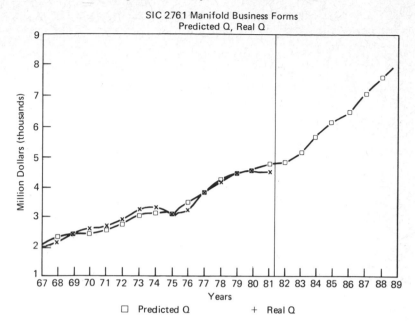

Figure 7-3. Actual and predicted value of shipments of manifold business forms.

Table 7-2 shows some important types of linkage models and the appropriate input variables. While industrial disaggregation is one important role of these functions, it is by no means the only one.

Linkage models are helpful in many applications to bridge the gap between variables forecast by a macromodel and the more detailed or specialized information required by the business user. Linkage functions may make possible translation of variables only available at the national level to the region. They may help to translate general wage trends into the corresponding figures for particular industries or occupations. They are often used to estimate needs for energy, transportation, or industrial capacity.

There are, however, considerable risks to the indiscriminate use of linkage functions. They seldom contain much structure, and often are estimated with greater attention to their good fit than to the appropriateness of the macromodel variables in the

Table 7-2　Varieties of Linkage Equations

Purpose	Dependent Variable	Macromodel Variables
Industrial disaggregation	Industrial output or real gross value added	Final demand variables Industrial activity
Regional disaggregation	Output or demand by region	Final demand variables and regional competitiveness
Sales and product line forecasting	Sales	Demand variables, prices
Price and cost forecasting	Price index	Material and labor costs Cost of imports and exchange rates
Wage forecasting	Wages and supplements	Wages, unemployment, consumer prices
Power and material input requirements	Quantities or calorific equivalents	Industrial activity, prices
Transport requirements	Ton miles	Industrial activity, personal income

equation or to the values of coefficients. So long as everything moves proportionately in the same direction, there will be good forecasts—but when underlying conditions change, such an equation can produce wild results. Consequently, attention to capturing the underlying structure and to realistic coefficient estimates is important. Most of all, the business forecaster must be on the watch for new developments in each of the market segments that can derail the best laid projections.

Operationally, the linkage equation may be mounted on a forecast vendor's computer or in a microcomputer. The use of the vendor's computer is efficient, but it is frequently quite costly. Use of the company's own in-house mainframe often encounters conflicts with the departments whose work is seen as the primary function of such a computer, such as accounting or payroll. The user's own microcomputer offers great advantages for estimating and operating linkage equations. Forecast data from the large macromodels is readily available by downloading over telephone lines or on regularly updated diskettes. The forecaster can experiment with the preparation of a variety of linkage equations and select those that are most appropriate from the perspective of structure and past forecast performance. As each new batch of forecast data comes in, the linkage forecast is updated. The microcomputer also serves to provide graphical presentation and projections so that a variety of alternative forecast assumptions can be readily compared. Once the microcomputer and the forecast data have been acquired, the added cost of running linkage equations is low and the possibilities are almost without limit.

Further Readings

The reader is referred to any recent textbook in applied economic statistics or econometrics, for example, Robert S. Pindyck and Daniel L. Rubinfeld, 2nd edition (New York: McGrow-Hill, 1983). Unfortunately, the subject of linkage equations is too applied and practical to get separate mention in most books. On the other hand, the instruction manuals and demonstrations of the forecast vendors provide numerous illustrations. For an article explaining the input-output based linkage function approach, see F. G. Adams, V. G. Duggal, and S. Thanawala, "Industrial Linking Functions for Macro Models," *Business Economics*, (September 1976).

Input-Output Economics, 2nd edition, by the Nobel Prize winner Wassily Leontief (New York: Oxford University Press, 1985), is a useful description of input-output and its applications. Development of input-output data has lagged far behind in the United States; the 1977 table did not become available until 1984. The latest input-output table for the United States is described in "The Input-Output Structure of the U.S. Economy 1977" in the *Survey of Current Business* (May 1984). A 1982 table is in the works.

Notes

1. Klein, Lawrence, R., *Economic Fluctuations in the United States, 1921–1941 (New York: Wiley, 1950)*.
2. Friend, Irwin and Paul Taubman, "A Short Term Forecasting Model," *Review of Economics and Statistics* (August, 1964).
3. Anderson, Leonall and Keith M. Carlson, "A Monetarist Model for Economic Stabilization," *Review—Federal Reserve Bank of St. Louis* (April, 1970).
4. From *The Future of the Office Products Industry* (Alexandria, Va.: National Office Products Association, 1985).

❖ 8 ❖

Modeling the Industry

Ultimately, business planners and decision makers require forecast data directly relevant to the industry and the firm: demand for particular products, the cost of energy and specific material inputs, prospects for wage and interest rates, and so on. The previous chapter discussed how some of this information can be derived through input-output or through linkage equations from a general macromodel of the aggregate economy. This chapter discusses a logical extension of this work: the model of the industry and of the business firm itself. These are the frontiers of business forecasting—they represent its greatest challenge and potential.

Relations Between National Models and Models of Industries and Firms

Developments in an industry and in the individual business firms that belong to it are greatly influenced by national and international economic settings. One way to view the relation between the business enterprise and the national economy is as a cascade. A picture of such a relationship between the national economic model and models of industries and firms is shown in Figure 8-1. On the top, the macromodel describes the environment in which the industry operates. At the next level, the industry models describe the operation of the market in

184

which firms, shown at the bottom develop their business strategy. The lines in Figure 8-1 between the blocks show directions of influence: solid lines indicate the effects from top down; dashed lines indicate feedbacks. Taking account only of the solid lines, we have a one-directional flow scheme; the industry and firm models are satellites depending on the aggregate economy. This is often a useful simplification. But what happens in major industries and firms does affect the national economy and a firm's decisions may have important impacts on the industry. The resulting feedbacks are shown by the dashed lines in Figure 8-1. But a fully interactive system of national, industry, and firm models reacting simultaneously with one another would be complex. And, more important, the impact of national developments on a particular industry and firm may be large, but the influence from a particular enterprise or industry to the national economy is likely in many cases to be small.

The national model must be designed to provide as many of the data inputs needed in the industry model as possible. One of the advantages of a complex macromodel is the consistent detailed forecast of the economy that can be fed into models at lower stages of aggregation. For forecasting on the level of the industry or firm, reliable and detailed econometric forecasts for the aggregate economy are a basic requirement.

External inputs affect the economy at each level. The influence of the international economy and the role of fiscal and monetary policy at the national economy level have already been noted. At the industry level a principal influence flows from the business cycle situation of the macroeconomy which dominates the movement of demand for certain products over the short- and medium-term. Exogenous factors operating at the industry level include foreign competition, industrial policy incentives, regulatory policy with respect to pollution, and prices of materials and supplies. Over the longer run, technological developments affecting the product or the production process may have significant impact at the industry level.

Firms operate within the constraints of the industry. They are affected by the situation of the industry in general and by firm-specific exogenous developments such as a transportation bottleneck, a fire at a plant, or a labor walkout. In turn, the indus-

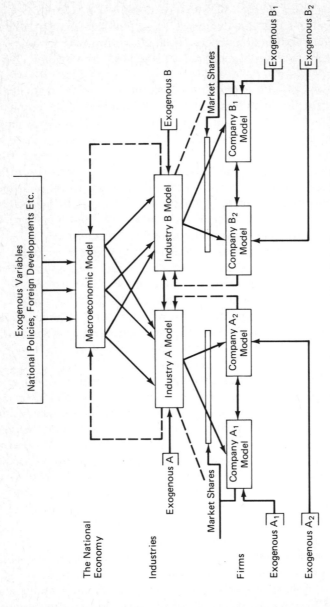

Figure 8-1. Relations between national, industry, and firm models.

try is affected (note the dashed lines). Decisions on the level of the firm about capacity, the introduction of new technology, or new products often influence—and sometimes revolutionize—the entire industry.

Business strategy by a specific firm and its competitors is the most important consideration at the firm level (note the reaction relationship implied by the two-headed arrow connecting each firm to its competitors). The horizontal box at this point in the chart represents the determination of market shares that are the heart of the competitive relationship between the firms making up an industry.

The issue here is only in part a question of forecasting the likely outcome. The objective is to determine what business strategy ought to be to achieve the firm's objectives given the forecast state of the nation and the industry. This has important implications for the model and its application. A flexible instrument for simulation that explores the consequences of alternative behavioral options is needed: What would happen if a new plant were built? What would be the consequence of a new pricing or advertising policy? The simulation system must ultimately spell out the bottom line consequences of alternative strategies. And, since there are many intermediate decision points and constraints such as inventory requirements, and cash

---

An interesting question is sometimes raised: If we modeled all the industries of the economy and summed them, could we be sure that the same results would appear as in the national model? Similarly, if models for all the firms in an industry were added up, would they yield results similar to those obtained in an industry model? The answer is that, generally, we cannot be sure. A constraint assuring such consistency could be imposed, but in most cases all the industries or all the firms need not be modeled. The purpose of disaggregated modeling at the level of industries and firms is not to get a better result for the aggregate economy but rather to get a fix on phenomena that cannot be well observed at the aggregate level.

needs, the simulation system must break out that type of information and inform the decision maker of the consequences of alternative strategies. This is a big order. Models of industries will be discussed here and firm models will be considered in Chapter 9.

Architecture of Industry Models

The structural outlines of national models are by now substantially standardizaed in accord with macroeconomic theory and the system of national income and product accounts. In contrast, the options for industrial modeling are diverse and largely unexplored.

As the potentials for different model structures are much greater at the level of the industry than for the nation as a whole, so is the need to recognize technological and commercial facts of the real world. Industries differ widely with regard to (1) the nature of the product (2) the nature of the manufacturing process, and (3) the industrial and commercial organization. The industrial model builder must understand the industry and the model must catch those special characteristics that make each industry unique. Thus, economics provides a broad framework of microtheory to describe the behavior of industries and firms and this body of theory is the backbone of industrial models. A model of the automobile industry, for example, shows a complex manufactured product made by few large firms. It calls for an entirely different structure than does a model of the market for an agricultural product like wheat or cotton.

Industry Data for Model Building

The empirical implementation of a model depends greatly on the data available. Industry statistics can be otained in astonishing detail—although often not precisely in the numbers which the econometrician would like to have. Many industries have adopted standardized accounting systems that show the flow of physical product from the raw materials to the final consumer. The Energy Department's accounts for energy and the petroleum industry and the American Iron and Steel Institute's figures on steel are outstanding examples. These accounts embody conventional measures and conversion ratios used in the industry, for example, the relation between barrels of oil and tons of coal expressed in terms of oil equivalents. However, important data on production costs and value of output are frequently difficult, if not impossible, to obtain.

Engineering data frequently offer unique opportunities for supplementing industry statistics. The technology of industrial processes has been studied in great detail by engineers responsible for design and costing of new production facilities. These data are invaluable to test the reasonableness of econometric relationships estimated from industry statistics.

On many occasions, the technological data must serve directly where industry statistics are not available or cannot be obtained. The input requirements of a new industrial process are known only in terms of engineering estimates. Information on technological change or on substitution between alternative raw materials may also come from engineering sources. The linear programming framework, which is usually based on engineering data, is a valuable tool for industry analysis.

Market Models versus Industry Models

It is apparent from our discussion of theory and information going into industrial models that they can take many different forms. A broad distinction can be made between what may be called *industry* models and *commodity market* models. These will be discussed as polar cases. However, many industries fall between these classifications and others combine attributes of market models at some stages and industrial models at others.

Structure of Market Models   Market models focus principally on the price mechanism that serves to clear the market. Typically, market models describe markets for primary commodities—agricultural commodities such as wheat, cocoa, cotton, rubber, or basic minerals such as copper, aluminum and other nonferrous metals. The purest examples of market models are for agricultural commodities where (1) there are many compet-

ing producers and consumers and (2) where the price is determined in a highly competitive market by the interaction of supply and demand. In many cases, though, special aspects of
industrial organization, such as the presence of dominant producing firms with some degree of monopoly power, must be
taken into account. Government intervention like that of the U.S.
farm program or the European Community's Common Agricultural Program (CAP) also play an important role. Massive
grain purchases by the U.S.S.R. and China also show how political or diplomatic dealings can replace pure market processes.

The rudiments of a market model can be summarized in four
equations (although many more equations may be appropriate
in real applications):

$$D = d\ (P,\ P_s,\ \text{GNP}) \tag{1}$$

$$Q = q\ (C,\ P,\ W) \tag{2}$$

$$P = p\ (D,\ I) \tag{3}$$

$$I = Q - D + I_{-1} \tag{4}$$

Equation 1, the demand equation, explains consumption of
the commodity *(D)* in relation to its price *(P)*, price of substitutes *(P_s)*, and to aggregate economic activity or income (GNP).
The latter is exogenous to the commodity model usually coming from the macroeconometric model of the overall economy.

Equation 2, the supply equation, relates output *(Q)* to production costs *(C)*, price *(P)*, and weather *(W)* or other industry-
specific natural conditions. Usually there are long lags between
changes in price and changes in product supplies since it takes
time to put in new acreage. In this connection it is important
to distinguish between the kinds of lags needed for tree crops
(very long), field crops (shorter), or livestock (in-between in
length). Minerals also have a long supply time horizon; it may
take seven or eight years to bring a new mine into production.

Equation 3 explains price on the basis of available inventories
(I) and demand *(D)*. Another way to characterize this equation
is as a demand equation for inventories. Inverting (3) by put-

ting I on the left-hand side and P on the right, we would have an equation for inventory requirements related to demand and price.

Equation 4 is simply the market clearing identity that says that inventories are equal to supply less demand plus inventories left from the previous period. This equation may also be seen as a supply of inventories equation, or a definition of inventory accumulation.

We have here a simple system of four simultaneous equations and four unknowns. Given the information from outside the equation system C, W, P_s, GNP, and the lagged data for I_{-1}, the equations can be solved for the endogenous industry variables: demand, supply, price, and inventories.

This example is, of course, an oversimplification of the reality of operational commodity market models. Such models are often quite complex. Each of the supplying areas and each of the markets is recognized separately. The forces affecting consumption, utilization of the product in each type of market, competitiveness against other materials, probable technological changes, and so on are taken into account. For a nonferrous metal like copper, the demand in the automotive industry and in residential construction, the competition between copper and aluminum, and the potential impact of glass fibers for communication in place of copper wires must be taken into account.

On the supply side, the available mining facilities and their uitilization is considered: What are production costs in various producing areas in local currency and in foreign exchange? Does the changed organization of the industry with the nationalization of most of the mining sites in the developing world affect its production potential? What is the status of speculative inventories? (Not just in terms of what the model predicts, but in terms of what they are in the real world!) The model may also recognize processing costs, trading relationships, contract prices, and futures prices.

Such models are not only useful for price forecasting, but also for exploration of alternatives. An interesting example has been the use by the United Nations of commodity market models for copper, manganese, nickel, and cobalt to investigate potential impacts of mining nonferrous metal nodules found on the deep ocean floor.

Industry Models   Industry models describe industries rather than markets. They emphasize the industrial process, that is, the requirements for raw materials, labor, and plant capacity. Industrial models apply particularly to large scale manufacturing industry such as petroleum refining or steel.

The reader should not confuse industry models with process analysis or linear processing models. The latter are a specific type of industry model describing a maximization process under capacity constraints. They may make up a useful part of an industry model. But our conception of industry models is broader, encompassing the operation of the entire industry and its relationship to the macro economy.

As is typical of most industries, output is determined directly by the requirements of the market as the relatively small number of large firms set up their production schedules in response to the needs of their customers. Price is determined to a large extent in relationship to labor and material costs.

The essentials of an industry model can be summarized in four equations:

$$D = d(P, \text{GNP}) \tag{5}$$

$$Q = I + D - I_{-1} \tag{6}$$

$$Q = q[(L,K), m(M)] \tag{7}$$

$$L = \frac{1}{q}(K, Q) \tag{7a}$$

$$M = \frac{1}{qm}(Q) \tag{7b}$$

$$P = p\left[\frac{(W \cdot L) + (P_m \cdot M)}{Q}, \frac{Q}{CAP}, \frac{I}{D}\right] \tag{8}$$

Equation 5 is the demand equation. As in the market model it relates demand *(D)* to price and to the economic activity variable (GNP) drawn from the national model.

Equation 6 can be seen as determining output *(Q)*. One special characteristic of an industry model is that production is adjusted to market demand requirements. The industrial manager sets output *(Q)* to meet demand requirements *(D)* and an inventory target *(I)*, given existing stocks (I_{-1}).

Equation 7 is a production function. It relates output of product to inputs of labor *(L)*, and capital stock *(K)*, and materials inputs *(M)*. Inverting equation 7, we see it as determining requirements for labor, given K and Q (7a), and, similarly, we obtain a demand equation for inputs of materials (7b).

Equation 8 explains price as a mark–up on costs of materials $(P_m{\cdot}M)$ and cost of labor $(W{\cdot}L)$ per unit of output, capacity utilization (Q/CAP) and inventories relative to demand *(I/D)*. In this equation the price of materials (P_m) and the wage rate *(W)* are information drawn from the national model.

In real applications, the models are considerably more complex. The need to bring together detailed knowledge of the industry with sophisticated econometric techniques is one of the factors that has long delayed industrial model building.

An Econometric Model of the Steel Industry[1]

A representative example of an industry model is a model of the U.S. steel industry produced at the University of Pennsylvania in 1982. The model was built as a simulation tool as part of a broader study of the problems of the steel industry and of industrial policy. Thus, the model was primarily intended as a means to examine how the industry would respond to alternative policies rather than for forecasting. Applications to forecasting and strategy analysis are not excluded, however. In view of its purpose, the model is highly aggregated: It treats the industry as a unit and it represents the operation of the market participants in accordance with economic theory, historical data, and institutional information. This is a descriptive model. It makes no attempt at optimization as would a linear programming approach. To give some introductory perspective it is helpful to highlight the variables of primary interest. The main external inputs are:

- Indicators of economic activity in the steel-using industries
- Prices of substitutes for steel products
- Factor costs, that is, wages and prices of material and energy inputs, interest rates
- Government and institutional policy with respect to pollution control, tax rates, protection, etc.
- Foreign variables, principally production costs in Japan and capacity utilization in Japan and the EEC

In turn, the main variables computed within the model are:

- Domestic demand by steel category
- Foreign trade in steel
- Production and the required inputs of raw materials and labor
- Price of steel
- Investment by the steel industry
- Revenues, costs, and estimated profits

The discussion of model structure below refers to Figure 8-2, a flow diagram of the interrelationships in the model.

Demand Block

Steel is an intermediate good, and the demand for steel is almost totally derived from the level of activity in the steel-using industries. In the upper left of the diagram is domestic demand for steel, measured in net tons and broken down by major steel product category [based on the classification system and data of the American Iron and Steel Institute (AISI)]. The equations for domestic demand $(DDOM_i)$ take the form

$$DDOM_i = f\,(DD_i,\ PREL_i)$$

where

$DDOM_i$ = domestic production + imports − exports for the ith steel product category
DD_i = steel user production index for the ith steel product category
$PREL_i$ = relative price index for the ith steel product category

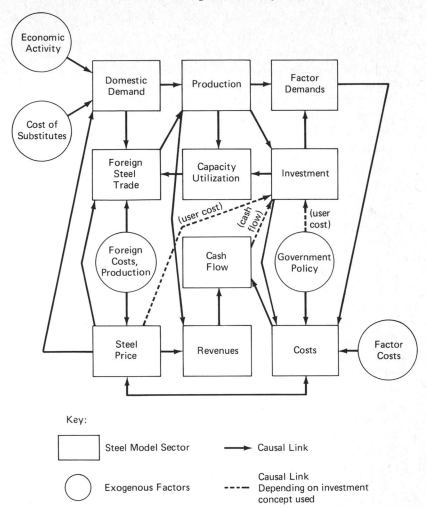

Figure 8-2. Steel model flow chart—basic model.

The steel-user production indexes (DD_i), similar to the synthetic market variables used in the input-output based linkage equation in Chapter 7, are constructed by weighting the production indexes of the steel-using industries by the pertinent

input coefficients.* This is the point where the principal linkages to the macromodel occur since the macromodel is used to
provide the input data for the steel user production indexes
(DDᵢ). The data on industrial activity going into this index are
forecast by the Wharton Long-Term Model.

Appropriately defined relative price variables enter the equations relating the price of each steel product to a price index of
competing materials. Time lags and first difference terms enter
these equations to allow for a gradual adjustment.

Table 8-1 summarizes the estimated activity and price elasticities for the various steel categories. Of the nine steel categories, three had activity elasticities significantly greater than one
(i.e., if economic activity in the industries using the type of steel
in question increases by 1%, the total demand for that type of
steel increases by more than 1%). These categories were semi-
finished steel, steel structural shapes, and steel plate. Two other
categories, steel pipe and tin mill steel, exhibited elasticities
significantly under one. The difference may be accounted for
by technological changes: for instance, automobiles in the mid-
1980s contain much less steel than automobiles in the 1960s or
1970s. Price elasticities vary from $-.06$ for steel wire to -2.08
for steel plates, depending on the ease with which each type of
steel may be substituted for by its competitors.

Imports and Exports

Steel imports have become such an important and critical
concern that they must be handled in the model. Exports, however, are exogenous. Most studies of the import question point

---

*Specifically,

$$DD_i = \sum_{j=1}^{n} a_{ijo} A_j$$

where

A_j = production index for jth steel-using industry
a_{ijo} = proportion of demand for the ith product category from the jth steel-using
industry in 1967.

The a_{ij}'s been calculated for 1967 using data on domestic shipments of steel
products by market classification compiled by AISI.

Table 8-1 Summary of Elasticities for Estimated Demand and Import Equations

Category	Demand Elasticity with Respect to		Import Elasticity with Respect to	
	(Demand)	(Relative Price)	(Relative Unit Cost)	(Relative Capacity Utilization)
Semi	1.51	−1.22	−2.06	—
Shape	1.57	−.48	−2.35	−.34
Plate	1.58	−2.08	−3.45	−3.83
Rail	.90	−1.27	−1.69	−3.36
Bar	1.00	−.83	−.99	—
Pipe	.76	−.77	−2.28	−1.10
Wire	1.18	−.06	−.79	−.42
Tin	.73	−1.26	−2.64	−3.31
Sheet	1.05	−.27	−5.05	−3.03

Source: Adams et al., 1985.

to two sets of causal factors: (1) those involving the expansion of domestic demand and (2) those concerned with the relative competitiveness of foreign and domestic steel. These factors have been built into equations.

Steel imports are determined as a function of domestic demand and a distributed lag of relative steel-making costs and capacity utilization in the United States and abroad. Import restrictions have been introduced in these equations where appropriate. The emphasis on costs and capacity utilization rather than just on competitive price reflects the fact that price information is difficult to get and to evalute—list prices do not reflect true competitive conditions. Unit cost is a good indicator of the competitive potential as is capacity utilization.

A summary of the import elasticities is given in Table 8-1. The sensitivity of imports as a share of domestic demand to relative cost is of a high order, confirming the hypothesis that costs play a significant role in determining the volume of imports. Capacity utilization in the United States, relative to that in Japan and the EC, also has a significant impact on imports for most of the categories, through export effort, and competitive pricing and delivery schedules.

Production and Factor Requirements

The underlying hypothesis of the model is that the industry will produce to satisfy steel requirements. Once domestic demand and imports have been determined, the total requirement for domestically produced steel can be computed. Since this model operates on an annual time frame, inventory changes are not considered, although in a model operating at a higher frequency they would be an important ingredient.

Production Shares

Technology in steel making is embodied in three different raw steel production processes: open hearth, electric furnace, and basic oxygen (the newest continuous casting processes are only now being introduced in the United States). A realistic description of the industry must be sensitive to the forces that determine the adjustment from the less efficient and older process (open hearth) to the more efficient and technically advanced processes.

One potential approach for this purpose would be a linear programming maximization model that would compute the minimum cost way of producing steel given the technical constraints and process capacities. Such an approach has great potential, but it is costly. Its cost and difficulty were beyond the needs of the present project.

A simpler approach estimated the equations to explain the share of steel production carried on in each process. The share of basic oxygen is related to the level of investment in steel (reflecting both the introduction of advanced technology and the cost differential between basic oxygen and other processes). For electric furnaces, which are frequently used when capacity utilization is at a high level, a relationship taking capacity utilization and relative costs into account is used. Finally, steel production by the open hearth process is largely a residual; it is declining every year.

The relative cost variables used in the production share equations are based on the relative uses of four key inputs: pig iron, scrap, fuel oil, and electricity. The weights are based on engineering data. Note that the sharp increase in petroleum costs during the 1970s affected open hearth the most, since it utilizes fuel oil.

Energy, Materials, and Labor Demand

The dominant form of technological progress in steel is the shift from inefficient to efficient processes. Engineering data provides us with the materials input coefficients for each of the three major production processes, and then serve as a basis for computing requirements of raw materials. With respect to labor inputs, the approach was to estimate a production function and to invert it into a labor demand equation, as we did in our conceptual discussion of industrial models, above.

Investment Block

Investment is likely to be the impact point of much business strategy and government policy. Investment is the key to efficiency and modernization of the industry. (Investment is also important from the perspective of the companies that supply capital goods to the steel industry.)

Two alternate approaches to investment functions were implemented in the model. These are (1) the neoclassical user cost theory of investment (which sees investment as determined by the productivity of capital in relation to its user costs) and (2) the cash flow method. One reason for considering the latter approach is that the steel industry has traditionally suffered from a cash shortage and had imperfect access to capital markets. Given limited cash flows, the impact of compliance with environmental regulations may well have been to divert investment funds from productive uses.

One of the goals of this model was to determine the effects of fiscal and financial variables on the investment decision. In the investment equation based on user cost, the key variable is the user cost of capital that embodies the interest rate as well as other factors affecting capital cost (e.g., corporate profits tax rate, depreciation rate, and the investment tax credit).

The alternate investment specification relates new capital expenditures to the financial state of the industry as measured by cash flow. Cash flow itself is computed from the financial sector of the model. It is interesting to note that this equation fits significantly better than the user cost based equation. An additional real dollar of cash flow results in an additional 22 cents of real investment within one year, 50 cents more within two years, and $1.41 more in the long run.

The reader should be cautioned, however, that in an integrated model system the fit of a single equation is only half the battle. As a system, the model did not work well for explaining cash flow. This variable represents the difference between two very large variables—revenues minus costs—and error accumulates there. Consequently, while the investment equation works better in the cash flow version, the model as a whole works better with the user cost investment equation.

The two investment equations also differ with respect to another important question, the impact of federally mandated pollution control investments. It has been assumed that the user cost based investment decision is concerned with productive capital so that mandated pollution control expenditures are assumed to be additional to productive investment. In the cash flow version, since cash flow is seen as a constraint, mandated expenditures have to be accommodated within the cash flow limitations and productive investment is reduced by the need to divert scarce cash into pollution control.

Price Determination

The traditional theory of steel industry pricing has focused on the markup over production costs. Production costs are estimated in the financial sector (see below). The underlying theory here is that the industry attempts to set prices to cover full production cost per unit of output, including capital costs, but that it is limited in its ability to do so by foreign competition. The latter is measured here by the estimated unit cost of Japanese steel. Prices of the individual steel products are then determined by linkage to the general steel price.

A number of alternate pricing hypotheses were evaluated in developing this equation. While the cost markup approach appeared to be appropriate here, for other industries with different industrial organization and price policies one might visualize different types of equations. For example, one might visualize price as determined simply by the intersection of a demand and a supply curve, but in that case the nature of the supply mechanism in the industry would have to be considerably revamped.

Financial Sector

The financial sector for the industry is formulated around the simple income statement for the major firms of the industry (Table 8-2). The approach used here is to explain the components of the accounting system with econometric equations. (This contrasts to the more customary simulation model approach discussed in Chapter 9.)

This means, for example, that a regression equation estimates revenues as a function of steel output and prices. An alternate approach could have focused on building up revenues from the sales of the individual steel products and their prices. Employment costs are expressed as a function of estimated wage rate and labor requirements. Other cost components are simi-

Table 8-2   Steel Industry Income Statement, 1979
(Billion $)

Revenues		57.35
Costs		56.16
Employment	19.09	
Materials	32.40	
Interest	.84	
Depreciation	1.88	
Income taxes	.42	
Other taxes	.81	
Other	.71	
Net income		1.20
Dividends		.61
Retained earnings		.59
Depreciation		1.88
Cash flow		2.47

Source: Adapted from American Iron and Steel Institute (AISI) Annual Statistical Report, 1979.

larly estimated by regression relations. Total costs, net corporate income, and cash flow can then be computed on the basis of the accounting identities in Table 8-2. This approach offers considerable opportunity for the analysis of industry strategy on pricing and investment behavior.

This summarizes the structure of the model. It is now our job to see how such a system may be used.

Testing and Validation of the Industry Model

Like the national model, the industry model must be tested to see if it adequately describes the principal characteristics of the industry.

Simulation over a Historical Period

The first aspect of validation rests quite simply on the ability of the model to reproduce historical industry data. This boils down to a comparison of actual historical and model-estimated values. The dynamic solution solves the model as a system, and its ability to give satisfactory results is of major importance. Even if each of the individual structural equations represents the underlying processes fairly well, the model may not hang together as a system. It may go astray when it is simulated as an interrelated system. Ideally, we seek a model that (1) tracks reality with reasonable accuracy, (2) follows the ups and downs of the business cycle, and (3) follows the overall trend of the industry variables. Some variables are much easier to track than others. Thus, demand for the industry's product may be tracked fairly well, particularly since it is explained in large part by variables outside the steel model system. Other variables are more difficult, especially, as noted above, the bottom line variables such as profits and cash flow.

An illustration of dynamic simulation for the steel industry model from 1970 to 1979 is shown in Figure 8-3. Table 8-3 presents error statistics. The pattern of movement, which compares dynamic simulation values to actuals, is reasonable (see Figure 8-3). The largest errors reported are for investment and imports with root mean square percent errors of 15.8% and

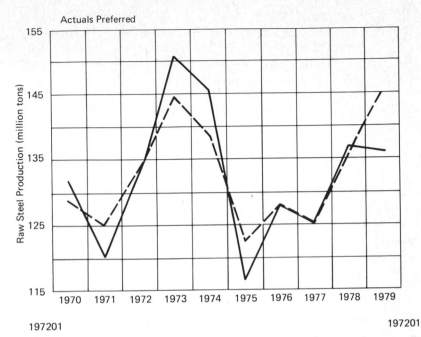

Figure 8-3. Steel production-actual versus simulated, 1970–79.

Table 8-3   Summary of Error Statistics for Dynamic Solution* 1970–79

Variable	Percentage Error	
	RMSE[a]	MAE[b]
Production	3.52	2.71
Capacity utilization	3.16	2.73
Employment	6.04	4.74
Domestic demand	5.37	3.48
Imports	15.91	11.47
Steel price	2.81	2.01
Investment	15.77	13.93
Cash flow[c]	1.33	.97

*The investment equation based on user cost has been used here.
[a]Root mean squared error.
[b]Mean absolute error.
[c]Errors reported are *levels* (billions of dollars), not percentages.

203

15.9%, respectively. Both of these series are noisy, however, and are subject to a wide variety of outside influences. Errors for the remaining variables are all 6% or below. Of particular note, however, is the behavior of nominal cash flow in the dynamic solution. The mean error turned out to be $1.33 billion for a series whose largest observation is $3.13 billion. As we have noted, the reason for this relatively large error is the fact that cash flow is treated as a residual difference. A 5% error in total cost results in perhaps a 50% error in cash flow.*

Multiplier Simulations

The ability of the model to track history is, however, only one test of its realism. Multiplier analysis is the other principal approach to model testing. The model is examined by checking (1) whether it responds sensibly in terms of sign and magnitude to a given exogenous changes and (2) whether these responses are transmitted suitably within the structure of the model. Thus, for example, in a steel industry model an increase in wages could be expected to increase the unit cost of steel production, to increase the share of imports in domestic demand, to increase domestic price, and, subsequently, to lower domestic demand and production. Some of the effects may be lagged, depending on the specification of the various behavioral equations. Such an analysis can also provide a springboard for an examination of alternative policy scenarios.

An example of a multiplier simulation is shown in Table 8-4. We assume that nominal wages of steel workers had been 5% lower than historically recorded wage rates during the period 1970–76. How does such a change affect the steel industry? The initial impact is through a reduction in industry costs. This increases cash flow and decreases the steel price. The price effect is largest after three years when prices are .7% lower than in the base solution. This price change stimulates domestic demand (eventually almost .5% higher than in the base solution)

---

*The simulation uses the investment equation based on the user cost conception since feeding cash flow back into the investment equation would cause additional error buildup so that the model would not operate properly.

Table 8-4   Multiplier Table[a]—Lower Wage Rate Scenario

Variable	Years					
	1	2	4	6	8	10
Price	− .26	− .42	− .68	− .68	− .54	− .37
Imports	−1.84	−2.83	−4.50	−3.20	−2.22	−3.27
Domestic demand	.01	.01	.05	.17	.36	.45
Production	.23	.45	.73	.53	.89	.92
Investment	.03	.14	.10	.26	.52	1.08
Employment	.12	.31	.42	.47	.70	.68
Cash flow[b]	.15	.13	.16	.21	.30	.47
Capacity utilization	.22	.45	.72	.52	.85	.86
Productivity	.11	.14	.31	.06	.19	.24

[a] Percent change from base solution.
[b] *Level* difference from base solution (billions of dollars).

and reduces imports (4.5% lower after four years). These two changes induce a small increase in domestic steel production, and that spurs an increase in domestic steel investment through the accelerator effect. Since the increase in output is faster than the productivity gain from the increase in investment, additional labor is required to meet the extra demand. After some years employment is up about 0.7% (some 7000 workers as compared to the base solution). Finally, labor productivity rises slightly in this scenario.

Such a simulation experiment can be very instructive. A broad battery of multiplier tests should be made when a model is first constructed. In the case of the steel model these might have included changed assumptions about

- Industrial activity in the economy
- Energy and other input costs
- Import tariffs and other forms of import limitations
- Tax incentives for investment

There is not an objective criterion on which to judge whether the model is operating properly in such multiplier simulations. Acceptance or rejection of the simulation performance of the model must be based on judgmental criteria, whether the individual elements of the model respond as they would have been expected to respond, and whether linkages of the system transmit impact in the directions, magnitudes, and with the time lags that an informed industry observer would expect.

Forecasting and "What If" Simulation of Industry Models

The final steps are in the application of the model for forecasting and for "what if" simulation. The forecasting application requires the steps discussed below:

Step 1: Adjustment of the Model to Recent Information and Industry Developments

As in the national model, this step involves adjusting the equation constants in light of recent performance. But it may also involve change in the behavioral coefficients of the model if significant technological changes or operating rule changes are known to be in process. For example, if it is known that a new technology is being introduced in some of the principal plants of the industry, this technological development should be integrated into the model before it is used for forecasting. Similarly, if it is known that consuming industries are changing their inputs, adjustments must be made in the model's demand equations. It is important in making model-based forecasts to recognize at least the same external information on industry developments and structural changes that would be used in a judgmental forecast.

Step 2: Forecast of the Macroeconomic Setting and Other External Developments

A vital stage of the forecasting process is establishing the prospects for the macro economy and other developments external to the industry that are likely to influence its operation. The easiest and most typical way for the industry analyst to establish an appropriate and consistent picture of the national economy is to draw on one of the national forecasts available from the econometric forecasting services. We have noted elsewhere that even these forecasts are subject to error. But many of them both reflect the best effort at macroforecasting and offer the advantage of consistency.

The forecast for activity in the automobile industry is consistent with the flow of consumer income and automobile purchases. Interest rates are derived from a model of the financial system. Production of steel-using machinery products is driven by investment expenditures. (If the analyst dislikes the assumptions underlying the macroforecast, the macromodel can be simulated to provide the analyst's own forecast. Forecast data can be downloaded from the mainframe macromodel into the industry model. Or, with the latest microcomputer technology, the satellite industry model can draw macromodel inputs directly from the PC version of the macromodel.)

Other assumptions going into the steel industry forecast should be consistent with the macro scenario. Projection of material and energy costs, and forecasts of exchange rates and foreign competitive conditions, for example, must be made with a consistent view of economic conditions in the United States and abroad. Finally, assumptions must also be made with respect to public policies. Presumably, macro policies are already built into the macroforecast, but policies that impact on the steel industry (in particular, industrial policies and pollution control regulations) must be projected realistically into the future.

Step 3: Forecasting

Forecasting with the model should not be seen as purely a mechanical process. As in the macromodel forecasts, the results must be evaluated for consistency and reasonableness in all their particulars: Does the model produce a reasonable picture of trends in labor and material inputs? Is the trend of steel prices in accord with cost and competitive factors? The evaluation of the forecast is a task for specialists from the steel industry. On occasion, adjustments in the exogenous assumptions, in the constants, or even in the coefficients of the equations may be appropriate in order to obtain an acceptable forecast. However, this is not a recommendation to adjust the model until it produces the particular forecast some expert would like to see.

The model should be used to learn something about industry prospects, not simply to support preconceived forecasts.

Step 4: Forecast Alternatives

Business planners frequently ask for optimistic and pessimistic alternatives. This represents a way of recognizing the uncertainty of the world and, in the case of industrial forecasting, visualizing the implications of alternative economic environments on the industry. The business planner would like to know what the best possible and the worst possible situation might be and what it implies for his industry.

Step 5: Simulation of Policy Alternatives

Examining policy alternatives is one of the most important uses to which an industry model can be put. The steel industry model described above was designed primarily to study alternative industrial policies. Five classes of polices were considered:

1. Fiscal policies
2. Monetary policies
3. International trade policies
4. Incomes policies
5. Pollution control investment policies

These classes are only a fraction of the possible studies for which such a model could be used.

In each case a changed policy scenario was imposed on a baseline solution. The effect of the policy is measured as the difference between the disturbed solution and the base solution during a historical period. A similar comparison could also have been made between two alternative solutions over the forecast period.

We will not discuss many policy scenarios here. But it is useful to consider one as an example of the operation of policy simulation. A protectionist scenario imposing a 5% import duty on steel will be considered for this purpose. The first question

Table 8-5 Effects of Tariff Scenario
(% Change from Base Solution)

Impact on	Periods after Start of Tariff		
	2 years	5 years	10 years
Imports	−12.26	−11.47	−19.52
Price	2.04	2.87	1.94
Capacity utilization	1.63	.66	.25
Production	1.65	.82	.72
Employment	1.06	.11	−2.31
Investment	1.12	4.78	1.91

is how to impose this change on the model in view of the fact that import duties do not appear explicitly in the model. The equivalent of a tarriff was imposed by adding 5% to the index of Japanese steel production costs which enters in the price equation and, relative to U.S. costs, in the import equations. (This is what a tarriff would do to the cost of Japanese steel going to the United States.) The results of the tariff scenario are summarized in Table 8-5.

The tariff caused an almost 20% decline in imports after 10 years. This is to be expected because of the high elasticities of steel imports with respect to the domestic/international cost variable. The effective reduction in foreign competition enables domestic producers to raise prices by 2 to 3%. The higher price reduces domestic demand for steel, partially offsetting the effect of reduced imports on domestic steel output. Employment increases during the first five years, but falls below the base simulation during the next five. This reflects higher levels of investment and a shift toward the more efficient basic oxygen process.

The tariff scenario shows that protection could effect some improvements, for example, in steel industry output and investment. But it has damaging effects on other variables like steel prices. Particularly notable is the effect on employment which improves early in the simulation and deteriorates later. Protectionism is not, after all, a long-run means to save steel industry jobs.

A Comment on Optimization Models

As noted above, process optimization models have considerable importance in their own right, but they should not be confused with the econometric industry model concept. Optimization has become a classic approach in the literature of industrial modeling. The standard case is the linear programming (LP) refinery scheduling model that seeks to determine how petroleum refineries can be utilized to produce a specified slate of product outputs at minimum cost. Given the prices of inputs, the capacity of the various interrelated process units and the required outputs, the LP's objective function is set to minimize the cost of meeting production requirements subject to the refinery's capacity constraints. The recipe for cost minimization that comes out of an LP model serves as a guide for planning the refinery's production activity.

The literature on programming and activity analysis is extensive and technical, but this is not the place to elaborate on the many types of programming models and their solution algorithms that have been developed in recent years. The applications have been widespread, and include refinery scheduling, transportation networks, modeling of product markets, portfolio optimization, spatial equilibrium analysis, among other things.

How do these modeling procedures fit with the industry modeling approach discussed above? There are clearly significant differences:

- Industry modeling is primarily but not exclusively based on econometrically estimated equation parameters. The optmization models are based almost exclusively on engineering or input-output type data.
- Industry modeling is primarily descriptive. No explicit optimization is involved, but optimization or optimal control methods can be applied. Optimization models are expressly oriented toward an optimum solution.
- Industry models describe dynamic developments. Often the applications of optimization do not consider dynamic solution over time, though they may.

The future does not lie exclusively with one or the other of these alternative approaches. Indeed, they are not alternatives.

There are many possibilities for merging optimization into econometric industry models. And here lie the greatest possibilities for introducing the optimization procedures already widely used in the business world into the broader framework used by the industrial modeler.

Industrial Models: An Appraisal

In conclusion, it is important to evaluate what industrial modeling can and cannot accomplish. First, it should be noted that industrial modeling is still a new science (or should we say art?). There have been industrial models of such industries as steel, aluminum, paper, petroleum, coal, textiles, tobacco, airlines, and so on. Some of these models are academic and others were developed in the business world. Engineering-based maximization models are widely used for refinery production planning, transportation scheduling, and other operating uses in business. It goes almost without saying that the results can be no better than the model. Typically, the purpose is not just forecasting. It is simulation of alternatives and, consequently, the structural integrity of the model is important. By their very nature, models are simplifications of the real world. The question of their accuracy or realism is, thus, not one of whether they are an exact replica of reality. Instead it is a question of whether the model structure adequately describes the principal relevant aspects of industry. The structure of such models appears to be adequate for many general purposes of forecasting and simulation.

But there are limitations. Our concern is particularly with the inability of the models to fully capture the impact of modernization and technical change. Some aspects of technical change are captured in the steel model through the shifts between production processes and through the impact of investment. But no doubt there are others. For example, in the case of steel we were unable to show explicitly the advantages of continuous casting. There are no statistical data for this process since it is so new in the United States. However, it could have been introduced into the model by using engineering data. The models may also not fully recognize structural or institutional changes. In the case of a recent model of airlines, it turned out to be difficult to model the deregulation process.

On a positive note, industrial modeling has a great promise. The ability to describe the operation of an industry in quantitative terms, easily making forecasts and simulating alternatives on a computer, often even on a microcomputer, is an important step. There are still many as yet unexplored potentials. The opportunities for industrial modeling are at least as many as the number of industries.

Further Readings

Little systematic material has been published on econometric models of industries. Walter C. Labys, *Quantitative Models of Commodity Markets* (Cambridge Mass.: Ballinger, 1975) and Walter C. Labys and Peter K. Pollak, *Commodity Models for Forecasting and Policy Analysis* (New York: Nichols Publishing Co., 1984) provide a comprehensive overview of different types of industry and market models and include a bibliographic list of many such modeling efforts. The reader is referred to individual industry studies, for example, F. G. Admas and James M. Griffin, "An Economic-Linear Programming Model of the U.S. Petroleum Refining Industry." This study, reprinted in Labys (1975) combines econometric demand and price equations with a linear programming production model. Other examples of industry models and their applications are in F. G. Adams, *Industrial Policies for Growth and Competitiveness*, Vol. II: Empirical Studies (Lexington, Mass.: D.C. Heath, 1985), which also includes a programming model of the world coal industry. A recent article is F. G. Adams and R. Santarelli, "Econometric Modeling of Industries on the Microcomputer," *Business Economics* (April 1985). The classic commodity model is Franklin M. Fisher, Paul H. Cootner, and Martin N. Bailey, "An Econometric Model of the World Copper Industry," also reprinted in Labys (1975). Other illustrations are in F. G. Adams and J. R. Behrman, *Commodity Exports and Economic Development* (Lexington, Mass., D.C. Heath, 1982). The deep sea nodule studies are summarized in F. G. Adams, "The Law of the Sea Treaty and Regulation of Nodule Exploitation," *Journal of Policy Modeling* (January 1980). Broader works on corporate modeling occasionally include material on industrial and market models, for.example, Thomas

Naylor, *Corporate Planning Models* (Reading, Mass.: Addison-Wesley, (1979).

Note

1. Adams, F. G., T. Alleyne, C. Bell, R. Koss, B. Pinto, and M. Puhakka, "Industrial Policy Impacts on the Steel Industry: A Simulation Study," in F. G. Adams, ed., *Industrial Policies for Growth and Competitiveness, Volume II* (Lexington, Mass: D.C. Heath, 1985).

❖ 9 ❖

Macroeconometrics and Models of the Firm

With few exceptions, the business firm has remained beyond the limits of true econometric model building. Business modelers tend to build corporate models following the somewhat different, perhaps more pragmatic tradition of systems simulation. The following classificatory scheme compares the principal differences between the macromodel econometric and business simulation modeling approaches.

Macromodel	Business
Econometric approach	Simulation modeling approach
Focus on macroeconomy	Focus on the firm
Emphasis on economic theory	Emphasis on business practice
Aggregate time series data in the national income accounts framework	Highly detailed data but few long-time series
Statistical estimation of coefficients and significance tests	Use of assumed coefficients, ratios, or engineering data
Sample period testing of model	Sensitivity analysis testing
Forecasting and simulation	Forecasting and simulation

These distinctions are largely self-explanatory, although the most important ones will be elaborated in the following discussion of corporate modeling. It is noteworthy, however, that the bottom of both columns reads *forecasting and simulation*. While the business modeling approach differs from traditional econometrics, the purpose is ultimately much the same. In actual practice, the econometric and system simulation approaches are not as sharply different as some of their proponents would maintain. Indeed, good simulation modeling has turned to statistical methods and, where appropriate, econometric modelers have extended their analysis to use engineering data (or even assumed coefficients based on theory) and to extensive simulation work. In any case, econometric inputs play an important role for business simulation modeling.

Corporate simulation modeling is a vast topic in its own right with an extensive literature and practice. Only a brief summary of this material will be presented here.

Corporate Simulation Modeling: The Potentials

Corporate modeling and simulation have been greatly influenced, as one would anticipate, by the immediate informational needs of business enterprise and by the organization of corporate decision making. The range of corporate modeling exercises is wide, reflecting the many aspects of business forecasting and decision making that can be studied quantitatively.

The most comprehensive and widespread business modeling takes the form of the corporate planning and financial model frequently used to forecast and simulate pro forma financial statements under a variety of assumed planning assumptions. The corporate planning model is a comprehensive framework for financial planning and analysis for the entire corporation, including its subsidiaries and divisions. There are also many specialized decision support systems with narrower scope for forecasting sales, modeling cash and credit requirements, scheduling production, transportation, and inventories, planning capital investment, reviewing marketing performance, evaluating production costs and input requirements, maximizing profit (or minimizing cost) in refinery scheduling, optimizing bank financial results, among others. Table 9-1 lists many of these model types and their data input requirements.

Table 9-1 Corporate Model Types

Model	Type	Coefficients	External Input Requirements	
			From Macromodel	From Other Sources
Corporate planning	Simulation/ accounting	Assumed: Acct. data Statistical estimation	Price indexes Wage rates GNP, personal income investment Interest rates	Detailed information on markets, competitors, etc.
Sales forecasting	Econometric single equation	Statistical estimation	GNP and final demands Input/output, inflation Personal income	Prices of competing products
Cost forecasting	Simulation/ accounting	Assumed: Acct. data Statistical estimation	Price indexes Wage rates Interest rates Capital goods prices Interest rates	Prices of metals and other inputs
Investment	Simulation	Assumed: Engineering	Capital goods prices Interest rates	Technological forecasts Long-run sales projections Capacity of plants
Inventory	Stochastic simulation	Assumed: Experience	Interest rates Prices	Sales estimates (volume) by type
Refinery scheduling	Maximization	Engineering data	Prices of crude oil Inputs wages and other cost factors	Capacity constraints Required product outputs
Portfolio management	Optimization risk analysis	Assumed: Financial Statistical estimation	Interest rates Financial flows	Exchange rates Financial market information

These business modeling systems have some important common characteristics. Informational needs are precise and detailed. The structural description of business operations must be shown explicitly in the model, so that it can be manipulated at each decision point and so that the alternative outcomes of different decisions can be considered. In most cases, but not in all, the structural relationships are assumed to be deterministic; this means that they are not estimated statistically as in an econometric model. Modeling of the firm often focuses explicitly on the actions of a particular economic agent, the manager. In place of many independent decision-making agents whose actions could be explained statistically, we have executive decisions made by management. When changes occur, they are likely to be abrupt. Traditional statistical procedures are seldom good vehicles for representing such developments. Moreover, many of the relationships are determined by technology, and this in turn is linked precisely to the machinery and production processes being used. Company engineers can often provide a fairly accurate guesstimate of the technical input coefficients appropriate to the equipment being used.

In the organization of the typical firm, analytical capabilities must be available at various organizational levels and information must be passed back and forth between these levels. Data produced in the most disaggregated sales district must be cumulated into (or made consistent with) the overall corporate plan and in turn the latter must be recognized in the divisional business simulation. This calls for an extensive corporate management information system, typically one based on the corporate income statement and balance sheet. In this framework, the impact of decisions at various levels is carried through to the bottom line of the corporation.

It has been said that the corporate "models using the deterministic simulation approach employ the computer as a large, fast adding machine to examine various effects and interactions of the input values upon the output values such as sales, costs, and earnings."[1] This is not a put down. The advantage of the computerized model system is to assure that simulations or forecasts are consistent in all their parts and to permit rapid, interactive operation of the model. While some corporate simulation models have feedbacks or call for simultaneous solution or maximization, even in the absence of these complex methods, computerization is essential for large complex systems. Many corporate simulation models are large and complex, yet they need not be and can be built within the limits of microcomputers.

Business simulation models are often bottom up systems (i.e., those aggregating information from the lowest level to the highest). An example of a bottom up system is projections made by the sales district and summed to produce a total. Conversely, an aggregate control total may also serve to assure the realism of the individual sales district estimates. Production decisions are made in the plants to meet sales and inventory requirements—frequently in great detail, because different products in various types and sizes may be produced. Costs are incurred at each level: for example, sales costs and organization costs at the sales district, production costs at the plant, overhead costs at the central staff offices.

This information is aggregated by the reporting system into tabular formats that are familiar to business executives and accountants as part of their traditional decision-making apparatus. Often such building up from the microlevel calls for detailed quantitative relationships linking each of the component values to the others. For example, production costs must be linked to the volume of production, the prices of material inputs, the quantities of these inputs, the wage rate, and the amount of labor associated with meeting the production target, among the other things. These relationships can be estimated on the assumption of constant ratios, historical data, or industry norms. Formal econometric estimation of such relationships is frequently not possible because of a lack of consistent data and, occasionally, inappropriate because of either changes in the production process or deliberate attempts to alter relationships.

The controversy over whether models should be small or large takes the form here of a choice between relatively small aggregated models and highly disaggregated detailed systems. The tendency to go to ever more detailed large models of business firms derives from the need for detailed structure and information. The computer eases the tasks involved considerably.

Today, the choice between the aggregate and the detailed approaches is influenced not so much by the cost of the computation as by the labor hours and length of time involved in developing the model and in maintaining it in operation.

An Example of a Corporate Simulation Model

This section presents an example of a deliberately simple corporate simulation model. To show a fully elaborated simulation system would require many pages of tables and would burden the reader with much company- and industry-specific information. This model fits easily onto the microcomputer and provides a good illustration of the linkage between forecast data from the macromodel and the corporate simulation system.

Our simulation model is concerned with a small cement producer we will call CEMCO. Fortunately, for purposes of presenting an example, cement is a relatively simple product—it doesn't have 57 varieties. Cement production involves first the making of clinker in a kiln using fuel, limestone, and other materials. The clinker is then ground into cement, bagged, and shipped to the customer. Shipping costs are paid by the producer.

The principal elements of CEMCO management information system are cost statements and an income statement shown in the schematic diagram of the model (Figure 9-1; more detail appears in Table 9-2.) The corporate simulation model describes the behavior of these financial statements. The cost of producing clinker and cement computed in the cost modules is fed to the income module (see the line from the cost blocks to the income block) which computes net income. The relationships within the modules (indicated by the vertical arrows) are accounting identities.

So far we have only an accounting statement. The heart of simulation model lies in the technical and behavioral linkages that explain each of the model's entries. Some of these relationships serve to link activities of CEMCO to the national or regional economic environment shown on the top of the diagram as "economic planning assumptions." Others are based on or-

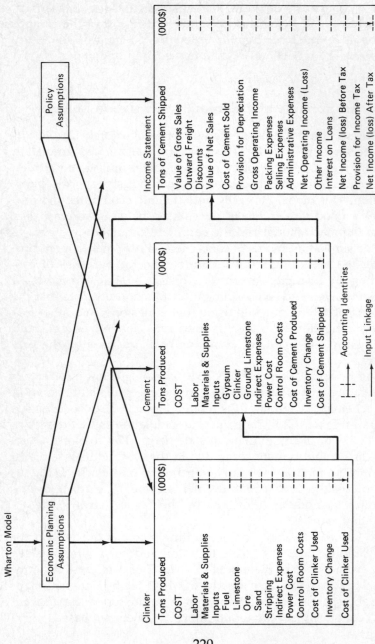

Figure 9-1. Principal relations of business simulation model.

Wharton Model

Economic Planning Assumptions

Policy Assumptions

Clinker (000$)

Tons Produced

COST
Labor
Materials & Supplies
Inputs
    Fuel
    Limestone
    Ore
    Sand
    Stripping
Indirect Expenses
Power Cost
Control Room Costs
Cost of Clinker Used
Inventory Change
Cost of Clinker Used

Cement (000$)

Tons Produced

COST
Labor
Materials & Supplies
Inputs
    Gypsum
    Clinker
    Ground Limestone
Indirect Expenses
Power Cost
Control Room Costs
Cost of Cement Produced
Inventory Change
Cost of Cement Shipped

Income Statement (000$)

Tons of Cement Shipped

Value of Gross Sales
Outward Freight
Discounts
Value of Net Sales
Cost of Cement Sold
Provision for Depreciation
Gross Operating Income
Packing Expenses
Selling Expenses
Administrative Expenses
Net Operating Income (Loss)
Other Income
Interest on Loans
Net Income (loss) Before Tax
Provision for Income Tax
Net Income (loss) After Tax

Accounting Identities

Input Linkage

220

Table 9-2 CEMCO Corporate Simulation Model—Panel A

	1985	1986
Planning Assumptions		
GNP (% change)	2.7	0.6
Inflation (% change GNP deflator)	5.4	5.5
Interest rate (Moody AAA)	15	14.4
Coal Price ($ per ton, Eastern coal)	39.16	41.98
Petroleum Price (refined $ per bbl.)	33.41	34.96
Wage Rate (% change)	6	6.2
Electric Power Rate (cents per KWH)	7.1	7.3
Business Fixed Investment, Structures	57.5	56.6
Residential Structures (bil. 1972$)	57.4	51.4
Cement Shipments, US Total (mill. bls.)	436.524	417.12
Policy Assumptions		
Discretionary Price Change (percent)	0	0
Total Price Change (percent)	3.4	3.4
Discounts (percent)	2.4	2.4
Wage Increase (%)	6	6.2
Change in Clinker Inventories	−10000	0
Change in Cement Inventories	−7500	0
Outstanding Debt	9,592,234	9,592,234
Provision for Depreciation	134,885	134,885
Dividend Payout Ratio	0.45	0.45
Clinker Capacity (tons)	480000	480000
Cement Grinding Capacity (tons)	520000	520000
Investment Tax Credits	0	0

ganizational decisions shown under "policy assumptions" and still others represent technical relations:

Cement shipments (in tons) are linked to the state of the economy as measured by residential construction, and business fixed investment. A regression equation links national cement shipments to these variables, and Cemco shipments are assumed to track national shipments assuming price or discounts are unchanged.

Shipments of cement are also related to the price quoted (here "Value of Net Sales" "$ per tons shipped" in Table 9-2C. From the perspective of CEMCO it is possible to increase sales by cutting price, but in all probability such a strategy would evoke a response from competitors. We assume that CEMCO competitors would lower their price if CEMCO cuts prices, but the competi-

Table 9-2 CEMCO Corporate Simulation Model—Panel B

	1985				1986			
	Units	$ per Unit	$ per Ton Produced	$	Units	$ per Unit	$ per Ton Produced	$
Clinker								
Tons produced	416,191				405,754			
Cost								
Labor	78.2	19589	3.681	1,532,152	76.3	20803	3.910	1,586,340
Materials and supplies			1.915	796,893			2.020	819,638
Inputs								
Fuel	58502.6	31.72	4.459	1,855,606	57035.5	33.19	4.665	1,893,000
Limestone	73416.2	10.97	1.935	805,533	71575.1	11.58	2.042	828,525
Ore	749.2	32.92	0.059	24,659	730.4	34.73	0.063	25,363
Sand	8240.8	5.49	0.109	45,209	8034.1	5.79	0.115	46,500
Stripping			0.116	48,192			0.125	50,842
Indirect expenses			3.426	1,425,970			3.708	1,504,398
Power cost			2.226	926,400			2.289	928,609
Control room costs			0.217	90,406			0.237	96,011
Cost of clinker produced	416191	18.14	18.143	7,551,020	405754	19.17	19.172	7,779,228
Inventory change (LIFO)	−10000	0.00	0.000	0	0	0.00	0.000	0
Cost of clinker used	426191	17.72	18.143	7,551,020	405754	19.17	19.172	7,779,228

Cement

Tons produced	475660				452851		
Cost							
Labor	13	19589	0.519	246,819	13	20803	0.579	262,122
Materials and supplies			0.206	97,920			0.217	98,351.
Inputs								
Gypsum	11106	27.43	0.640	304,637	10573	28.94	0.676	305,980
Clinker	426191	17.72	15.875	7,551,020	405754	19.17	17.178	7,779,228
Ground limestone	5228	10.97	0.121	57,366	4978	11.58	0.127	57,619
Indirect expenses			1.080	513,684			1.197	541,936
Power cost			1.414	672,435			1.454	658,223
Control room costs			0.034	16,100			0.038	17,098
Cost of cement produced	475660	19.89	19.888	9,459,981	452851	21.47	21.465	9,720,558
Inventory change (LIFO)	−7500	17.95	−0.283	(134,591)	0	0.00	0.000	0
Cost of cement shipped	468160.10	19.919	20	9,325,389	452851	21.47	21.465	9,720,558

Table 9-2 CEMCO Corporate Simulation Model—Panel C

Income Statement	1985				1986			
	Units	$ per Unit	$ per Ton Shipped	$	Units	$ per Unit	$ per Ton Shipped	$
Value of gross sales	468160	37.81	37.810	17,701,228	452851	39.11	39.110	17,711,071
Outward freight			6.063	2,838,550			6.397	2,896,742
Discounts			0.889	415,979			0.919	416,210
Value of net sales			30.858	14,446,698			31.794	14,398,119
Cost of sales								
Cost of cement sold	475660	19.92	19.919	9,325,389	452851	21.47	21.465	9,720,558
Provision for depreciation			0.288	134,885			0.298	134,885
Gross operating income			10.651	4,986,424			10.031	4,542,677
Packing expenses			1.695	793,623			1.788	809,892
Selling expenses			1.320	618,085			1.321	598,205
Administrative expenses			0.194	90,593			0.212	96,209
Net operating income (loss)			7.442	3,484,124			6.709	3,038,370
Other income			0.288	134,885			0.298	134,885
Interest on loans			3.073	1,438,835			3.050	1,381,282
Net income (loss) before tax			4.657	2,180,174			3.957	1,791,973
Provision for income tax			1.164	545,043			0.989	447,993
Net income or loss			3.493	1,635,130			2.968	1,343,980
Dividends			1.572	735,809			1.336	604,791

224

tors would not follow a CEMCO price increase except when underlying cost conditions justify such an increase. We have assumed a price elasticity of -0.1 in the downward direction and a high elasticity (-3.0) in the upward direction, and that only with respect to deviations of cement prices from movements of standard costs. Consequently, there is little gain to CEMCO from an independent price change announcement. If input costs rise for all cement producers, CEMCO can make a price adjustment without losing market share.

Discounts, frequently offered by cement producers for competitive reasons, also affect volume of sales. We have assumed a price elasticity of discounts of -0.5.

Production of cement is linked to shipments of cement. This means that production schedules are set to meet shipment requirements and to maintain inventories at desired levels.

In turn, production of clinker is determined by input requirements into cement grinding. There is room for inventory changes.

Inputs of materials into production of clinker and cement are assumed proportional to the volumes produced.

The dollar costs of these materials inputs are determined by quantities required and by prices assumed as part of the planning assumptions of the model.

Inputs of fuels are also closely tied to production acitivity and the cost of fuel used depends on quantity and price. Within the limits of available production equipment, the manager has possibilities for substituting between various fuels depending on their price.

In cement production, labor is largely a fixed cost. This is generally true for maintenance labor in the cement industry but even for production labor the correspondence between production and employment is weak. We have assumed that the manager has some leeway in deciding how much labor to use.

The wage rate is a company policy variable, and labor cost equals wage rate times employment.

Indirect expenses are allocated between various functions on a fixed proportion basis.

Inventories are costed on a LIFO basis.

Interest cost, of course, depends on the outstanding loans and on the relevant rate of interest.

Dividends are linked to past dividends and adjusted toward a desired payout ratio applied to net after-tax profits.

The accounting identities serve to compute net profit (in total and on a per ton of cement shipped basis).

The model system provides a picture of the principal forces, outside and within the company, that affect its financial performance. Many dimensions of CEMCO results are influenced by the economic environment. The linkage is from the Wharton Model to the economic assumptions that feed into the model. Some important examples are:

The economic situation affects the demand for cement.

Energy and materials prices affect production costs.

Interest rates affect borrowing costs.

An important consideration is that performance is affected by management decisions and the model offers the possibility of modifying some critical decision parameters. Some examples of such decision opportunities for management are:

As we have noted, there may be a little leeway for modifying the volume of cement shipped through price changes. An increase in price could improve results but only if competitors also increase prices, since otherwise prices increases could be very costly in terms of lost business. A price cut may secure some additional business but this is not likely if competitors cut their prices correspondingly. In this regard, discounts have an advantage in that they may be hidden from the competitors and so do not always produce a matching price cut by other cement suppliers.

There is only limited possibility for increasing or reducing the number of employees. Wage settlements will affect the rate paid. A critical consideration in evaluating the impact of wage increases is whether the company can make offsetting adjustments in employment or whether it can pass the wage increase along to customers in the form of higher prices.

The possibility of modifying fuel costs has been noted by selecting the cheapest fuel that can be utilized in the kilns. Further modifications in fuel inputs can sometimes be made but only at the cost of making investments in new firing facilities.

Construction of new facilities may ease capacity constraints. But if takes time to build new plants and it costs money. New facilities can be financed from debt or from equity.

The solution of corporate planning models (in this case carried out in the LOTUS 1-2-3 program) is typically quite straightforward. Like the CEMCO Model, corporate planning models are typically recursive. This term means that the direction of causation is unidirectional; there are no current feedbacks. (Even simultaneous systems do not pose insurmountable solution difficulties, however.) Exogeneous and policy variables determine sales, these determine production, and that determines cost. An accounting identity translates this information into profits. The results achieved in one year affect the firm in later years so that business simulation models frequently display interesting dynamic properties.

Testing and Multiplier Analysis

How is an industrial simulation model tested? Running the simulation model over a historical period is one way to see whether it provides a realistic picture. Sample period simulation, however, as carried out with macromodels, is not possible since we do not have a long time series of all the variables and since CEMCO, as most firms, underwent rapid structural changes in recent years.

An approach to testing the model, which is specifically suited to simulation systems, is sensitivity analysis. The behavioral coefficients of the model were largely assumed on the basis of cost and engineering data or they are simply fixed ratios observed in a few years (in some instances only one year).

The question then becomes "How sensitive are the results of the model to the values of the coefficients assumed?" One at a time, the parameters of the model are altered slightly and the results on the model solution are tabulated. This type of analysis can serve two purposes. (1) it can provide insight into the likely accuracy or inaccuracy of the model; and (2) it can provide useful information while the model is being constructed. If disturbing the values of a coefficient only affects the outcome of the analysis a little, we need not worry whether that particular relationship is being measured with accuracy. Conversely, if a parameter greatly affects the result, special effort should be put into getting as accurate a value for that parameter as possible.

Multiplier analysis differs from sensitivity tests in that the coefficients are not disturbed. Instead, the exogenous variables—planning or policy assumptions—are altered one at a time and the impact throughout the model system is observed. Do the results correspond to what experienced business managers would expect? To give an example, an increase in fuel prices should raise production costs and would affect profits unfavorably except for an offsetting adjustment in the price of the product.

The CEMCO model has been sensitivity tested and has undergone multiplier tests. Unfortunately, the sensitivity analysis shows that the results are quite sensitive to the values chosen for the parameters. And, in particular, the variables most important to the business planner (e.g., the net profit) are also the most sensitive. This not an unusual problem with business simulation models, and suggests that great care must be taken in establishing values for the critical parameters, relating them closely to what is known about these relationships in the particular firms being modeled.

However, the multiplier tests show a model that responds well to external forces. We will see some of these results in our discussion of applications in the next section.

Application of the Simulation Model

Finally, how is the simulation model used? Simulation models are particularly useful for making consistent planning projections and for simulating the effects of alternative assumptions around the baseline forecast. We will consider first a planning projection from 1984 to 1986. (The results of this model projection are summarized in Table 9-2.) A number of steps are necessary for such a projection.

Step 1: Lining Up the Model

The model must be lined up with the latest data. Beginning with the known exogenous inputs for the latest known year (1983 in our example) and taking one element at a time, we line up the model. Lining up may involve simply adding constants to the relationships to put the results in line with known data, as in the macromodel. But it may also be necessary to modify some of the parameters assumed. For example, if a new kiln has been installed that is known to use fuel more efficiently than previous equipment, the coefficient for energy inputs should be adjusted to reflect the change.

Step 2: The Planning Assumptions

The economic environment in which the company operates represents the inputs that are assumed to feed into the model. These need to be consistent internally—it would not make sense to introduce estimates on the outlook for the GNP and for inflation that are inconsistent with the assumptions for interest rates. This is the point where the macromodel plays an important role. While a company is not likely to have a macromodel forecast of its own, it can draw on the forecasts available from econometric forecasting firms and other sources. Many corporate planners prefer to make a forecast of their own, frequently one that reconciles the diverse feelings of various groups in the company, the financial people, the sales and marketing departments, and the production groups. It is important in that case to make sure that the assumptions are consistent, an aspect where an econometric model is helpful.

Step 3: Company Policy Assumptions

It is unlikely that the corporate plan will recognize the myriads of decisions that must be made in running a business. Many of these are made in response to changing conditions and are not initially part of the planning process, though often they may call for recomputing the planning model. The company plan must reflect the policies outlined by the company's managers. What is the direction in which the company's business should be expanded and at what rate? Should the company seek short-run increases in volume by undercutting its competitors' prices? What will be the company's wage policy? How large a share of profits should be distributed to the shareholders (dividend policy) and to what extent should needed capital be raised through selling equity or through borrowing?

Step 4: The Baseline Projections

The planning and policy assumptions are then introduced into the planning model to provide a set of projections. But it is unlikely that this first round of projections will be satisfactory. To begin with, there may be anomalies in the result. There may have been some glitches in entering the data or an assumed relationship may give strange results when it is projected into the forecast period. More important, however, the results of the model forecast may be unacceptable to some of the participants in the planning process. To some extent this may be the result of the exogenous assumptions. In that case, the model projection may serve as a way of persuading the participants that external conditions produce a certain result that must be lived with or for which remedial steps will be required.

Unacceptable results also could be the result of policy assumptions. In that case, the policy assumptions themselves must be reviewed and the model must be used to consider what would happen if other policies were followed. Can unacceptable results be blamed on the coefficients assumed? If arguments are provided to justify different coefficients, they may be changed. But such changes should not be made simply to bring the projections into line with desired outcomes. This must not be an exercise in wishful thinking.

We visualize here an iterative process of forecast adjustment. The first round projection is presented to corporate decision makers and division managers. These managers review the result and suggest modifications. The model is simulated once more and the results are again distributed on the computer network. A number of rounds of discussion, simulation, and revision may be necessary until a satisfactory baseline planning projection is obtained. The model provides a convenient tool for considering the implications of alternative assumptions and modifications. Most important, it assures that the planning projection is consistent with the structure and technical, behavioral, and institutional relations of the company.

The baseline forecast of CEMCO's cost and income statement for 1985 to 1986 is shown in Figure 9-2. The underlying economic planning assumptions, shown in Figure 9-2A, were transferred from the most recent Wharton Econometric Model forecast. The forecast period is a time of slowing growth and moderate inflation. Interest rates were forecast by the Wharton macromodel at high levels in view of the predicted conflict between imbalance in the federal budget and the need for monetary restraint. This particularly affects residential construction, which shows a significant decline between 1984 and 1986. (Since the macromodel does not directly produce a forecast of national cement shipments, a regression bridge equation links this variable to business fixed investment in structures and to residential construction.)

The lower half of Figure 9.2A shows the company policy assumptions. This section offers numerous opportunities for altering company policy, but for the purpose of the baseline forecast no policy changes have been assumed: discounts remain at their starting point level, prices are moved in line with standard costs, and the dividend payout ratio remains at 45%.

Figure 9.2B summarizes the cost statements of CEMCO. The top shows the cost of producing clinker. The requirements for and prices of fuels and other materials determine input costs. Wage rates and labor needs determine labor costs. The costs of producing the cement itself are shown below. The production of clinker is determined by the needs to produce cement.

Figure 9.2C shows the income statement. The governing values here are the quantities of cement shipped and the realized price (net value per ton). After allowing for movement of standard costs, discretionary price changes, and discounts, realized price (net value per ton) determines the volume of shipments. That in turn determines the production requirements and the costs measured in Figure 9-2B and summarized here in "cost of cement sold."

The forecast projects relatively stable volume of shipments at approximately 4.5 million tons throughout the forecast period. But the rise in costs is not fully offset by increases in prices so

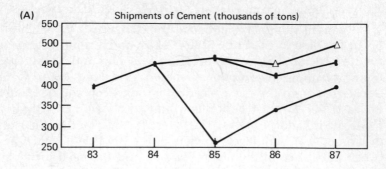

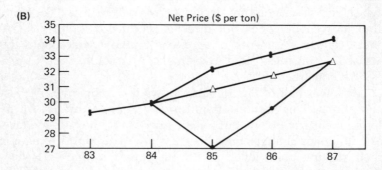

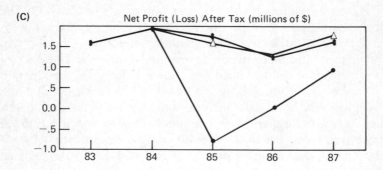

- ● Baseline
- △ Recession
- ▮ High Oil Price

Figure 9-2. Scenario simulations of CEMCO model.

232

that projected net income (before tax) falls significantly from $2.2 million in 1985 to $1.8 million in 1986. (The baseline estimates are shown graphically in Figure 9-2.)

Step 5: Alternative Forecasts

Business planners are aware that the outcome of business operations may differ from business plan projections. Policy must be formulated to allow for various eventualities. The corporate simulation model can be used to prepare an optimistic and a pessimistic view of the future. The simulation model can serve to examine the consequences of specific "what ifs." For example, what would happen to profits if one of the kilns broke down and CEMCO were forced to buy clinker in the open market at high cost? What would happen if short-term interest rates rose to sky high levels as they did in 1981–82? What would happen if there were another energy shock causing energy prices to rise sharply? What would be the consequences of alternative wage bargains with the labor unions?

As conditions change, there will be many occasions to rerun the model either to monitor what is happening or to test new decision alternatives. The response of the model to the economic environment or business policy can be readily tested through simple simulation exercises similar to the multiplier runs considered with respect to the macromodel in Chapter 5. The results of some simulations are compared to the baseline solution in Table 9-3. Note that in each case (1) the exogenous change has been introduced starting in 1985 and (2) only one variable has been altered. The results convey an impression of the impact of various forces on CEMCO financial performance:

Residential construction increases 10%. Residential construction is one of the important markets for cement. A 10% increase in residential construction accounts for a considerably smaller impact on only about 2% on CEMCO shipments. Nevertheless, the impact on net profits is somewhat greater, between $50 and $100 thousand.

Price increase of 10%. We have assumed a discretionary price increase of 10% above and beyond increases in standard costs that other producers might also join. Consequently, the elastic segment of the demand curve applies; other firms do not increase price

Table 9-3   Effects of Assumption Changes—
CEMCO Simulation Model
(Changed Assumptions Begin in 1985)

Alternative Simulations	1984	1985	1986	1987
	Shipments of Cement (Thousands of tons)			
Baseline	453	468	459	504
Residential construction + 10%	453	474	466	517
Cement price + 10%	453	306	296	329
Cement price − 10%	453	473	457	509
Discounts + 10%	453	491	475	528
	Net Price ($ per ton)			
Baseline	29.94	30.86	31.79	32.88
Residential construction + 10%	29.94	30.84	31.77	32.86
Cement price + 10%	29.94	35.13	36.21	37.45
Cement price − 10%	29.94	27.29	28.10	29.05
Discounts + 10%	29.94	27.05	27.86	28.81
	Net Profit (loss) after Tax (Thousands of $)			
Baseline	1971	1625	1343	1825
Residential construction + 10%	1971	1679	1446	1926
Cement price + 10%	1971	1165	909	636
Cement price − 10%	1971	453	159	463
Discounts + 10%	1971	427	264	673

and CEMCO volume of shipments drops sharply. The effect is to reduce profits to a quarter or less of the baseline forecast despite the higher price per ton.

Price reduction of 10%. A price reduction of 10% is also damaging to CEMCO performance. Volume shipped increases only very little despite the lower price since other firms can be expected to cut prices as well.

Increase in discounts of 10%. Since discounts are not announced, competitors may not follow them and the response in terms of quantity may be somewhat larger. The model projects shipments somewhat greater than in the baseline simulation, but the impact on CEMCO's bottom line is still severely damaging.

Numerous other alternatives can also be tested by simulating their effects in the framework of the CEMCO model. In a real world simulation study, it is not sufficient generally to modify only one variable as in the exercises above. "What if" simulations are likely to involve scenarios that call for changing numerous input variables at the same time: changes in the underlying economic conditions as well as the management's responses. Two simulation scenarios are shown here, and the results are summarized graphically in Figure 9-2.

1. *Recession simulation.* We have assumed that a sharp recession occurs in 1985 and 1986. For the cement industry the principal impact is through a drop of residential construction by 50% and of business fixed investment in structures of 40% between 1984 and 1985. Residential construction, which typically leads the cyclical recovery, is increased 30% in 1986. By 1987, the economy is back on its original track. We have also assumed lower growth of GNP, an inflation rate cut by 1%, and a modest reduction of long-term interest rates to 12 and 13%, in 1985 and 1986. In order to stimulate its volume of business, CEMCO responds to this situation by increasing discounts by 10% in 1985 and by 5% in 1986. Such a scenario contains numerous offsetting changes. In real-life simulation these changes should match as closely as possible those found in the economy, as depicted by a macromodel simulation, and the likely policy responses.

   The simulation shows a drastic fall in cement shipments. At the same time, price realizations are sharply reduced. However, CEMCO is not able to reduce its fixed cost so that the impact of the recession on the bottom line is magnified. Figure 9-2C shows that CEMCO is turned from a profitable company to one sharply in the red as a result of the recession situation. Fortunately, the economy recovers in 1987 and CEMCO is back on its feet by 1987.

2. *High oil price scenario.* The impact of higher oil prices, assumed here to rise $10 a barrel beginning in 1985, extends across the entire economy. Consequently, we have assumed that business fixed investment in structures and residential construction—the variables impacting on cement consumption—will be reduced in 1986 and 1987. At the same time, CEMCO can offset some of the fuel cost increase through rebuilding its kiln facilities. But this costs money and takes time. We have assumed that CEMCO will take out a loan of $2 million for a fuel efficiency investment program. This program will reduce fuel consumption by 10,000 barrels a year beginning in 1986. An energy saving investment tax credit of 15% is assumed to be

available in 1985. The investment is depreciated beginning in 1985.

This simulation shows somewhat slower cement shipments in 1986 and 1987, a consequence of the slower economy. The net price of cement rises substantially because of the higher fuel cost. Finally, while after tax profits fall below the baseline simulation in 1985 (even allowing for the investment tax credit), the improvement in fuel efficiency allows a modest increase in profits as compared to the baseline forecast in 1986 and 1987.

These simulations are only two examples of the rich possibilities for scenario simulation for which such a model can be used. The CEMCO model is a simple example of a corporate simulation model. In a real-world situation, simulation models become very detailed and complex providing an interactive picture of the corporations operations. (This has also frequently been their disadvantage. The requirements in terms of information, the difficulty of establishing realistic system parameters, and the problems of building and operating an extremely large system have sometimes been barriers to the continued active use of such a model).

Templates for Business Modeling

As noted in Table 9-1, the corporate simulation model can serve many purposes besides the cost and income statement simulation illustrated here. An obvious extension is the development of a balance sheet model. Another useful extension is a sources and uses system for cash and liquid assets that might include portfolio optimization features. Inventory models, investment and capital planning models, production planning systems, personnel planning and payroll systems, production scheduling, and numerous other aspects of business operations can be closely linked into the corporate simulation system.

Modeling is not just for manufacturing firms like the one in the Cemco example. Models can readily be extended to the operation of service companies, banks, fast food restaurants, construction projects, retail and wholesale trade, transportation, and so on. Airline operations and their responses to varying economic activity and interest rates, pricing strategies, labor and fuel costs, and equipment purchases can be studied readily in simulation models, for example. The structure of such a model must be linked closely to the technical and business characteristics of the firm and embedded into its accounting system.

The concept of simulation modeling is not limited to larger nationwide companies. Successful and useful models have been built for firms as small as automobile dealerships. A number of points are important to note in connection with shifting from the national or world scale company to application by smaller firms:

1. The smaller firm does not have a specialized economist or econometrician, and the model must not be so complicated as to require one.
2. Smaller firms usually have a regional or narrow product focus. The macromodel inputs must be detailed on a regional or a product-specific basis. It is not sufficient to link a regional company to national variables, as we did for expository purposes in the CEMCO example. In some respects, regional developments may parallel what happens on the national scene (e.g., interest rates and materials prices), but in others region-specific inputs are necessary. Product demand may also parallel what happens in a broader category. But that information is frequently not helpful when the company deals only with highly specific products sold in narrow markets. This may mean regionalization of the national model; regional brakdowns are available. It may call for specialized linkage equations. It is important to monitor specialized markets and to introduce anticipated developments that may affect the firm as they appear on the horizon.
3. Each company is unique. The model must be adapted to the individual company. This applies to all sizes and forms of companies. Indeed, it is more of a challenge for large complex corporations with a multiplicity of products and production sites. But the large corporation is well equipped in its planning and accounting departments to build up a company-specific model. The smaller firm does not have this facility.
4. The model must be user friendly. This may not simply mean ease of learning how to use it and speed and simplicity of operation. It may also entail whether the system fits in with existing programming systems used by the firm's planners or ac-

countants, and whether it can readily be accommodated on the relatively simple microcomputer equipment the smaller firm will be using.

The development of model templates is an approach for meeting the joint need for specificity and for simplicity.

The basic framework for the model system linking macro-model outputs and basic company simulation model is relatively standard. It is built around the accounting system. Most industries have a fairly standard set of accounts for monitoring the firm's production operation and financial performance. That makes it possible to set up templates. Such templates would contain the following elements similar to those in the CEMCO example.

Macroeconomic variables. A set of standard variables (which could be modified) to be drawn from the macromodel. A template for these variables once adapted to the specific needs of a firm, would be used repeatedly to interrogate the computer data bank for the forecast variables required.

Company policy options. The template for company policy represents a framework that may be different for every industry or type of firm. Not all the options in the template will be utilized, but it should offer numerous possibilities.

Product demand. The template for product demand brings together elements from the economic environment, competitive conditions, and company pricing and promotions policy. Standard templates can be developed for many products. The model for a diversified company may have to draw on a number of templates.

Production and cost statement. This represents the determination of sales, the production response, and the calculation of costs in each department of the enterprise. The template must be industry-specific since each industry has its own organization of production and input framework. The firm with many products may have to draw on a number of standardized templates to develop its production and cost module. It is important to recognize that the template only sets up the table and a set of standard relationships linking its component parts. Some of these are accounting identities and are truly standard. Others are behavioral or technical coefficients and must be adapted to the specifics of the company the template is being applied to. In the case of CEMCO, for example, the template called for a relationship between production of clinker and inputs of fuel. The coefficient of that relationship—the amount of fuel required for each ton of clinker—depends specifically on the equipment being used.

Income and loss statement. The income and loss statement assembles information from the cost and production statement. The accounting template here is again fairly standard; it must allow for the information from the various company departments or divisions.

Macro Econometric Information and the Corporate Simulation Model

Econometrics does not often serve as the vehicle for building the business model. However, an important function of econometrics is providing the input data into the business model and supplying the linkages between the national or industry model and the business simulation system. Corporate models can be seen as extensions of the national model. In effect, the company model operates in an environment whose characteristics are determined in the macromodel. This is the satellite relationship considered in Chapter 6.

The mechanics of such a relationship are simple. When this type of work was still in its infancy, not so long ago after all, data from the macromodel output was transferred by hand into the assumption file of the corporate model. This is no longer necessary. On one extreme, the corporate model is mounted directly on the time share system of the econometric forecasting firm. This is a convenient way to operate the corporate model for many companies lacking suitable computational facilities, even though it is generally expensive. Fears about confidentiality have largely been dispelled by security measures that allow secret company data to be segregated from other material. Once the corporate model has been mounted on the central computer, the transfer of the appropriate forecast data can be arranged automatically. Each time the baseline forecast is changed, the data are fed into the corporate model and a new corporate forecast is prepared. Alternative forecasts, and even alternative assumptions that differ from the econometric model forecast, can be easily inserted into the corporate model and the impact evaluated. The results are transferred by telephone to the client's computer terminal.

As will be considered in more detail in Chapter 10, the potentials of the microcomputer have now broadly changed these perspectives. In most cases, the corporation will no longer rely on terminals linked into a consulting firm's mainframe computer. Many corporate simulation programs can be mounted and operated on desktop microcomputers. Since the computations involved are relatively simple (except in the case of the linear programming models), the microcomputer offers an excellent means for corporate modeling. Computer programs such as Excel or Lotus 1-2-3 can do the more simple corporate models, and other programs, such as Interactive Financial Planning System (IFPS), are widely available for more complex systems.

Entering macromodel data into the corporate model is also becoming simpler. The forecast vendors are offering their forecast output on diskettes so that the required data series can readily be transferred to the corporate simulation model. Alternatively, if somewhat more detailed data are required, or if the delay involved in preparation and distribution of diskettes is to be avoided, data can be downloaded from the forecast vendor's mainframe computer through a telephone connection and introduced into the microcomputer version of the corporate model. These techniques are still new, but they are spreading rapidly. They offer great flexibility at remarkably low cost.

This offers a vision of dramatic expansion. What was largely material useful to major corporations and banks now feeds readily into the planning and decision making of smaller firms. Whereas until now the econometric model was largely a tool for the economist or the sophisticated planner, econometric information is increasingly going into personal computers on the desk of the divisional manager. It goes into the manager's divisional model and guides his or her budgeting and decision making. As compared to a few thousand business economists, there are several hundred thousand managers. The potentials for expanded use are enormous.

Further Readings

The literature on business modeling has become very extensive. Yet some of the early books still provide a broad overview, for example, Albert N. Schrieber, *Corporate Simulation Models* (Seattle: Graduate School of Business Administration, University of Washington, 1970). A pathbreaking econometric model of a firm is B. E. Davis, G. J. Caccappolo, and M. A. Chaudry, "An Econometric Planning Model for American Telephone and Telegraph Company," *Bell Journal of Economics* (Spring 1971).

Thomas H. Naylor has written or edited numerous books on business simulation. Among the most useful are: *Corporate Strategy: The Integration of Corporate Planning and Economics* (Amsterdam: North-Holland, 1982); and Thomas H. Naylor, John M. Vernon, and Kenneth Wertz, *Managerial Economics: Corporate Economics and Strategy* (New York: McGraw-Hill, 1982). Broader ranges of corporate modeling are described in books on decision support systems—the new buzzword— for example, Ralph H. Sprague and Eric D. Carlson, *Building Effective Decision Support Systems* (Englewood Cliffs, N.J.: Prentice-Hall, 1982), and Peter G. W. Keen and Michael S. Scott-Morton, *Decision Support Systems* (Reading, Mass.: Addison-Wesley, 1978).

A good summary article is Carey Leahey, "Linking Business Decisions to Macroeconomic Models," *Business Economics* (October 1984).

Note

1. Dickson, G. M., J. Mauriel, and J. C. Anderson, "Computer Assisted Planning Models: A Functional Analysis," in A. N. Schrieber, ed., *Corporate Simulation Models* (Seattle: Graduate School of Business Administration, University of Washington, 1970).

❖ 10 ❖

Econometric Forecasting for Business—Perspectives on the Future

It has been more than 30 years since most major business corporations set up economics departments—the National Association of Business Economists (NABE) held its first national convention in 1958—yet today there is little agreement on the role and organization of a business economics forecasting effort. This is partly because business forecasting has been undergoing rapid change. The content of the work is stretching vastly beyond the traditional emphasis on the macroeconomic environment. The methodology has moved toward econometrics and other quantitative techniques with computerization of data and modeling. Business forecasting is becoming more closely integrated with the business planning process. Even the nature and training of business forecasters are changing. Prospects are for further rapid development and for greater integration of econometrics and simulation methods into the affairs of the company. But the need for judgment at critical points today is no less than in the past.

The Changing Role of the Company Economist

The traditional role of the business economist was quite limited. Often with little or no staff, the economist's job was to keep the board and the company executives informed on general economic trends and to represent the company's interests on broad economic matters before trade associations and

Congressional committees. Frequently, the economist had little active involvement in the company's business affairs. "On tap but not on top." Most often, the economist had both advanced graduate training in economics [a Ph.D. or an "ABD" (All But Dissertation)] and some teaching experience. On occasion, such a "pure" economist became interested and involved in the economics of the business, and the position of chief economist sometimes proved to be a stepping stone to senior management responsibility. But, perhaps more frequently, the business economist remained just that—an economist serving as the "court seer" in the large corporation.

At the opposite extreme there were always some business economists who effectively functioned at various levels in the corporate planning or finance departments. As firms have increasingly turned toward formal corporate planning procedures, the need to integrate the economics and planning functions has been recognized. Plans must be based on a consistent set of assumptions about the economic environment. The techniques of econometric and simulation modeling have turned out to be useful for many aspects of business decision making and planning. Today, many corporations include economics entirely in the planning function. There the economist's job is to determine not what will happen at the level of the economy in general, but what relates to the industry and firm.

What then is the current role of the business economist? Few firms, except those operating on a world scale, can afford economists for the sake of their macroeconomic views alone. In most cases, the business economist serves to translate the macroeconomic environment to the level of the particular firm by

- Establishing specific economic prospects for the sale of the particular products generically (beer) and for specific brands (Budweiser beer).
- Forecasting the cost of inputs such as steel or petroleum.
- Projecting interest rates for corporate financial decisions.
- Predicting exchange rates for international transactions, and so on.

When econometric methods were first introduced, most major business firms aspired to building and operating their own macromodels. At the time, though, the large effort required to build more than a minimum model stood in the way of much private company macromodel building. Some large industrial firms like General Electric and some large banks build macromodels for their own use. Of the many firms that planned or implemented models only a few continue to maintain models to meet the special needs of their economists—IBM is one of the few U.S. companies to carry on a truly large-scale macromodel operation for its exclusive use.

This does not mean that interest in macroeconmics and in traditional macroeconometric models has disappeared. On the contrary! Most businesses subscribe to the macromodel services provided by specialized forecasting firms like Wharton Econometrics or DRI.

A survey of business economists carried out by Thomas Naylor in 1980 showed that "nearly 90% of the (business) econometric models included in our survey use national macroeconomic variables as input variables. Therein lies the rationale underlying the fact that 90% of the firms in our sample subscribe to some type of econometric service bureau which provides macroeconomic data and forecasts."[1]

The Naylor survey showed that interest in econometric models among corporate economists is high—58% of the respondents were "very interested" and 31% "somewhat interested" in econometric models. But by 1980, most of the model construction effort in business appears to have been focused on the industry or on some specific aspect of the firm—for example, marketing, finance, or corporate activity. According to Naylor, applications of econometric models in business fell into a wide variety of fields as shown on Tables 10-1 and 10-2.

This survey indicates a far broader and more business-oriented use of econometrics than one might have supposed. Yet, it is probably only the tip of the iceberg. The potentials for practical applications of econometric and modeling approaches are great, and business econometrics is likely to be extended far beyond its present limits. Econometric forecasts are being used broadly throughout various corporate divisions and departments, and they will probably be utilized on a greatly more decentralized basis in the future.

Table 10-1   Activities That Have Been
Modeled with Econometrics

Activity	Percentage of Respondents
Marketing	43.8%
Finance	41.1
Corporate	31.5
Production	17.1
Manpower	11.0

Source: Naylor (1981).

There remains a need for central coordination, however. The more widespread and decentralized the role of econometric forecasts in the operation of the company, the greater the need for coordination from the center. It will not do to run an entire company on the basis of one badly conceived or erroneous forecast. Nor is it satisfactory to let each division of a firm work with a different forecast, and perhaps pick the forecast vendor in a purely subjective manner. There is clearly a continuing need for coordination by an expert economics staff.

Table 10-2   Applications of Econometric Models

Application	Percentage of Respondents
Long-term forecasts	75.2%
Financial forecasts	38.6
Industry forecasts	56.7
Sales forecasts	52.9
Strategic planning	51.6
Budgeting	37.6
Profit planning	31.8
Balance sheet projections	31.2
Marketing planning	31.2
Cash flow analysis	30.6
Cost/price projections	29.3
Capital budgeting	21.0
Market share analysis	19.7
Risk analysis	17.2
Supply forecasts	17.2
Merger-acquisition analysis	8.3
New venture analysis	8.3

Source: Naylor (1981).

The Changing Role of the Forecast Service

Today's computer and telecommunications equipment puts data banks and econometric models at the disposal of practically anyone. When the forecasting services began in the late 1960s, they made available on their central computers not only data and macromodels, but also storage space for the clients' industry and company data and the software systems with which to manipulate this information. Business econometrics went into a highly centralized phase. Such a situation is shown in Figure 10-1A. Clients are linked by terminals and phone tie lines to the host mainframe via a data transmission system such as Tymshare or Telenet. Subscribers can manipulate the data, the models, and their own linking equations and company models on the service company's mainframe host computer. At one time DRI operated the largest Burroughs mainframe computer system in the country!

Until recently, the advantages of centralized services outweighed their high communications and operating costs. But we are on the threshold of a new period: the age of distributed processing and microcomputers. The microcomputer revolution represents a giant step; business economists are drawing away from the central mainframe computer and the decentralization of econometric manipulation has important consequences for the development of business econometrics.

Figure 10-1B shows a variety of possible solutions: (1) The client can continue as in the past, operating on the central computer and communicating by terminal and phone line. (2) The client can choose to simply draw data from the central computer by phone line or by a diskette sent through the mails and use it in his own computer. The procedures for downloading through modems or diskettes (already available from Wharton and its competitors) permit users to draw out historical and forecast data, combine it with their own company data, and manipulate it on their own microcomputers. Statistical packages for this purpose are becoming available. These program packages include the typical features to which practicing econometricians have become accustomed on large econometric service mainframes—data base management, model esti-

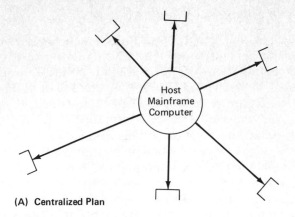

(A) Centralized Plan

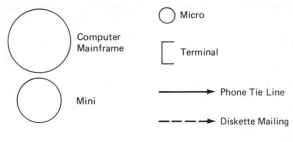

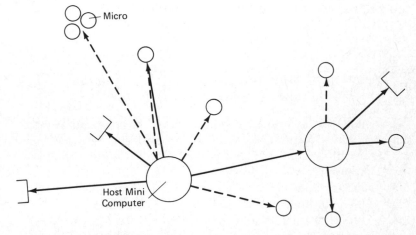

(B) Distributed Processing

Figure 10-1. Relations between forecasting service and clients.

247

mation, model solution, model simulation, and report writing.

The latest development is spectacular: the macromodel itself on the microcomputer. It has been possible to shoehorn the Wharton Model, Wharton's PC Mark 7, onto a standard microcomputer and get surprisingly good speed and flexibility for simulations. And the model can be combined with the data management, equation estimation, and graphics capabilities that have made the microcomputer so persuasive to many business users. It is possible to run at minimum cost, in house, often in less than an afternoon, what would earlier have taken several days on the vendor's mainframe computer. Not only is the cost greatly reduced, but the uncertainty about what that cost might be, a serious matter for many managers, has been eliminated. Not surprisingly many firms are rapidly turning to this new methodology. The day is not far off when the econometrician can do everything, or almost everything, on the microcomputer.

The central computer retains a role but simply as a source of data updates and standard macro forecasts. In Figure 10-1, part B replaced the mainframe central computer with a smaller host computer, a minicomputer, and with linked computer systems including microcomputers, some of them freestanding, at some of the client companies.

Relation of Microcomputer Models to Company Planning and Monitoring System

The next step is to enter economic forecast information into the company's planning or financial model. The data transfer can be done automatically and passed along through the company's computer system to planners in subsidiaries and divisions at many locations. This permits a high degree of company-wide coordination with great convenience and speed.

The coming microcomputer revolution will take econometric computation largely in house. Econometrics will be cheap and convenient. If it were not for the continued high cost of the econometrician, even the smallest business enterprise would not want to be without it.

However, it is also important to stress that the implications of the changing computational environment extend far beyond the physical, organizational, and cost aspects considered above. There are important consequences for the kind of work and for the way that work may be done.

To begin with, econometric and related quantitative efforts are likely to be extended much further down the corporate ladder and to enter more and more into business decision making at all levels of the corporation. Forecast projections for particular market areas, plants, and products will be linked to the company's econometric or simulation modeling and forecasting system. Data required for specific operating models of various sorts will be drawn from the same source. Financial reporting systems will monitor actual performance against the forecast on a continuous basis and report the results to corporate decision makers at various levels of the company. Smaller firms will also be able to take advantage of the new technology. Networks of microcomputers will extend econometric and simulation modeling into areas of company operation and planning not heretofore touched by such techniques.

This may also mean that econometric computations and modeling will be carried out in environments and by people with less academic training and experience than they do now. While this has the advantage of extending the technology into new areas, it also carries some significant risks, which will be considered further below. The new age of econometrics in business will clearly greatly extend this already burgeoning field.

The Changing Business Econometrician

This brings us to the next phase of the econometric revolution: the econometrician. The academic economists who activated the first phase of economics in business are often superceded by business staff people with backgrounds in management and with training as MBA's or industrial engineers. The new business economists are an altogether different breed. What they lack in formal education, they make up in energy and enthusiasm. They have readily accepted computers and econometrics. They are eager to try new techniques, for example, to stretch econometric methods from their traditional macroeconomic applications to product line forecasting and corporate simulation models. Their academic training and experience in business gives them a clear grasp of what the business needs—what to forecast, what factors to take into account, and how to relate the forecast to corporate operations. Since they see their careers within the corporate hierarchy, they do not seek to establish outside academic standing. To be sure, a Ph.D. still counts, but more as a mark of advanced training appropriate to a company chief economist than as an essential requirement for practicing the econometric craft.

Unfortunately, however, the new economists' enterprise and enthusiasm are not always based on a solid foundation of economics and statistics. This poses some serious risks. Business forecasters do not always appreciate the limitations of econometric tools and the forecasts they produce. The cost may not only be an occasional poor forecast. The risk is that unrealistic expectations will not be fulfilled and that econometric techniques will go unjustifiably into disrepute.

Another risk is in the area of theory. As we have noted, there has been much turmoil among economic theories in the past few years. Competing doctrines—monetarists, supply siders, rational expectationists, and old-fashioned Keynesians—clamor for recognition. It takes a solid grounding in theory to wander securely through the thickets of alternative doctrines without being seduced by the latest currently fashionable idea!

Training for Business Econometricians

How will appropriate training for the business econometrician be provided? There are already a number of developments suggesting that the business econometrics revolution's needs for education will not go unmet.

1. *Formal graduate education is still an excellent approach to training a business econometrician.* There is no doubt that basic knowledge of mathematics, statistics, and economic theory can only be acquired in this way. But it is also true that the economist practicing in business needs knowledge of the business—mar-

keting, accounting, industrial organization, and finance—that is often not a part of the more specialized "general" economics programs. This lack is now being made up by business economics Ph.D. programs at Wharton, NYU, and UCLA, for example. These programs are intended to match more academically oriented programs in quality and rigor, but they contain course materials that are particularly relevant to the economist and econometrician whose career will be in a business environment.

2. *Increasingly, courses in applied econometrics and in basic economics and statistics are being offered as part of the MBA program in many business schools.* This is an important development, belated perhaps, but necessary since many of the future econometric practitioners in business are going to be MBAs rather than Ph.Ds.

3. *The econometric consulting firms are providing more and deeper training.* So called "hand holding" has always been a part of the business of forecasting and computer time sharing. But most of this has been carried out by customer service people who were basically computer jocks. They could show the customer how to sign on and sign off, what control messages were needed, and little more. The forecasting firms have learned to build up their customer training and consulting to include applied econometrics and simulation modeling: how to use the macromodel, how to build the product line linkage system, how to design the company simulation system, and how to link all that together into an operational whole.

4. *An effort is being made by the National Association of Business Economists to develop short courses in applied econometrics.* Courses on forecasting methods have also been offered by some of the leading business schools and by specialized training schools.

5. *A promising development has been the employment of many bright young people, fresh with undergraduate degrees in economics, by economic consulting firms.* Less than ten years ago, there was little that a student with an undergraduate degree in economics could do without going to graduate school. Now, many students find their first jobs as research assistants in the forecasting firms that have become a training ground for future econometricians. Some of these young people will return full time to the university,

others will take only a few essential courses on a part-time basis. But many of them will go on to become forecasters and model builders in the world of business econometrics.

Perspectives on the Future

The world of econometric forecasting for business is undergoing rapid change. At this point, we must ask where it is going. One might be tempted to pose the question: "What will econometric forecasting look like in the year 2000?" But the changes are too rapid and the time too distant to say anything useful. We face many imponderables, even if we look ahead only the few years until 1990.

What elements are likely to remain fairly fixed? There is little doubt that the fundamental framework of detailed macroeconomic modeling will not change in a revolutionary way. Demand oriented macrotheory and the national accounts will remain the backbone of the macromodel. The new approaches to theory (Chapter 2) will be built in to the extent that they can be validated. We can expect to see new approaches to technical change in the economy's production function, improved management of the policy variables, and improved treatment of the monetary sector. The international economy can be expected to be more closely integrated with the domestic economy with respect to commodity trade, international capital flows, and the exchange rate. There will undoubtedly be other model refinements, in some cases leading to more detailed macromodels and in others to specialized sector models. New complex theory-based developments are possible, even likely, but it is not probable that the basic framework will suddenly turn out to be entirely different or that magic simple formulas for prediction will relieve corporate economists of much of their work.

The trend toward model disaggregation that we have noted at length will continue. Here the fixed element is likely to be the continued use of the input-output method, though with more up-to-date tables, more detailed breakdowns, and probably with better systems to adjust the input-output coefficients.

The basic approach to macro forecasting is also likely to

undergo only qualitative changes. Computer systems will make possible greater mechanization of the forecast effort, an improvement practical forecasters will adopt with enthusiasm.

Industrial Econometrics

The biggest changes will undoubtedly occur in the ways in which needs for forecasts and other planning variables are met within the company. The proliferation of inexpensive computer equipment within the company networked to central data systems, the growing emphasis on detailed formal planning procedures, and the use of management information systems all point to the rapid extension of econometrics and modeling down the corporate ladder. We can expect to see much more forecasting and simulation focusing increasingly on detail for the industry, the firm, and the divisions within the enterprise. The consequences of these developments are not going to be simply organizational or methodological. They are likely to alter the traditional character of econometric work. The focus will become industrial econometrics rather than macroeconometrics.

The work will involve current and projected company data that can be related to evaluation of the future of the enterprise, its performance, and its planning and decision making. The emphasis is likely to be more frankly empirical and technical, that is, based on accounting and engineering data, and less tightly bound to the theoretical precepts that guide traditional economics. The work is likely to be carried out by industrial engineers and MBA's.

The Role of the Forecast Vendors

In this new world, is there still room for the large forecast vendors like Wharton and DRI? Clearly, their role is changing. As we have noted, mainframe computation, even macromodel simulation, is rapidly being replaced by the microcomputer. Many small new entrepreneurial firms are going to be offering econometric software and versions of macromodels on microcomputers. There are already signs of a shake-out among the forecasting companies. In the end, the economies of scale of large data base suppliers and macromodel forecasters will probably prevail. It it not a job for a small firm to assemble and keep updated the vast data sources required by the business forecaster and planner. It is not a job either for a small company to develop and maintain large-scale models. The newcomers may find a niche by supplying classroom models, simple ones for demonstrations and experiments on the campus. But serious business users will require the detail, up-to-dateness, and service support available only from the large vendors. The future according to Wharton or DRI will continue to be the basis for business planning.

The Role of the Economist

Is there in this picture no longer a place for the economist? Can the economist be replaced by the technician or the business manager? Recently, some major industrial firms and banks have evidently been answering these questions in the affirmative. At least partially as a consequence of the forecasting revolution, they have closed down their corporate economics staff and transferred its functions to the divisional level. Sometimes the economists have moved as well, but more often the forecasting effort has been integrated into planning and budgeting. It is too soon to tell whether this represents a wise move.

New developments will leave their mark on business econometrics. The content of the field is changing. It will greatly increase its relevance to the current affairs of the business enterprise. Computerization on the scale envisioned here will improve the ease and automaticity of econometric operations. The practioners will have different backgrounds and incentives. But our opinion, perhaps a biased one, is that the economist will continue to play an important role.

In the brave new world of business econometrics, economic judgment may well be more important than in the past. The tight and comprehensive linkage of detailed company information in a coherent relationship to the forecast of the economic environment means that there is much at stake. While much of the work will be done by computer, the central questions of a good economic forecast, one that is based on the most recent information, the evaluation of external developments, and projections of policy response, cannot be done mechanically. Informed judgment will continue to play a critical role in the forecasting process. This is not to say that judgment should replace formal forecasting procedures, or that a sharp pencil on the back of an envelope can take the place of the computer. It does say, however, that there is no replacement for the critical evaluation of a forecast prepared by an experienced and highly trained economist. This will still be true in the year 2000.

Further Readings

Little has been written on the organization of the business forecasting effort. A number of brief pieces have appeared in *Business Economics*, the journal of the National Association of Business Economists (NABE), for example, Thomas H. Naylor, "The Politics of Corporate Economics" (March 1981), and "Experience with Corporate Econometric Models: A Survey" (January 1981). *Business Economics* has begun publishing a series of brief articles on the job of the economics staff of major corporations. The first is by James F. Smith, "The Business Economist At Work: Union Carbide Corporation" (April 1985). Other articles have appeared in the *Journal of Forecasting*. NABE and the Conference Board have a continuing interest in these questions.

There is need for a good textbook on the practice and organization of business forecasting.

Note

1. Naylor, Thomas H., "Experience with Corporate Econometric Models: A Survey," *Business Economics* (January, 1981).

Index

257